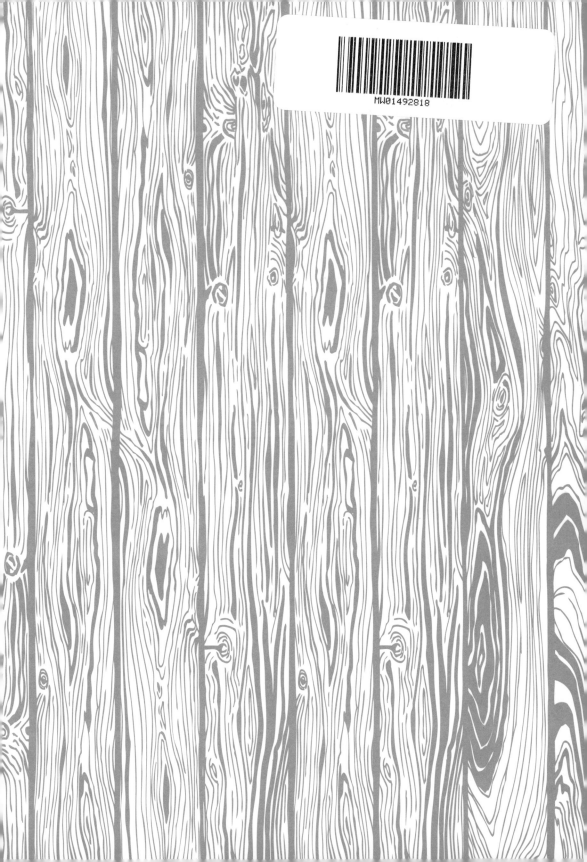

FIELD&
STREAM

THE BEST
AMERICAN

HUNTING STORIES

edited by
ANTHONY LICATA

weldon**owen**

© 2014 Weldon Owen Inc.

415 Jackson Street
San Francisco, CA 94111
weldonowen.com

Library of Congress Control Number
on file with the publisher.

ISBN 13: 978-1-61628-676-7
ISBN 10: 1-61628-676-8
10 9 8 7 6 5 4 3 2 1
2014 2015 2016 2017
Printed in China by 1010 Printing International

Cover and interior design by William Mack
All interior illustrations by Kelsey Dake

CONTENTS

THE WAY OF THE HUNTER

THE COMPANY WE KEEP

INTRODUCTION

For over 100 years, *Field & Stream* magazine has published the best in long- and short-form writing from the nation's greatest writers, thinkers, and outdoorsmen. In this collection, we bring together the best of the past decade of contemporary writing in celebration of the sport of hunting.

From *Field & Stream*'s talented experts and renowned writers like Bill Heavey, Rick Bass, Steve Rinella, and Philip Caputo come some of their most harrowing and touching words on the art of the hunt. Go with Susan Casey on her first elk hunt, travel to the black forest of Germany with Dave Petzal, and tag along with one of the youngest, most deserving hunters to ever leave an impression on Bill Heavey.

These stories are rich in philosophy and wisdom, humor and empathy, and the deep thread of experience that runs through all those who love the outdoors. Read them by the campfire, and then go out and make your own great memories.

THE
ART OF
HUNTING

CASTAWAY IN DEER PARADISE

BILL HEAVEY

Stalking along a hillside of broken conifers behind my guide, Michel Quevion, on the first day of the hunt, I'm playing a high-stakes version of *Dancing With the Stars*. Maintaining my interval of exactly two steps behind, I mirror his every move—Ginger Rogers with a .270 and Muck boots trying to keep up with this Fred Astaire, a Québécois whose English sounds like it has just gone through a garbage disposal. Not that he speaks much. My job is to avoid costing us points with the judges, who are wearing antlers and will vanish at the first misstep. When Quevion steps, I step. When he slows, I slow. When he stops, I stop. And I hardly dare breathe until he is moving again. I've done this dance many times over the years, but I've never felt such urgency to get it right—nor such dread about missing a step.

I can't yet put my finger on what it is about this guy that ups the ante. We are a few miles from the southeast coast of Canada's Anticosti Island—3,000 square miles of essentially uninhabited sub-boreal forest in the Gulf of St. Lawrence. Visibility at the moment ranges from 10 yards to more than 100, and the yellow grass in the conifer forest's understory is loaded with beds and piled droppings. I don't know what these deer are eating, but they are processing large quantities of it. We've already bumped a few, which fled without snorting—their white flags erased in midair on the second or third leap, as if sponged up by the forest. I couldn't say whether they were buck or doe, but all looked uncommonly round and sleek. Not that it matters now.

Quevion and I have not spoken in 40 minutes, but he did shoot me a momentary glance a while back that spoke volumes. The uppers of my boots had brushed each other midstep, sending out the faintest whistle of faced neoprene. Quevion turned and cocked an eyebrow, prompting me to fall to my knees and roll my pants legs outside my boots, the way he wears his. I vowed never to make that mistake again. The problem right now, however, is that my arms are killing me. Somewhere down on my body—dangling from a pack strap, binoc harness, or belt—is some loose plastic snap or buckle that keeps hitting my rifle. I compensate by extending my arms, carrying it farther out. Felt gun weight naturally increases proportionally to the gun's distance from your core, however, so my Model 70 Featherweight .270 now feels like pig iron. I'd be perfectly happy to stop for the 20 seconds it would take me to find and fix the problem. But I've already used up one stop to fix my pants legs. I'm not about to stop for a second wardrobe malfunction.

Keeping my interval and focusing on Quevion's boots, I become aware of the force field of energy he emits: a combination of mental focus, physical awareness, and sheer predatory determination. He seems to intuit the presence of deer before his physical senses have located them. When this happens, he suddenly stops midstride and simply waits for his eyes or ears to confirm what he already believes. As he stands there, hands motionless at his sides, his concentration is such that the tips of his fingers twitch involuntarily, as if that much electrical current must find an outlet. I recognize that I'm in the presence of an increasingly rare phenomenon in the modern world: a man making a living at a task he seems born to be doing. And it makes me redouble my efforts to win his approval, even as it triples my dread at disappointing him.

I've come to Anticosti Island after a couple's therapist advised that my treestand and I ought to see other people. Like nine out of 10 American deer hunters, I do my field work 20 feet up, where I sit motionless for hours on end—a lawn dwarf in a Lone Wolf. Lately, I've found myself lusting after something more physical: an old-fashioned, boots-on-the-ground white-tail hunt. A little research revealed that Anticosti, where a hunter can take two deer of either sex, is arguably the best place in North America for that.

I glommed on to a party already booked for a five-day hunt that included Ric Riccardi, brothers Jack and Paul Reilly, and Steve Burnett. I met Burnett, my entrée to the group, through David E. Petzal.

"Heavey," Petzal told me, "he's the only human I know of even half as strange as you. I think you two would hit it off." The hell of it is that Petzal was right. Burnett and I have become fast friends.

Riccardi has come to Anticosti camps run by Cerf-Sau Outfitters for 22 of the past 26 years. "Three things make this place special," he tells me. "The ground here is quiet enough to make still-hunting effective. I mean, if you're walking in Rice Krispies, you're not going to see much. Second, it's the only place I know of where I can walk all day and never see another hunter. Third, every time you take another step, there's the chance you'll see a shooter buck."

Cerf-Sau has camps in the Bell River and Chaloupe River territories, with a combined area of 425 square miles on the southeastern part of the island. We're staying at the Chaloupe River camp, where we settle into a roomy cabin with hot water, electricity, and a woodstove. We take meals and pick up boxed lunches in the main building with other hunters, almost all of whom are American. The Reilly brothers are sharing another guide, Francois. Riccardi, the veteran, knows the island so well that he prefers to hunt solo. Burnett and I, the Anticosti newbies, are hunting with Quevion.

We've been warned by the others in our party that Quevion is a hellacious guide.

"The best I've ever seen at spotting whitetails," says Riccardi.

"He doesn't talk much," says Jack Reilly. "But everybody around here listens when he does."

Paul nods. "He wants you to get a deer even more than you do."

On this, our first day, Burnett had Quevion in the morning, and I got him after lunch. When I asked how the morning had gone, Burnett piped up,

"Good!" Then added, "And sort of humbling. He's a great guy. It's just that he's so damn competent you feel like a moron. Don't even take your binocs. They're just extra weight."

At a certain moment on the hillside where Quevion has stopped, seeking confirmation of his deer intuition, his fingertips cease twitching. Then two fingers of his right hand gesture me forward.

"Dere's a good buck in dot ticket," he whispers. "See his hantler?"

Quevion points toward a clump of stunted firs full of the swaying antler-colored grass that so often fools the novice into thinking the grass holds a buck. The difference this time is that hidden in this yellow clump there actually is a pair of swaying deer antlers, and they belong to a buck. He's feeding calmly, facing away and nearly screened by brush. I mirror Quevion as he takes a half step to the right, which reveals a small window to the buck. We wait. The deer is quartering away sharply, but if he will stay put and turn our way just a few inches, a shot almost behind his ribs will take out the opposite shoulder.

"Now," Quevion says at last.

The shot is only 70 yards, but my rifle and scope choose this moment to transform from pig iron to rubber. Quevion moves in front of me, squats slightly, and taps his left shoulder. My first thought is that this is a totally inappropriate time to indicate his desire to deepen our relationship. Then I understand that he's offering a rest, so I place the fore-end on his shoulder. He inserts fingers into his ears. When the crosshairs settle on the buck's flank, I press the trigger.

The blood trail is heavy and short. Seventy yards into it, as we search for the next splotch of red, Quevion grunts. Not 4 feet away, in the middle of a bush, lies my buck—a 7-pointer with a kicker on the left side.

"His hantlers looked bigger when first I saw," says Quevion apologetically. "From de light on dem. But you make de good shot. Both lungs."

He shakes my hand, and a wave of something washes over me. It takes me a moment to sort out my feelings. I'm elated to have taken a buck, of course, and I'm greedy to devour my guide's compliment. Beneath that, however, lies a stronger emotion: relief. The thrill of victory is sweet, but it's the tip of the iceberg. The real adrenaline rush is in having escaped the agony of defeat.

By the time I've retrieved my knife and a Butt Out from my pack, Quevion has finished field dressing the buck with a small blade. He cuts slits in the hocks and inserts the front legs through them. Then he binds the arrangement with twine, kneels, and asks that I give him a hand both for support as he rises and to keep the buck's antlers from poking him in the head. With a practiced motion similar to that of lifting a canoe, he rolls the deer onto his back, grabs my hand, and stands. Then he's off and striding down the hillside toward the road, stepping over fallen trees and plowing right over everything else. Stumbling to keep up with a guy hauling 120 pounds of dead deer on his back, I feel both proud and slightly foolish. It's as if I've just won the trophy for Most Promising Hunter, 12-and-Under Division.

For thousands of years before chartered airplanes began ferrying American hunters here from Montreal, Anticosti was a hunting ground visited by native peoples living on the mainland. The Innu, for example, called it Notiskuan ("where bears are hunted"). Accounts from as early as 1542 note the abundance of black bears; in 1797, one Thomas Wright, who spent a winter on the island, reported that bears were "extremely numerous: 53 were killed within six weeks and many more were seen." The island went through a number of hands before being sold in 1895 to chocolate maker Henri Menier, who promptly set about creating a private game preserve, importing buffalo, elk, caribou, moose, foxes, and 220 whitetail deer. The big winners in this zoological version of *Survivor* were—drum roll, please— the deer. Within 50 years they had grazed the native black bear population into extinction—a rare documented instance of a prey species killing off a whole class of predators.

Today, there are a few moose on the island and a great many foxes (red, black, and hybridized), but none of the other introduced critters could keep up with the whitetail eating machine. The deer population fluctuates, but the absence of non-human predators and the relatively mild maritime climate (cool summers and long but generally mild winters) has resulted in a herd that numbers around 120,000. That's about 40 deer per square mile. At that density, of course, you aren't breeding monsters. In fact, biologists say the average size of an Anticosti whitetail has decreased over the past

25 years as the deer do to their preferred forage what they did to the black bear. But the deer are sleek and round and fun to hunt, and Cerf-Sau claims that success rates on two deer run about 85 percent (exclusive of outdoor writers, of course). Further, the venison is uncommonly tasty, perhaps because some of the deer feed on seaweed that washes up on the beaches, in effect pre-brining themselves. While big racks are not the norm, they do exist.

By the end of the third day, our group has only two bucks hanging in the meat house, an unusually poor showing, according to Riccardi. "It's partly the weather," he tells me. "We're still in the 40s and 50s in late October, which is not normal. I've never seen so few deer moving up here."

On the next-to-last morning, Quevion and I are once again stalking, this time in open country studded with patches of evergreens along a stream valley. It's windy enough that the deer don't hear us, and they're feeding so intently that several times we come upon animals 10 yards away with their heads in the grass. I put one rounded, swaybacked body in my scope, waiting for what I'm sure will be an antlered head when it finally looks up. It turns out to be a big doe. We pull this trick three times—all does. At lunch we switch, Burnett and Quevion circling back toward the road one way and me the other. Having absorbed something of the rhythm and rhyme of this kind of hunting, I'm pleased at being able to stumble on a few deer on my own. Once again, however, they're all does. I'm waiting at the truck when Quevion and Burnett show up. Up the road, we stop for Riccardi, who hasn't seen a buck all day.

"See anything?" he asks Burnett.

Burnett, who has what I take to be the same tired, slightly dazed look that I imagine I'm wearing, shrugs. "Killed a 9-pointer," he says in a monotone. "Biggest deer of my life. Too far to drag him out, though. They'll have to get him with the four-wheeler later."

Riccardi and I exchange irritated looks. We're all beat, and Burnett thinks it's a good time to jerk our chains? Quevion's expression looks the same as always, so there's no information to be gleaned there. Burnett, I notice, is in an uncharacteristically good mood during cocktails. Then, halfway through dinner, when we hear the crunch of truck tires on gravel outside, he rises from his seat and murmurs, "That's probably my buck."

A truck backs up to the meat house. In the bed is a four-wheeler and, overhanging both sides, a very long buck with a heavy 9-point rack. It's a beast, requiring two men to wrestle it onto the scales where it clocks in at about 185 pounds. Burnett's own body seems to go slack as heavy slaps of congratulations rain down upon him.

This buck is a honker. The rack, typical of Anticosti bucks, while not especially long tined, is impressively thick. The tines are fat as Vienna sausages and taper to sharp points. It's all business, this rack, like a compact .45, and there's no doubt that it could hurt you. The guides all say it's the highest-scoring rack of the year so far and likely as not to remain that way.

Back in the cabin, the tale unravels. Burnett is now openly giddy but confides that he almost blew his chance at this trophy. He and Quevion were skirting the edge of an open area when they saw the buck chasing after two does.

"'It's big' is all Michel said," Burnett begins. "Then he dropped to all fours and started, like, running after it. Like a dog, man! Booking. I'm doing my best to keep up, but I can't. Meanwhile, my gun is whacking me in the shoulders and face at every step." They stalk to within 250 yards and Burnett misses it—twice. "By then I couldn't even look at him. I just wanted to crawl into a hole. I couldn't even think." Quevion sees that the buck is so preoccupied with mating that it moves off only a short distance. "Michel sort of shook me and said, 'He didn't leave.'" The guide just motors forward again on all fours and Burnett follows as best as he can. "So I'm still whacking myself with my own gun as I crawl—on hands and knees—soaked and scraped up and just scared to death. I've screwed it up twice, and now I'm going to get to put the final nail in my coffin. And when I finally get to where Michel is, the buck is still there." Quevion has Burnett use his back as a rest. "I'm working at 10 percent of brain capacity now. I'm flooded with shame and fear and adrenaline." At 125 yards Burnett gets the buck in his crosshairs and pulls the trigger. "All I heard Michel say was 'He's down.' By then I was afraid to believe him. And that's how it happened. I hit him in the neck and dropped him in his tracks. Obviously, I shouldn't have taken those first shots, but you see a buck like that, and it just fries your mind. You can't think straight. And once I'd missed, all I could think about was having to drive back in the truck, because having Michel sore at you is just the worst thing in the world, and—"

"Wait," I interrupt. "It's not the worst thing in the world."

Paul Reilly, who has been listening the whole time without saying a word, weighs in: "Oh yeah? Up here it is."

HORN OF
THE HUNTER

DAVID E. PETZAL

It begins with music. The hunters stand assembled and are serenaded by six drivers, who play a tune called the Begrüssung ("greeting") on German hunting horns. Originally designed to enable the trackers to signal one another, they look a bit like French horns, but are keyless, and their shafts are wrapped in green leather. The tone is deeper and more resonant than that of a bugle. The greeting is for 40 writers from 19 countries assembled outside the town of Laubach on a bitter cold February day. We have come from America, Europe, Great Britain, and Russia, and we are about to participate in something with roots going back to when Germans hunted with spears.

Unlike most American hunts, which are more or less grabasstic, a German hunt is tightly organized and, after the serenade, begins with a briefing from the *Jagdmeister* (hunt master), in this case a gentleman named Ruediger Krato. Herr Krato, using actual horns and antlers to demonstrate, shows us what we may and may not shoot. German game populations are very carefully managed, and the biggest and best animals are left strictly alone. There is no lecture on gun safety; the German system of gun ownership and hunting license qualification is infinitely more rigorous than ours, and anyone who gets through it is guaranteed safe.

A German hunting license—a *Jagdschein*—is issued not by one of the country's 16 states, but by the federal government. You get one after a year of intensive study in the fields of game biology, ballistics, marksmanship (rifle and shotgun), handling of meat, and everything else connected with the sport. You pay a considerable amount of your own money for the instruction, and I understand that about 60 percent of the people who take the oral, written, and range examinations flunk on the first try. It is a lifetime license—unless you do something like drive drunk, in which case it will be taken away, along with your guns, and you will never get it back.

Holding a *Jagdschein* permits you to hunt, but it also obliges you to kill a certain amount of game (to limit crop damage), aid in searches for lost persons, kill troublesome wild animals, and help the police and game wardens should it be necessary. You become, in effect, a game warden yourself. Hunting in Germany has been called a sport for the rich and famous. Not so. Over 700,000 deer (and that's just deer) are harvested every year, and it's not just the rich and famous who are taking them. According to the German Hunting Association, 74 percent of the country's hunters work for a living. That said, public hunting, as Americans understand it, does not exist. On private land large enough to qualify as an estate, hunting rights belong to the landowner. Smaller properties can be grouped together under a system of shared hunting territories, and hunting rights here are controlled by a hunting cooperative that leases those rights.

We are broken down into groups of roughly eight people, assigned to vans, and driven by a guide to our stands. The hunt begins officially at 9 a.m. The stands are made of timber, and we sit 15 feet off the ground. We have been told that the hunt will end at 11; furthermore, we are not permitted to leave the stands for any reason until our guide comes to get us.

I am sharing a blind with Shannon Jackson, who handles public relations for Zeiss in the U.S. Shannon is a good person to be in a blind with. She takes up very little room, sees game very well, knows how to sit still, and is bloodthirsty.

The land on which we are hunting is a hilly section of hardwood forest with clumps of evergreens scattered throughout. There are clear-cuts here and there, and the stands are sited either on these or on open fields.

At 9 a.m., pandemonium breaks loose. First comes a volley of rifle fire from all points of the compass from people who have gotten something in their scopes right away. Then come the dogs. Each driver—there are about a dozen—handles a pair of small dogs that course through the woods on their stubby legs, making a high-pitched racket. Adding to the general cacophony, the drivers yell, whistle, blow horns, and bellow for their dogs.

This causes the local game animals to go elsewhere in a hurry, and there is an impressive variety of them. At the bottom end of the scale are foxes, raccoons, and a coon-dog hybrid. In the middle, roe deer (a small deer about the size of an American antelope). Larger specimens include mouflon (pronounced muff-LON), wild boar, and red stag. The first animal of any size that I see is a mouflon with a huge full-curl left horn, but no right horn. He canters through the clearing with a yap-yap dog on his heels, or hooves, as it were. Since he is not legal (you can't shoot anything bigger than a half-curl), I don't pull the trigger.

A minute later a driver walks through and asks if I've seen anything. I say yes, and describe the sheep; the driver says, "*Ja*, I know him." And that is quite true. All these woodsmen know every major animal on the property.

My turn to pull the trigger comes when a big sow (legal, because she does not have a string of piglets trailing her) chugs into the clearing and pauses for a second. At the shot she goes down, scrambles up, and staggers for 20 yards before she drops for keeps. Minutes later, three drivers show up, gut her, and take her away.

At 11, our guide arrives and leads us back to the van. We go back to the inn for lunch, and by then it's good to get back inside; we have been sitting on frozen snow, and it's something like 20 degrees F outside.

The second drive starts at 1:30. Shannon and I are in a stand where you can shoot on three sides. After the starting din, a couple of pigs streak across our clearing just as fast as a pig can go. Then, from down in the woods near the road where we walked in, I hear a loud grunt and breaking branches.

It's time to pound some pork, I think, but what steps into the open is not a boar but a red stag.

He is perhaps 30 yards away, and I have to choose instantly whether or not to shoot. That morning we'd been told to check the ends of the antlers: If each antler forks into two points, the stag is almost certainly legal; three points and it's an emphatic nein. This fellow has two points. I shoot, hitting him high in the lungs. He goes down hard, but then struggles up and makes it into the woods.

A few more high-speed hogs and dogs run by us, and then a pair of pigs pause on a ridge 70 yards away. One is very, very big, and the other is medium-sized. *"Das Viertel hat sich zur Holle,"* says the big pig to his friend ("The neighborhood has gone to hell").

"Bang," says my rifle. The porker makes it perhaps 30 yards and drops.

By now it is 3:30, and the drivers come to collect us. After looking for a few minutes we find the stag, a nice, legal 8-pointer about the size of a small bull elk. I breathe a sigh of relief that can be heard in Frankfurt.

It is time to go back to the inn for the closing ceremony. In the U.S., a big-game animal gets slung in the back of a pickup, or over a packsaddle, and that is pretty much it. The Germans do something much better.

On an open field, the drivers lay a bed of pine boughs that form a rectangle roughly 20 yards long by 40 yards wide. At each corner of the rectangle is a section of tree trunk that has been cored and split; fire is put to it, and the wood becomes a giant torch. The day's kill is laid out in order of importance from bottom to top: foxes, roe deer, boar, mouflon, and red deer. The total is 12 red deer, 65 wild boar, 15 mouflon, 13 roe deer, 16 foxes, and three raccoons. Not one person has shot something he wasn't supposed to. I don't know if that would happen here under the same circumstances. *Jagdmeister* Krato, standing at attention and saluting smartly, renders this accounting to our host, Dr. Ralph Nebe, who is vice president of sales for Zeiss.

The last act of this pageant, like the first act, is music. There is a *Jagdhorn* tune for each species. The drivers play six different tunes with a few minutes' silence between each. It's how German hunters pay their last respects. There, in that bitter cold evening with the torches snapping and smoking, I sense that I am participating in something very old and very fitting.

Weidmannsheil means, roughly, either good luck or good shooting. The reply is *Weidmannsdank*, a hunter's thanks, and I would like to say *Weidmannsdank* to the drivers, and the dogs, and the animals whom we saluted. I will never forget it.

MORTALITY

THOMAS MCINTYRE

The yellow gravel road turned on itself, switching back up the escarpment. Rotting snow began to bank along the sides, the melt running down. The Land Cruiser, shiny black at first light in the town and in the village where the pavement still ran and where we stopped for eight-treasure tea, was now powdered with yellow and, as the road grew wet, was becoming mud spattered. It climbed the road steeply, engine revving, and the gravel crunched wetly under the tires. Finally, at the top of the plateau where the March Qinghai sky was shattered blue was a green sign with white numerals, showing more than 4,500 meters of elevation. I gestured to the driver to stop, and I got out with the interpreter to take pictures. The old man stayed in the vehicle.

I gave the camera to the interpreter, and I stood with the sign behind me. The interpreter snapped three photos. He handed the camera back. I nodded and said, "*Xie xie.*"

"'Thank you.' Yes," the interpreter said, as if I were an apt pupil. We got back into the SUV. The old man, silent for many miles, stared out the passenger-side rear window.

"It's not here," he said.

I turned in the front passenger's seat to look at him. The night's bourbon still weighed on him; and he wore sunglasses, so I could not see his eyes but I could see two deep furrows between his brows. His hat was the felt one he'd had for a half century and had once dabbed with fresh elephant blood. I'd seen that hat with an orange cover when I was 20 years old as he laid it on the ground on the Roan Cliffs beside his .300 and opened his Case knife to dress a 4x4. I'd seen it long before that in San Joaquin Valley dove fields and out among the Joshua trees in the desert by the ghost mining towns where we'd shot jackrabbits when my father did not go. And he wore it two days ago as we drove to see the Great Wall, and again he stayed in the car.

"What's not here?" I asked the old man.

"My rifle," he said. "I left it farther back."

"Farther back where?" I asked. "It's still in the gun case in the rear."

"No," he said, recalling another place from a lifetime of hunting. "It must be somewhere. Else. I must . . . " He stopped.

The driver did not speak English and the interpreter did not quite understand, and for a long time no one said anything in the car.

A military-olive truck met us late in the day, and we crossed country without any roads and only a visible two-track over the steppes, skirting a blue lake with broken ice and waterbirds, and here and there on the plateau, distantly separated, a house surrounded by walls made from sun-dried earth.

At last light we came to the camp of three yurts and a kitchen tent, surrounded by stony summits. Along with the Chinese camp manager were two Tibetan girls who did the housekeeping. They were tall and slender, with anthracite black hair and white, white teeth. One was named Spring Flower. They draped white silk *hadas* around our necks. And there was one more Chinese man who did mechanical work and tended trophies.

A Texas hunter and his wife were already in camp. He said he had taken an exceptional Tibetan gazelle but had not seen a blue sheep he wanted. He was packing to leave in the morning, and on his folding bed I saw some 20 empty cartridge cases in a pile.

When I went into my yurt, the old man was sitting up in his bed under the woolen blankets, his breathing like a ragged bellows. He asked if there were oxygen tanks in the camp, and for the doctor. I went out and told the interpreter. He came back with the mechanic, now in a long white coat and a white hat like a chef's toque. They stood on the carpet covering the ground, and the interpreter listened to the old man and talked with the handyman-physician who nodded, then went out. The interpreter patted the shoulder of the old man, who jerked because he hated being touched, and told him to rest. Before I lay down, I said that maybe he should drive out in the morning with the Texas hunter and his wife and get to a lower elevation. He didn't answer, or maybe I didn't hear.

The next morning, headachy from altitude, I sighted in my '06 on a cardboard box with a black cross inked on the upturned bottom. I took a picture of the old man with his new silk scarf and then shook hands, though I don't know if he remembered.

Miles from camp on the snow-patched yellow steppe, gazelles ran in slanting herds, fleeing when they saw us approach from a half mile away. We drove and spotted for hours, until a very good lone buck with ribbed black twinned S's curling back on its head stood for us at 300 yards. I was out quickly, uncasing my '06 and opening the bolt. I sat away from the vehicle and chambered a round. The buck vanished straight down with the shot.

Tomorrow it would be real hunting, riding ponies with the herdsmen onto the summits to look for blue sheep scattered among the rocks. The old man, too old for car hunting, was far too old for that. He had come here for one final journey to a place he'd never been for game he'd never hunted. But he'd come too old, I thought, this man who had known me since I was born, not considering, at the time, that someday I too would be too old.

When I returned with the gazelle, the black Land Cruiser was gone. Now there was an extra tag in camp.

PEOPLE OF
THE CARIBOU

BILL HEAVEY

The single-engine Caravan touches down on the gravel runway at Arctic Village, women driving red Arctic Cat quads suddenly appear, each at the head of her own dust cloud, and converge on the aircraft. Several appear to have small children strapped to the racks, so I'm pretty sure this is not an attack. I unfold myself through the plane's rear door and stand there blinking in the bright 5 p.m. sun. The women fall to, unloading boxes of frozen food and cases of soft drinks onto the ATVs. All are destined for the town's two-room store. One of the women, seeing me idle, gives me a nudge. "Get busy," she says. I do.

I've come to Arctic Village, one of 15 villages scattered throughout northeast Alaska and Canada belonging to the Gwich'in American Indians, to see what life is like among one of the last subsistence hunting cultures in North America. The Gwich'in, an Athabascan tribe who count the Navajo and Apache tribes among their relatives, believe they have been following a single group of caribou—the Porcupine River herd—for 20,000 years. I hope to follow along for a week or two.

If I was expecting museum American Indians (you know, the ones in the diorama: two women fleshing a hide by a brook, with a hunting party of braves returning in the background bearing caribou slung on poles), this is the wrong place. They have satellite TV, snowmobiles, video games, and the more popular varieties of Doritos: Nacho Cheese, Cool Ranch, and the new Pizza Cravers. They watch the CBS Evening News and Oprah. The young boys hang around the village with the same low-slung jeans and sullen looks you see on kids in Fairbanks.

On the other hand, they live on tribal land—the status of which is still in dispute—run largely by and for their people. And it's not like where most of us live. Arctic Village is one of the most isolated communities in North America, 120 miles by river from its nearest neighbor, another Gwich'in settlement. Alcohol is not allowed here; neither are unsponsored outsiders. There are no roads—the only reliable way in or out is by charter plane—and therefore no cars. There is no running water other than at the Washeteria near the school, which supplies treated water and has showers and clothes washers. There are no motels, restaurants, or theaters. The one store sells little more than a few canned goods, frozen food, and the more popular calibers of rifle ammo.

It's a tough place in which to survive, let alone make money. Most people live well below the poverty line, and the only paying jobs are seasonal, working on firefighting crews and building the few houses that go up each summer. Meanwhile, with the cost of air freighting outside goods effectively tripling prices, a gallon of gas will set you back $10, a pound of ground meat about $6. What this means, among other things, is that no one can afford to eat "store food" year-round, so about two-thirds of the meat eaten in this community of about 130 people is bush meat. It's primarily caribou—at least in good years, when the animals pass near the village—but also ground squirrel, hare, ptarmigan, porcupine, muskrat, beaver, lynx, Dall sheep, and moose, as well as waterfowl and fish from the Chandalar River and nearby lakes. The proper name of the village is Vashraii K'oo, "place with high creek banks," and it was a seasonal fish camp for thousands of years before being settled.

Economic necessity aside, however, many Gwich'in prefer bush meat and even say that if they don't get it regularly, they feel weak, even sick.

It's not an easy place to get a handle on. The common saying here is that the American Indians have to live in two worlds, which, while true, only takes you so far in understanding who they are. You could just as easily maintain that they live between two worlds.

In my 11 days here, I will come to see that the physical act of hunting is key to beginning to understand the people. The food value of the meat, while important, is just the hunt's most obvious product. On another level, hunting is how they connect to the land and the animals, to one another and to one another's families, to their ancestors and their nomadic culture, and to their spiritual life. If you overlay the map of Gwich'in traditional homelands with the map of the range of the Porcupine River herd, you find that the two match up almost exactly—except for one place, Izhik Gwats'an Gwandaii Goodlit, the grounds where the caribou give birth each spring. This place, literally "the sacred place where life begins," is off-limits to them. No one in Arctic Village has ever seen it, much less entered it. As Charlie Swaney, one of the town's chief hunters and my host, puts it, "That place belongs to the caribou. It's where they take their first breath, first step, first bite of food. The forage there is better, there are few bears or wolves, and the winds keep the bugs away." A good chunk of this sacred place lies on the North Slope in Sector 1022 of the Arctic National Wildlife Refuge, the very place that oil companies have been trying for decades to drill wells. They assure the American Indians that drilling will have no impact on the caribou.

The Gwich'in, who refused to take part in the Alaska Native Claims Settlement Act of 1971, an act of Congress wherein the U.S. paid nearly $1 billion for taking Alaska Native lands, don't buy it. As a woman told me one night, "We're not conquered. They never conquered us. They think they bought us, and they didn't even do that. Now they want to buy us again. Money, it goes away as soon as it comes. That land is what has always kept us alive. We can't sell that."

At the airport, of course, I know none of this. All I know is that I should have brought sunglasses, and I'm in a place as foreign as anywhere I've been in the world. Within 10 minutes of landing, the plane is long gone and the loaded quads have rumbled off one by one. My boss, one of the last to leave, wants to know where I'm staying. I give her Charlie Swaney's name. I learned of Charlie through a mutual friend and persuaded him to let me come on a hunt. The village looks to be a mile or so away over rough gravel, a good hump with a 60-pound duffel on your shoulder. The woman sighs and rolls her eyes. "O.K., get on," she says. A few minutes later, she lets me off outside Charlie's house. I thank her and introduce myself. Her name is Joyce.

"He know you're coming?" Joyce asks.

Of course, I tell her. Why? "Because his best friend died day before yesterday. Albert Joe. Accidentally electrocuted himself. He was gonna go hunting with you guys. Now the whole town's getting ready for the funeral." She guns the four-wheeler and is gone.

I stand there while six or eight dogs, chained and standing atop little houses scattered in the nodding foxtail grass, howl at me and my intruder's scent. Even if I'd known what I was getting myself into, everything has changed. Albert "Joe" James, 67, I will learn, was a beloved figure in the community, a sort of unofficial grandfather. He had climbed a power pole with a transformer on it just as work had been ending on Wednesday. Somehow he touched the wrong wire. To Charlie, 20 years his junior, Albert Joe had been about as much as one man can be to another: longtime hunting buddy, closest friend, best man at his wedding, father figure.

I turn my attention back to the dogs, which are smaller and skinnier than I'd expected. They look nothing like the big sled dogs in the Disney movies my 10-year-old, Emma, watches obsessively. They do not know that I've watched too many Disney movies myself, that I secretly pride myself on my ability to connect with strange dogs. Several, especially one with a part of its right ear missing, look as if removing a portion of my lower leg would make their day.

The house is unpainted plywood on the outside. Leading up to the front steps like a carpet is the 12-foot-long rubber track belt from a snowmobile. Rusting steel drums full of junk lie in the grass along with derelict snowmobiles and four-wheelers, scrap lumber, rusted machine parts, ends of rope, and sections of old blue tarp. It occurs to me that my yard would look something like this if the county stopped picking up trash. A telephone booth–size wooden frame with blue tarp walls must be the outhouse.

An ample woman in a brown Columbia Titanium jacket shuffles out of the house and yells at the dogs. "You must be Marion," I say brightly. I am way out of my comfort zone and so double-down on the only resource I have, a defensive screen of desperate extroversion. I introduce myself to Charlie's wife and nearly force my welcome gifts—a carton of Marlboro Reds and an oversize tub of Folgers coffee—upon her. I tell her I'm sorry to hear about Albert Joe, who turns out to have been her uncle. There are, I'll find, basically three families in Arctic Village—the Tritts, the Franks, the Johns—and virtually everybody is related.

"Charlie's sleepin'," she says. "He went out hunting Wednesday and got back late last night. Ya goin' ta stay here?" Marion asks this last in a tone that is less than wholeheartedly inviting. "If it's convenient," I say, in a tone so desperately ingratiating that even I find it offensive. Evidently it is not convenient. She thinks, then directs me to the nearby house rented by her son, Rocky, who has gone upriver to hunt moose. She says to get settled and come back in a couple of hours.

I hump my stuff up to the unlocked house and go inside. It's a one-room affair, with a mattress on the floor, a card table and three stools by the window, and a centrally located woodstove but no wood. Pop-Tarts wrappers and Rockstar drink bottles litter the floor, where the dust is thick enough for a vacuum cleaner proving ground. It's straight out of the 19th century except for two bare electric bulbs overhead and, on the far side of the room, a brand-new Nintendo Wii hooked up to a small monitor. Other than that, the place is empty. I unroll my sleeping bag on the bed, lie down, but can't rest. I get up and look around again.

On the shelves above the bed I find a pint Ziploc. Inside are a 1-ounce bottle of Pic X-100 insect repellent, a whopping 98.11 percent DEET, with the top duct-taped shut against accidental discharge; a 7.5-ounce can of Huberd's Shoe Grease ("Since 1921. The original pine tar and beeswax waterproof/conditioner"); a 1.5-ounce bottle of industrial-strength military-surplus athlete's foot ointment (20 percent zinc undecylenate, 2 percent undecylenic acid powder); and a 1-ounce tin of Bag Balm, "Vermont's Original" since 1899. I study these objects like an anthropologist excavating an ancient site, hoping for insights into the collective psyche of my hosts. What I come up with is this: Death by mosquito-inflicted blood loss is an itchy way to go, so be prepared. You will be using your feet a great deal, so take care of them. Bag Balm, developed to moisturize cow udders, contains a mild antiseptic and is good for all manner of cuts and abrasions. I happen to know that it was used by Allied troops in WWII to keep weapons from corroding and was also taken to Antarctica on the Byrd Expedition in 1928, where it was reputedly used on the frostbitten feet of sled dogs.

I meet Charlie later that evening. Marion and some other people are sitting at a table talking when Charlie shuffles out of the bedroom, looking like he just woke up. He is 45, with the black hair and high cheekbones typical of Gwich'in. He is taller and lankier than anyone else I've seen here and seems at once open and reserved. There is something in his carriage—an unstudied and easy commingling of humility and dignity, humor and seriousness. It's a quality I've encountered before in certain soldiers: leadership. He is a guy you would want nearby in a tough situation and whom you would follow. Still half asleep, he touches my hand and accepts the box of Winchester .270 Ballistic Silvertips I brought with a smile. "I like these 130-grain bullets," he says. "Flat shooting." He has already taken out several hunters after caribou, returning with six bulls one trip and one bull last night. "You can feel the whole mood in the village change when they see that meat come in," he says. "People know they're gonna eat good." They had seen two bulls the other day but only got one before the fog rolled in, forcing them to spend the night up on the tundra. He'd brought a tent but forgot the poles, so they slept inside the collapsed tent and got soaked. He returned to the news about Albert Joe. I tell him that I'm sorry for his loss, that he should make me the least of his worries, and that we'll talk about hunting after the funeral.

"He just got careless," Charlie says, the understatement of the year. He shakes his head, presses his lips together hard.

The sudden death has struck a hammer blow. Albert Joe was a beloved, profane, silly, and public man, still full of life at 67. Lately he had devoted more time toward weaning the village boys off video games and getting them up into the country to learn the skills by which the Gwich'in had defined themselves: how to hunt and fish and run a trapline, how to predict the weather by what the clouds were doing in the far-off mountains, how to find your way in the endless steppe of tundra, how the caribou behaved and why.

And the behavior of that Porcupine River herd is changing. It has been 11 years, since 1999, that the animals have shown up in any significant numbers, 11 years since the villagers have set up their traditional September camps on the ridge 4 miles southeast of town. Many of the children have never experienced those camps, which are normally a highlight of the year, a time to renew old friendships, to remember what life was like once for the Gwich'in. This year is shaping up like it might be better. Some caribou have already been brought in, and a number of hunters have reported glassing animals on distant mountains. Tents are going up on the ridge. The hope is that this year will be different.

"There's something wrong with the earth, and it's telling us the only way it can," Charlie says simply. "We've had more rain this year than I can remember. The winters are getting colder, and the summers are getting hotter."

I ask what they do when the caribou don't show up. "There are moose upriver sometimes, which they didn't have in the old days. We eat more store food, more noodles. We set nets under the ice on Old John Lake for whitefish, pike, and lake trout. Sometimes you can catch grayling upriver. But it's not the same without caribou. Fish is better than store food. But it doesn't make you strong. Once you get used to wild meat, you don't feel as strong unless you have it."

"The land is turning into a bowl of water," says a woman at the table. "We've had so much rain that the river's eroding the banks. It's getting wider."

"The willow is growing tall," notes a man who has not spoken until now. "Twenty years ago, it never grew above your knees, and now it's over your head some places!"

"Tell him about the polar bear," says another woman.

Polar bear? I thought polar bears were coastal animals. We're 100 miles inland. The bear was first sighted up on the ridge two weeks ago, Charlie says. Since then it has been seen three times outside of town, including once by Charlie himself. The villagers are accustomed to large predators. They've lived with brown bears and wolves for millennia. Usually, it's the young, curious bears that are troublesome, especially if they smell meat in a hunting camp, and no one leaves the village without a rifle.

(Indeed, when I walk up to camp one afternoon, mostly for the exercise, I encounter three teenagers, two girls and a boy, just outside the village. "Oh, good," says the boy, handing me the rifle he has been carrying across his shoulders. "You can give this back to my mom. She was worried about not having a gun in the tent tonight." The boy hands me a bolt-action .30/06 with open sights. "Chamber's empty but the magazine's full. You know how to shoot one of these things?" I tell him that I do. "O.K., good to go, then. Oh, yeah. The safety's broke." And with that the three resume walking and chatting. I find later that children are taught to shoot well before they write their age in two digits.)

People seem afraid both of this individual animal and of the new and unknowable threat it implies. Alaska Fish and Game back in Fairbanks has been alerted. They're supposed to be sending an agent out to investigate, but no one knows when. Several people at the table openly state that they'll shoot the animal if it comes near the village.

Charlie says, "They're having trouble finding seals, and they've gotta eat. So they're following the caribou now."

The next morning I encounter Charlie carrying a gas can. "Go down to the river," he says. "We just heard on the radio that they're bringing two moose in." He's going to gas up his Argo, an ATV that is like an eight-wheeled tank that never goes fast but goes through anything. Charlie has the only one in town. It's a somewhat public vehicle, and the only thing big enough for the job at hand.

The East Fork of the Chandalar runs wide, shallow, and muddy past the opposite end of town. I go down and sit on a bench by a log church built in the early 1900s. Grass is growing on its roof. By the water are a number of 20- and 24-foot johnboats with 40- and 60-hp engines. A fish net stretches across the creek that joins the river here. People come and go, smoking cigarettes. Two hours later, the boats finally arrive, one so loaded it has barely 4 inches of freeboard. The hunters are tired and dirty but smiling. They land with two young bulls quartered and skinned. The Argo, well lined with the blue tarp the Gwich'in adapt to endless uses, is backed up to the boats, and four young men from the village jump to form a bucket brigade. They grunt as they transfer huge hunks of moose flesh from shoulder to shoulder. In less than five minutes, the Argo is loaded and on its way, eight hooves sticking up out of the well at crazy angles.

It takes 15 minutes to walk back to Charlie's, where women are already cutting meat on makeshift tables of plywood laid atop sawhorses. A woman named Alice Smoke, 75, opens a bone the size of a baseball bat with a 21-inch bow saw and scoops out some marrow with her knife. "Better than Chinese food," she tells me, smiling as if she has waited a long time for this moment. She offers me a sliver. It's white and jellylike, surprisingly mild and less rich tasting than I'd expected.

Sitting nearby is Maggie Roberts, the same age, who cuts me a piece of sinew from a leg. "Babiche, we call it," she says, chewing some herself. "Good for constipation." I'm happy to report that moose sinew tastes fine, which is good, because you could chew a piece for a week without appreciably altering its structure. Meanwhile, Maggie volunteers that when she was little her parents still traveled seasonally, following caribou, moose, Dall sheep, small game, and fish. Her father didn't want to live in Arctic Village or any village. Once alcohol came, there was trouble too often. Mostly they were living in cabins by then, she says, rather than wooden-framed skin huts used in the old times. "If we found a place with a lot of caribou, we'd stay there," she says. "You'd make a rack of dry willow and hang meat on it. We'd make a fire underneath it and smoke it. We didn't have tarps in those days. We'd make a roof of spruce bark so it wouldn't get wet when it rained." Then they'd move again, with the family's dogs carrying everything: food, blankets, tents, the various parts of their stove, the caribou skins the family slept on. Dogs were seldom used to pull sleds. "That didn't happen until after the white people came. The Russians, I think, were the first ones here. We traded furs with them. Before that we didn't have pots and cups."

Sometimes, she remembers, the men would go up in the mountains to hunt. "The dogs carried the meat down, maybe 40 pounds each, in leather packs on their sides. The men would send them down from the mountain. 'Go to grandma,' they'd say. And they'd come to us. And the women would send them back with tea or tobacco if we had any. 'Go to grandpa,' they'd say. Just those words. And the dogs, they knew what it meant, they'd do it."

She works as she talks, guiding an Old Hickory butcher knife through a haunch, the haunch growing smaller as the pile of boneless meat grows bigger. Occasionally she stops to give the blade a few strokes on one side only with an 8-inch tool file, the common practice here. Every house I've been in has the same carbon-steel knives, made by the Ontario Knife Co., and at least several files with which to sharpen them. She tells me about the time her mother made new boots for her father. He had been working waist-deep in the river tending his fish traps that fall, and would frequently have to come out to dry off and warm up. So her mother decided to make him better boots. "We didn't have rubber in those days. I mean that we knew what it was, but we didn't have any ourselves. So she took skins she'd tanned, the skin from the lower leg is the strongest part, and she sewed them good, real tight with babiche. And then melted the moose fat, you know, and just worked that in for a long, long time to waterproof them. After that, he didn't get wet."

She just vaguely remembers going hungry once or twice when game was scarce. It wasn't famine-hungry, she says. They didn't have to eat their dogs or anything. But the children got only a bite or two of ground squirrel each and some broth. Their mother kept the cabin warm and told them to drink water and not to move around too much. Maggie says she was very small and just barely remembers this. "But my father, he was always talking to us about the famines in the old days, about coming across a tepee and the whole family lying inside like they were asleep. But dead. 'So you have to learn to do things for yourself, to hunt and fish and trap,' he'd say. In famines, you know, people would try to eat anything. They'd even boil old hides. Usually they couldn't eat that, but they would try. My parents, when they'd butcher a caribou, they'd throw the hooves with some of the leg attached over a branch or a tree. That way they could be found, even in the snow, if there wasn't anything else to eat. You could make soup from that and it would keep you alive."

I stand there looking at this small woman quietly chewing moose sinew as she cuts meat. She is a person who doesn't take up space or call attention to herself. And it occurs to me that she knows more about animals and plants, about hunting, trapping, and fishing, about dogs, shelter, and survival, than I will ever know.

The only male fool enough to hang around a group of busy women, I am soon pressed into service loading cardboard boxes—which are falling apart under the weight of meat packed into garbage bags—on ATVs and helping deliver it to various houses. Sometimes there is somebody home, and sometimes I just follow my assigned partner into the unlocked house and dump the meat in the electric chest freezer that most people have. The mood throughout the village does seem brighter with the arrival of the moose. It's as if the meat is doubly nourishing, strengthening both the body and the bond between the one who gives and the one who receives. It does not feel like charity. It feels like community.

Four days later, one day after the funeral, we are finally going hunting. I ride along with Charlie and two other men, Jonathan John and Roy Henry, up to the camp on the ridge. The plan is to go out on top the next day to hunt. At this time of year, the beginning of September, the bulls are just coming out of velvet. For now, their priority is bulking up. In a month, with the start of the rut in October, they'll stop eating, focusing only on mating. They'll lose 30 percent of their body weight and some will die in the violent sparring over females. And their meat will become so rank that not even the dogs will eat it. I've never seen caribou fight. It's hard for me to picture these herbivores, which sometimes congregate in peaceful herds numbering in the tens of thousands, turning fratricidally violent.

At camp that first night, I get my first taste of ground squirrel, a meat that I find almost addictive. They're found in the drier ground near ridges and the tops of hills, where they live in extensive colonies. The Gwich'in catch them in small steel leg-hold traps, and dispatch them—after grasping them firmly behind the head to avoid their formidable buckteeth—by pinching their hearts through the skin. The animal is thrown whole on the fire until the fur is thoroughly singed, which is not the most appetizing smell. After the singed fur is scraped off with the back of a knife, the animal is gutted, scored at the four limbs, and placed in water to boil for an hour or so. Singed ground squirrels are a little like Ball Park Franks; they plump when you cook 'em. A blackened, bloated ground squirrel is a fairly grotesque and accusatory thing to ponder for any length of time. The expansion of fat tissue caused by cooking contorts the face into a death grimace. And although quite dead, it looks as if it would love to make use of its yellow incisors one last time. If you can get past this—and it's not hard if you're hungry—you are rewarded with meat so sweet and rich that it needs nothing more than salt to make a satisfying meal. The people at camp are amused that I take such a liking to ground squirrel. One young mother teases, "You're like the elders. They love these things. We usually take them back to town for them." I protest that I'm an elder, too, but am offered no more ground squirrel.

Nothing up here happens in a hurry. The Gwich'in themselves joke about "Indian time." But I have now been here long enough that I'm losing some of my natural impatience. Besides, "When you hurry is when you make mistakes," as Charlie says. With daylight lasting until nearly 10 p.m., there's seldom a compelling reason to rush. Before departing the next morning, we have a big breakfast of pancakes with syrup, fried caribou, and coffee. This is followed by a few cigarettes, which leads to another pot of coffee and another round of cigarettes. Finally, a little after noon, Charlie, Jonathan, Roy, and I load the Argo. We each bring a sleeping bag, rain gear, and extra layers. The weather is in the high 50s, but it can change fast anywhere, and change almost instantaneously up top. Charlie brings a tent, a cooler with a few provisions, and some wood. "Not much to make a fire with once you're up on top," he says. The others each have rifles. I'm unsure as to whether I'll be allowed to shoot and figure it's best not to push, so I don't ask.

Once we reach the ridgetop, the trail turns and follows the crest for a ways, then drops slightly into the tundra and passes a tiny lake. A half mile on, we climb to a saddle between two hills, then hike to the top of the taller one. Just below its summit, we sit in the lee of a windbreak constructed of carefully piled stones. And then I realize where I am. In front of us lies an endless tundra steppe, a larger swath of the earth than my eyes have ever swallowed at a single glance. It is literally hundreds of square miles of gently rolling land, rising to three or four waves of mountains of the Brooks Range in the north, each taller than the one before it. The lower country is ablaze with fall yellows and reds. The top 6 feet of the tundra is alive with the stunted plant life that survives here: blueberry, cranberry, salmonberry, willow, lichen, grass, and moss. Beneath that lies permafrost. It's a place that probably looked pretty much the same 5,000 years ago. It has never felt the blade of a plow or dozer, never been broken by roads or roofs or cut by wires or pipes. I make out no definite trails of any kind—animal or man— just faint changes in colors that help you decide how you might want to travel from one place to the next. There are at least three weather systems in play, competing with one another: a rainstorm, fog, and bright sunshine. Between the fog and the sun is a short, wide rainbow, the most vivid I have ever seen, jutting up from the ground like the broken-off stub of a sword. It's like being in God's upstairs workshop. I could drink it in all day.

Charlie sits, anchoring his elbows on his knees and raising his 16X binocs, while Jonathan mans the spotting scope I'd seen on Charlie's kitchen table. Wordlessly, they put the Vise-Grip to the scenery, squeezing it for caribou. I already tried the binocs in camp and found that I couldn't hold them steady enough to resolve an image. God only knows how Jonathan free-hands the spotting scope. No one speaks for a good while. Roy, an old friend of Albert's who has come in for the funeral and stayed on to hunt, exchanges a shrug of shared uselessness with me. Neither of us brought optics and we're not going to spot anything these guys don't.

At last Charlie grunts and asks Jonathan what he makes of the group on the second mountain range where the gray of the rock face meets the uppermost yellow of the willow. I haven't given much thought to Jonathan until now. He's a taciturn man in a Navy ball cap and scraggly facial hair. He says little and sounds a bit like Oscar the Grouch when he does speak. Turning the scope to the indicated spot and cranking it to higher power, he finally deigns to make use of its tripod. "Yah, some nice bulls in that group," he murmurs. "Two real big ones on the right I had in silhouette for a moment there. They're moving pretty good." Charlie and Jonathan both try to show me through their respective optics, but I simply can't see anything that could be caribou. "It helps if you already know the country," Charlie says. "That way, you know when you're seeing something that wasn't there before." He tells me to look for "little black dots." If the dots move, they're caribou. This is the shortest glassing lesson of all time and fully covers the topic.

I ask how many and how far off these ones are. Charlie thinks and says, "There's about nine in that group. And they're about, oh, 25 mile or so." Jonathan nods in agreement. "Yah, about that."

"So they'll be here in . . . " I ask, letting my voice trail off.

"Two days," Charlie answers. "If they keep coming this way." Charlie identifies four more groups of bulls, none of them numerous. One of them he estimates is 40 miles from where we're sitting. He watches long enough to see how the closer groups are behaving, and from this deduces where they're headed. "It's only in the past couple of days that their antlers have gotten hard," he says. "They're real careful of them until that happens. They'll keep to themselves, sort of quiet and out of the way. But now, they don't care about anything but finding the best feed to fatten up. They'll go anywhere." He sights one group that he thinks is coming our way. If they keep coming, they'll pass through some time tomorrow. He knows a better spot from which to keep tabs on them. If they do as he expects, it's also a better spot to intercept them. He says it's a rock dome about 12 miles away, farther out into the tundra. We get back into the Argo for the four-hour ride, having to stop several times to winch our way across streams.

When we arrive, we climb up the dome to glass the group and look for other caribou. Charlie hands me his .270 and we stalk our way forward. He whispers that the caribou like high places like this. The winds give them relief from flies and mosquitoes, which can bleed them to death in the worst times. "Be ready," he says. "You never know when you're going to jump one up here." I am a lousy offhand rifle shot and have told him this but am happy to be holding a rifle. I decide I won't take any shot over 100 yards unless I can get to a sitting position. I stay as close to him as I can in case I need to give the rifle back in time for a shot I won't take. It's hard. Charlie covers ground.

The light has gotten angular by now, the tundra seeming to glow from within rather than reflect light. I ask how he keeps track of where he is out here. He says it's all by triangulating known features. "But when the fog socks you in, you can't do anything but wait. Me and Albert once got stuck out here for eight days. We weren't in any danger or anything, but after six days we had to start rationing our food." I ask if he ever uses a GPS. He frowns at the mention of this, as if I've asked why they don't employ Predator drones. "We don't have anything like that up here," he says, slightly irritated. I can't tell whether I've suggested something far beyond his fiscal means or whether it's something else, that maybe he is thinking that as an American Indian it is necessary to register your land, send in a map or something, before a GPS unit will display where you are on country your people have been inhabiting for millennia.

We glass until it's too dark to see. Charlie can't locate the group he was watching and seems comforted by that. If they're coming this way, they'd be below our line of sight, having come into the lower part of the tundra, with its hills and valleys. He seems to think we're where we need to be. I'm thinking of something Jonathan said last night around the fire about people in the old days. "My grandma said we used to live just like animals. Because animals were all what was in their brain." Charlie, I suddenly realize, is like that. He doesn't talk much about caribou, but when he does his observations are always presented in terms of what they need at a particular moment and why.

We get water from a pool in the moss at the base of the dome, make coffee and a pot of instant macaroni, and fry up some caribou. I am exhausted. We haven't walked that far, but traveling in the Argo is like riding a slow-motion mechanical bull all day. The tent is absurdly small, about right for two men staying at a tropical nudist resort. We squirm into our bags fully clothed, rifles lying between us in what I've come to think of as "Alaska camp ready" condition: the bolt closed, the chamber empty, the magazine full. It's so tight in here that whatever position you land in when you hit the floor is the one you keep for the night, despite the rock in your back. I'm so tired that for once it doesn't matter.

I wake and open the tent flap the next morning to see a cow caribou 60 yards off and running away. Charlie is gone. Jonathan and Roy are still asleep. I climb up the dome to look for Charlie. I walk for an hour, trying to stay downwind of where I think he might be, before I see him returning. He has killed a cow farther on for camp meat, which explains the other cow I saw running. He saw the group again and says they should be passing close to here in a couple of hours. We walk back to camp, have a quick cup of coffee, and all head up in the Argo to get the cow. Jonathan and Charlie make short work of field dressing the animal, making it look as easy as slitting open the mail. Jonathan removes a lacy membrane of fat covering the stomach so that it's a single piece, almost like a doily, and hangs it on a bush to dry. "*Icha'ats'a chu*, we call it," he says. "Old-timers used to use the stomach as a cooking pot," he continues, rolling the carcass so the guts spill downhill. "They'd clean it out and put pieces of meat in it. Then they'd dig a hole and put hot rocks in, some dirt, and then that stomach. In an hour or so, it'd be ready. That was before we had pots." This is the most I've heard Jonathan say so far. We load quarters into the Argo and return to camp, where Jonathan starts to fry up some of the meat, and Charlie uses the moment to stand atop the Argo and glass for our bulls. The group must have changed course or moved faster than he thought, because the next thing I see is Charlie jogging across the tundra with the .270 in one hand. The fact that he said nothing tells me how dire the situation is. I take off after him. By now, he has slowed to a brisk walk, which is good, because I sure as hell can't run in this stuff. At every step I sink 4 inches into the ground. It's like running in cement. He is headed for a rock outcropping about a mile away, which must be where he hopes to shoot from. Even a brisk walk winds me, and I start removing layers as I heat up. Within 200 yards, I've removed my parka, vest, hat, and fleece pullover. Meanwhile, Charlie is pulling away from me steadily, long legs scissoring away.

He drops to a crawl as he gains the top, by which point his lead has increased to 300 yards. When I'm within about 200 yards, he looks back long enough to give me a single, emphatic "down" motion. I stop, hit the wet ground, and freeze. The last thing I want is to be responsible for a busted stalk. After a minute, he looks back again, seems pleased that I've obeyed, and motions for me to approach low and from further downwind. I dogleg in that direction, walking in a Marx Brothers crouch, and finally come up behind him. When I finally get to him, he is calmly smoking a cigarette. "You shouldn't have done that," he says quietly. "You'll get tired." I ask in a whisper how far the bulls are. "About 100 yards," he says. Then he stubs out the cigarette and stands.

When he does, I rise to midcrouch and see three bulls calmly walking along. They stop when they see Charlie. All three look large and fat, with dried scraps of velvet still clinging to their antlers. A few hundred yards behind them are a few cows with calves. Charlie drops the first one with a neck shot and drops it again with another when it rises. He puts two shots into the next caribou, which staggers, stands still for a long moment, and topples over dead before it hits the ground. The third bull, farther off, takes a bullet and stands, seemingly not bothered by the lead insect beneath its skin, as if trying to remember something. I hear the click-clack of Charlie reloading the magazine, and at the next shot see the bull rock slightly as it absorbs another bullet. The animal turns and begins walking directly away from us. There is no shot at this angle, and neither of us speaks as we hope and pray for it to turn. After another 40 yards it does, offering a quartering-away shot at about 175 yards. Charlie's first shot is high, splintering antler just above its head. The second shot appears as a discoloration, a red blossom behind its ear. The bull falls in a heap.

Charlie shows no elation. If anything, he seems somewhat subdued. I can't tell whether it's because he didn't kill as cleanly as he would have liked. Maybe, as with many hunters, the final act of the hunt, the killing, while necessary, is the part he enjoys least. Maybe it's some combination of the two or something altogether different. In any case, he is suddenly all business. He hands me the rifle and a handful of shells. "I'm going back to get the Argo," he says. "I don't want any crows or bears on that meat." With that, he is gone, walking in that same ground-covering stride. I put four in the magazine, one in the chamber, and engage the safety. I look around. The cows have altered course away from me. In the distance I see another group of caribou on the heels of this one, though they're too far to distinguish bulls and cows. No birds or bears come. I mark and memorize the location of the downed animals, which are surprisingly easy to lose track of in the low brush. The easiest way to pick them up again, I decide, is to look for the only things in sight that don't respond by moving slightly in the wind.

Half an hour later, the Argo arrives and we spend about two hours dressing and cutting up the caribou. Roy and I work together silently, skinning the caribou and using the skin to stack the meat on. We've got about as much meat as we can carry with four men on board, so we leave the skins behind. By the time we load everything, Jonathan and I, riding in the back

46

of the Argo atop meat and gear and guns, are sitting noticeably higher than Charlie and Roy in front.

I lost my Filson waterfowler's hat, my favorite, on the walk, and the sun is powerful. I can feel my skin burning, but there's nothing to be done about it. We ride for four hours, stopping only for water. Shortly before we get back to camp I see a hat on the trail and ask Charlie to stop. It's a camo military-issue boonie hat. Charlie thinks he knows who it belongs to, one of a group of younger guys who were up here drinking a few days back. "Keep it," he tells me. "Anybody drinking on a four-wheeler deserves to lose it." I do, and am happy to have the protection.

We finally reach camp about eight o'clock. I suddenly realize how beat and bloody I am. My hands are covered with dried blood; my shirt and pants are stained with it. It's strange, but after you've had blood on you for a while, it doesn't feel dirty. Almost the opposite. I am hungry, too. I attack a plate of fried meat and rice without washing, using my hunting knife to cut the meat. After dinner, awaiting the cup of coffee that I hope will keep me awake long enough to dig my sleeping bag out and find a place to unroll it, I wash my plate and the knife in a tub of warm, soapy water. Back at the fire, Jonathan shakes his head. "Don't wash your knife like that," he says. "Soap and hot water, they're bad for a hunting knife."

Charlie nods in agreement. "Rolls the edge."

"Rolls the edge?" I repeat, dumbly. My knife is a Benchmade Rant with a blade of 440C stainless steel. It's almost indestructible. But I'm more interested in what these guys think than in winning an argument.

"You can't see it, but if you put it under a microscope you'd see that hot water and soap roll the edge," Charlie says. He and Jonathan both seem vaguely uncomfortable, almost embarrassed at having to tell me something so obvious. But they seem to be doing it out of a sense of duty, as if I'm now inside the tent and must be taught certain things.

"When it's all over, your trip," says Jonathan, "you gotta make a conclusion about it, right?" That's right, I tell him, I do. I ask what he thinks it should be. "Well . . . " he muses, the tip of his cigarette glowing as he takes a puff. "This world, this country, it's rough, you know? You see it. So you got to be tough. Not just in your body but also in your mind. That's what I'd say."

I'm about to say something when Joyce, the woman who told me to get busy the first day and had me loading boxes, says, "You got a new hat!" I did, I tell her. I lost mine and found this one. "It suits you," she decides after a moment. "You're starting to get Indianized." This somehow starts a discussion on the merits and faults of wearing floppy-brimmed hats while riding four-wheelers. The verdict is that they can obstruct your vision at crucial moments.

I bid everyone good night, find an empty tent, and am almost instantly asleep. When I wake late the next morning, Charlie is already gone. "He took some other guys out up top," Marion tells me. "There's still a lot of people in the village who need meat."

HOW I CAME TO BE FILLED WITH NEW ZEAL AND ENTHUSIASUM

DAVID E. PETZAL

When I told people I was going hunting in New Zealand, many of them looked at me blankly because they were not quite sure where New Zealand was, or what it was, or if it was part of Australia. So let's start with the differences between the two countries.

Australia is a continent, most of which is uninhabitable desert. It is home to seven or eight of the worst snakes in the world, a spider that can drive its fangs through your shoe, great white sharks, saltwater crocodiles, two species of deadly jellyfish, a lethal octopus, plagues of rabbits and frogs, and Mel Gibson. It is the only culture to have coined a word for beer vomit.

The first humans to arrive in Australia were the Aborigines, who got there 70,000 years ago. Then, in the 18th century, the British offered their worst criminals the choice of hanging or being sent to Australia—"transportation," they called it. Most chose the gallows.

New Zealand lies 1,300 miles south and east of Australia. It comprises two islands—North and South—that extend 1,000 miles from the top of North Island to the bottom of South Island. It's home to 4-million-plus people, 12 species of big game, huge trout, and some of the most gorgeous scenery anywhere on this planet. There is not, as far as I can tell, a single dangerous creature in the joint.

Sometime between the ninth and 13th centuries, New Zealand was colonized by the Maori (may-OR-ee), a Polynesian people who evolved a complex culture involving elaborate wood carving, hunting down and killing all the moa (a large, flightless bird that was good eating; when a Maori host asked if you'd like some moa, he was not referring to quantity), and making war on one another nonstop.

New Zealand was visited by Europeans as early as the 17th century, and they gradually began to settle there. But it was not until 1840 that the British, aghast that there was still a place on earth they had not stolen, declared New Zealand to be part of their empire. For a while the Brits and Maoris had an excellent time killing each other but finally got tired of it and settled down to farming and getting along.

There were (and are) no predators in New Zealand, and it proved to be heaven for raising sheep. Over the years, game was also imported from different parts of the world, and it all flourished. Now, the same islands that once held no large animals are home to healthy populations of red deer, chamois, tahr, wapiti (American elk), fallow deer, sika deer, rusa deer, sambar stag, goats, Arapawa sheep, and wild boar.

Tahr and chamois are mountain animals, hunted on the South Island, which has a range of steep alpine peaks running down its spine. The North Island, which is warmer and not quite as mountainous (although it is plenty steep), is home to the rest. Last spring I went to the North Island to hunt what is regarded as the premier New Zealand trophy, the red deer.

Cervus elaphus, or red stag or red deer, has proved so adaptable that it thrives not only in New Zealand but in Scotland, much of Europe, and Argentina. Typically reddish blond, though subtle color variations occur, the animal somewhat resembles our elk. A good-size bull will weigh 400 to 500 pounds, and if you get one in the rut when it's worn down from fighting and fornicating, it may go only 300.

The antlers lack the height and width of wapiti headgear but are far heavier, have more points, and are frequently palmated. They're scored by the SCI system, ranging in seven medal grades from Silver (300 to 320 points) to Gold (345 to 365) to Super Gold (400 plus). A few very rare animals score in the 500s, and they look like something out of the last Ice Age. A Silver rack is an awe-inspiring trophy; a Super Gold will give you heart failure. Red deer antlers make a spectacular showing because of their variety and their massiveness. I saw a Gold animal shot one evening whose main beams went 11 inches at the base.

In April and May (autumn in New Zealand), the bulls go into rut and advertise their availability by roaring. It is not really a roar, but more of a cowlike moan, part bellow and partly the sound you hear coming from a fraternity-house bathroom on a Monday after a party weekend. More or less nonstop, the roaring is complemented by bellowing from the rutting sika and fallow deer that also roam these hills.

Alpine Hunting New Zealand is the creation of Shane Quinn, a taciturn Kiwi who started the operation in 1992. The Alpine Hunting lodge is two hours by car north of Palmerston North, a medium-size town an hour's plane ride south of Auckland. There are six guest rooms, a kitchen, and a combination tool-butcher-helicopter shed. (The chopper is used to haul carcasses; the country is so steep that it's the most practical way.) If you need a cat fix, Alpine has two, plus an elderly dog, Sassy, who gimps around looking for attention.

Six guides work in rotation at Alpine. Mine, David Blayney, is a 42-year-old former soldier, gun nut, and exceedingly tough character who also happens to be extremely funny. (When he dropped me off at the Palmerston North airport for the start of my trip home, he delivered a hysterical monologue on what guides go through while waiting for their clients to deplane: Is it that one? Oh God, don't do this to me . . .)

Alpine showed me more and better game than I've seen anywhere else in my life, period. I saw animals all day long, and some of them were very big indeed. Shane's operation has produced six world-record red deer heads, three No. 1 chamois heads, three No. 1 sika deer heads, and top-ten trophies for other species. The way they do it is no secret: The number of hunters is strictly controlled, and Alpine does not hammer the hell out of the herd.

• • •

Blayney's hunting technique turned out to be the same as that used by Don Malli, a Wyoming rancher friend who is the best mule deer hunter I've met. "We get above them and wait for one to make a mistake," Blayney explained. The country is steep (North Island is volcanic) and cut by cliffs, gorges, high bluffs, and escarpments. There are no level spots.

The area we hunted was carpeted with black-green manuka, sagebrush-on-steroids-like plants that grow to 8 feet. The animals duck into it whenever they sense trouble, and if they take two steps into the manuka, you won't see them again.

Guides and hunters get around on six-wheelers. You could, if you were in very good shape (the lodge is 4,000 feet above sea level) and willing to waste a lot of time, walk the entire hunt. Since I was not inclined to do so, I opted for the six-wheeler. During my first evening at Alpine, we took a 15-minute ride to the top of a high ridge, and it was there that my ability to estimate distance failed me.

There we were on the top of the ridge, David the guide with a spotting scope and David the geezer with binoculars, listening to the roars emanating from below. I looked straight down the cliff and wondered out loud how many yards it was to a pale-tan stag I was glassing below. "Six hundred yards and change," I said. David smiled.

"Three hundred and change," he said. His rangefinder said it was 330 yards, and this was the way it went for the whole hunt. You are always looking straight downhill, or across a gorge, and never across flat ground, so you had better bring a rangefinder and trust it.

We rode and looked, then looked some more. Our break came just before noon on the second day of hunting. We were glassing at the head of the Ohinewairua Valley, and nothing much was happening. I had sighted in my .338 on the previous day, and my Teutonic scope had not behaved in its customary flawless manner. I explained to David that Teutonic scopes sometimes work better if you scream at them in German (the same is true of Teutons), so I yelled at it in *Deutsche*.

At that moment a very, very good red stag leaped to his feet 300 yards below us. He had been hidden so well in the manuka that, had it not been for my Hunnish hissy fit, we never would have seen him. He checked us out for a second and took off down the trail at a rapid trot, not panicked but not wasting time, either.

I wanted to go after him, but David said no, we would have lunch and check out my rifle and give him time to settle down. That was what we did, and the scope, having been cursed out in its native tongue, now worked perfectly. I am not making this up.

In the early afternoon, we took the six-wheeler down to where we had seen the stag earlier and set out on foot, picking our way through the shrubbery, slow and careful. Then David froze and pointed.

"There," he whispered, "on the far side of that ravine, lying down looking to the right, 190 yards."

The stag was looking back the way he had come, assuming we would approach from that same direction, but we were one ridge over, farther away than he thought we would be. He was almost completely hidden, and I had nothing to shoot at, but then nature gave me a rare assist, as the wind suddenly shifted and blew from us to him. The wind said, Red alert: geezer with gun. Being a smart stag, he didn't bolt but simply stood up and started moving slowly away from us.

He walked for 40 yards and turned broadside, and that was all I needed, as I held right on and squeezed the trigger. He was a 10x11, between 8 and 9 years old, and in fine shape. David guessed his weight at 450 to 500 pounds. He had been eating, not rutting, and his hide was unscarred and his antlers unmarked. Later, when Shane Quinn measured him, he scored 352 points, putting him solidly in the Gold Medal bracket. David took his cape and head and carried them up a 100-yard incline that I could barely manage without the load.

Later that day, the helicopter went to get the rest of him, and as I watched, I saw his body soaring up into the evening sky, moving closer to where his spirit had gone a few hours earlier.

AN IMPROBABLE ELK HUNT

SUSAN CASEY

If you had asked me a year ago, "So, when's the elk hunt?" I would have been certain the question was meant for someone else. Because the two key words in that sentence—elk and hunt—meant nothing to me, and when combined spoke of blood and guns, and those were things I didn't spend much time with. I'd seen an elk once, but that encounter took place on Main Street in Banff; it was a tourist-addled nuisance cow looking for handouts of Cheetos and hardly a majestic ambassador of the species. Hunting wasn't part of my upbringing, at least not the type that results in homemade jerky. As for rifles, I'd never held one.

But then at a cocktail party last June, hunting entered my life in an unexpected way. It happened during a conversation with Sid Evans, *Field & Stream*'s editor-in-chief. As the crowd milled around us and the canapés were passed, I described my new infatuation with spearfishing. Stalking dinner felt surprisingly satisfying, I told Sid, and of course he understood. What was it like to go after something bigger, I asked. Did you have the same primal feeling, but amplified? This idea interested both of us and within minutes the gauntlet went down: Could *Field & Stream* take a hunting know-nothing, a gun ignoramus—in other words, someone like me—

and send her on one of the toughest hunts in North America? Specifically: If the correct efforts were made, the appropriate expertise recruited, could a person go from never having laid eyes on a .300 Win. Mag. cartridge to making a 300-yard shot on an elk? In a matter of months?

The next morning Sid e-mailed to see whether I was serious or "was that just the beer talking?" Elk hunts are brutal, he cautioned. The Rocky Mountain elk fires on all sensory cylinders—smell, hearing, vision—and has an almost eerie knack for staying one step ahead of its pursuers. Elk hang out at high altitudes, in crags and gullies and dark folds of timber, in steep and slippery places where humans fumble around at a disadvantage. Elk hunting would be a commitment. A large one. I would need to learn every nuance of the animal from scratch. The hunt would require peak fitness levels, so that running around at high altitudes was, literally, no sweat. I would need to become a very good shot in a very short time. The magazine would understand if I wasn't up for it, he wrote. "After all, I realize that you haven't killed so much as a squirrel."

"I'm in," I e-mailed back. "How soon can I go?"

My enthusiasm came from a mix of curiosity and guilt—I eat meat but know nothing about what it means to kill for it. I love animals, but I also know that sentimentalizing nature is wrong. Dying, killing, becoming prey—these things are all part of the game, and to ignore them trivializes life. Bluntly put, the modern relationship to the wild is a fake one. For many, meat is a section at the grocery store. And at Safeway there are no big brown eyes to consider, no blood. Hunting struck me as a more honest approach, and a necessary one if the goal is to understand the true nature of, well, nature. If this seems like an improbably heavy philosophical reason for going on an elk hunt, consider that I was an improbable elk hunter, and on the day I agreed to become one, the improbable stuff was only beginning.

We have a fairly limited amount of time to turn you into a killing machine," David Petzal said as we drove to Camp Fire, a private men's shooting club in Chappaqua, N.Y. It was a warm Friday in July, and Dave, a laconic man with a salt-and-pepper beard who has been *Field & Stream*'s resident rifle expert for 25 years, was taking me to his off-site office for a lesson.

That morning I shot my first target, a cardboard bighorn ram, with a .22

at 100 yards, firing prone, and then kneeling, and then offhand (for purposes of humility). Dave has a slow and deliberate way of speaking and a way with language that is dryly hilarious, and he delivered instructions in a courtly drawl. As he moved through the basics—the importance of inhaling, exhaling, and then squeezing, not pulling, the trigger; of relaxing, focusing, and keeping steady hands—we both noticed that mine were shaking. A lot.

"Do you drink coffee?"

"I'm afraid so. The stronger, the better."

He looked at me and shook his head. "Caffeine is not your friend. How much do you weigh?"

"I don't know. About 105 pounds."

"Think of yourself as 105 pounds of inert matter. With a trigger finger."

The .22 felt light, the gun equivalent of training wheels, and it fired with an insubstantial pop, but Dave was testing a beast of a weapon, a synthetic-stocked .338, and its booming recoil was a reminder of what lay in store. My serious gun, the elk-dispatching one, was a magnificent Dakota Arms .300 Win. Mag. rifle borrowed from its owner, Paulette Kok, a friend of Dave's. Its stock, handcrafted from a blank of English walnut, had been shortened to 12 1/2 inches. The Dakota was elegant and lethal and sat imposingly on the rack. To be honest, it frightened me.

"Slam that bolt! Harder! Abuse it!" I was lying on my stomach, shooting the .22 at a fluorescent orange gopher. When hit, the steel target made a bright pinging noise that I liked. Dave felt I wasn't being authoritative enough with the action. He wanted to hear it snap open and shut smartly and see bullet casings flip into the air. "Use your palm," he told me. "Stop grabbing the bolt with your fingers." By now, my third lesson, we had ranged farther afield, driving another 60 miles north to Tamarack, a manicured hunting club in New York's Dutchess County.

On this range I could practice 300-yard shots by climbing a hill and grazing the top of a cornfield. It seemed impossibly far. "You should be able to make it," Dave said firmly. "The mistake people make is not trusting their rifles. These things are deadly accurate from a long way off."

For the time being, 75 yards was challenge enough. Today I would warm up with the .22 and then move to the bigger gun. After a 30-minute session of small-caliber gopher abuse, Dave handed me three .300 cartridges, threw his pack down, and put on earmuffs. The Dakota had a heft and a certainty about it, and as I lay prone, pressing my cheek along the stock and adjusting the scope, I almost felt comfortable. Breathe, exhale. Squeeze. BOOM! The gunshot felt smooth, a profound bass explosion with a silky kickback and unspeakable power. My legs jerked in a spasmodic froglike gesture. It wasn't a very pretty demonstration of form, but I had managed to hit the target in a reasonable spot, and Dave seemed to have faith.

"You flinched," he said. "But I'll take it. You're 105 pounds of what?"

"Inert matter."

As the summer passed, Saturdays at Tamarack became routine. It made for a long day—two hours on the train, another hour in Dave's truck, two hours on the range, and then back again—but I was seeing results. My hunt was set: October 20 in western Colorado, a state with a healthy population of 30,000 elk. Over the weeks I shot and shot and shot and began to rend paper in a more consistent manner. Perhaps I had become a little cocky, or perhaps I was simply being careless on the day I split my forehead open with the scope. It was a kneeling shot, and the impact rocked me off my heels. Blood ran down my face; I wiped it off and felt the cut, a clean and deep half-moon. Noting that I didn't seem bothered by the carnage, Dave had nodded his approval, mentioning that when an elk is gutted, the volume of liquid that comes pouring out is "disgusting. With an antelope you're up to your wrists in blood. With an elk you're up to your shoulders."

I suppose it was inevitable that eventually, when talking about the elk hunt, I'd hit a raw nerve in someone. But I didn't expect the most hostile response to come from my own brother, no stranger to a good hamburger. On Labor Day weekend I'd arrived at the family cottage in Ontario's lake country with a bandaged forehead and stories about learning to shoot. This didn't sit well with my brother; our conversation started out testily and deteriorated from there. "I just don't believe in hunting," he said, crossing his arms and glaring.

I'd heard this line before, and often from meat eaters, not all of whom recognized the irony. My question to them was always the same: Would it be a problem if I bought elk steaks at the store? For that matter, what about ground beef? Commercial meat producers feed hundreds of animals per day through machines with names like the Belly Ripper, the Hide Puller, and the Tail Cutter, and though the slaughterhouse cows are intended to be dead by the time they meet these grisly renderings, often they are not. To eat meat and then denounce the elk hunt was hypocritical, but there was no budging him. The argument ended bitterly as he and his wife left, packing up their DVD of nature photographs from a recent hiking vacation.

"I hope that elk's scream haunts you for the rest of your life," my brother had said as he'd left. Those words echoed in my head. Such furious anger from someone I loved caught me off guard. It seemed unfair and misplaced. Killing is the most profound act imaginable, but in centuries past, it wasn't optional if you wanted to survive. And even now, while others do the dirty work, out of sight and mind and conscience, that predator DNA ticks on inside us. What I was proposing to do here was perform the necessary act of getting my own food, rather than subcontract that task to a middleman.

Back in New York, I e-mailed Dave about the family dustup, and when I arrived at the train station that Saturday, he greeted me with a wry smile.

"So now you're seeing the other side of big-game hunting," he said. As we drove north to Tamarack, he described an altercation he'd had once in the Johannesburg airport.

"I had just checked my guns back out from the police and some middle-aged lady marched up to me with smoke coming out of her ears and said: 'You're going hunting, aren't you?'

"'Yes ma'am, I am.'

"'What are you hunting?'

"'Eland.'

"'What's an eland?'

"'It's the largest of the antelopes and it's a beautiful silvery gray with gentle brown eyes and heavy spiral horns,' I said and then lied: 'There are hardly any left and so I'm going to kill one for myself before they're all gone.'" He paused. "And as she turned beet red, I said, 'That's what you wanted to hear, isn't it? Now kindly go away.'"

I knew that Dave was trying to teach me more about hunting than the mere mechanics of shooting. He'd described how it feels when the animal goes down, what it means to actually end a life. During these conversations I'd felt bluff and full of adrenaline, untroubled by potential remorse for the elk. But Dave, with his decades of experience, was more sanguine: "Any of three things will happen when the moment comes," he told me. "One, you'll pull the trigger. Two, you'll get buck fever and freeze. Three, you'll decide you're unwilling to shoot. Not from panic, but from a conscious choice."

The date was September 10. Summer was sliding by, hunting season was around the corner, and even the trees had a brisk fall energy. I picked up my rifle. Lying prone, I emptied the magazine and killed the paper elk three times. "Very nice," Dave said and turned to fire off a few rounds himself. He was testing a gun that he appeared to like. It was black and sort of cruel looking with none of the warm woodiness of the others I'd seen, but something about the way it shot pleased him, and at that moment I realized that rifles, like high-end sports cars or fine wines, each have a unique personality. I felt that this was especially true of the Dakota—I was fond of it beyond reason. Yet even though the gun and I were having a lovely relationship, it was never a small deal when the .300 went off. It was loud but also percussive, and I felt its reverberation in my sternum, underneath the center of my chest, somewhere in the vicinity of my heart.

Smith Fork Ranch sits like a jewel in the West Elk Wilderness, 100 miles southwest of Aspen. This is country that can only be described as nature showing off: white-topped mountains towering on the eastern horizon, verdant valleys to the west, piñon-studded mesas to the south, lush rivers swirling through all of it, and canopies of aspen turned alchemically to gold.

The ranch's buildings—several log structures, a barn, a riding ring, and four one-bedroom log cabins—were so in tune with their surroundings that they might as well have sprouted from the ground. In 1974 Smith Fork's owners, Marley and Linda Hodgson, restored a venerable but fading guest ranch, enlisting local artisans for every part of the job, right down to the light fixtures. The result is a five-star retreat that's deeply rustic, but the sort of rustic that involves a choice between 15 different kinds of single malt Scotch.

On the evening I arrived I sat with the Hodgsons in the ranch library, nursing a glass of tequila and looking at the head of a soulful-seeming 6x6 bull elk. A fire roared beneath him. Though tomorrow would be spent horse packing to Smith Fork's 10,000-foot camp in the West Elks, I was thinking about how much I wanted to stay right where I was, shooting at elk from the porch perhaps, when the door opened and two men in cowboy hats came in: my guides. Levi Kempf, 26, was fresh faced and blond with a shy smile. A seasoned hunting guide, he also ran the ranch's flyfishing programs. Chuck Gunther, 41, Smith Fork's head wrangler, was the kind of authentic cowboy that casting directors dream of. He had deep-set eyes, dark hair, and a lavish mustache, topped off by an imposing black Stetson and a black bandanna at his throat.

Over dinner they explained that Saturday was the first day of Colorado's second rifle season. There are four such seasons in a year, each a weeklong opportunity to fill a tag. For weather reasons the second and third ones tended to be the most popular, and both men mentioned that tomorrow, Friday, would be a frenzy of hunters jockeying into position for the opening bell. On the way up the mountain I'd see all kinds, Chuck explained, from do-it-yourselfers whose gear was patched together with duct tape to experts whose deployment was less a sporting endeavor than a military campaign.

I could feel myself becoming hyper with excitement and wanted to go back to my room to repack my gear for the seventh or eighth time. "Make sure to keep your hunter-safety card and permit accessible at all times," Chuck advised, explaining that the local game warden was a zealot with an uncanny knack for showing up when least expected. He was even known to have set up roadblocks for illicit elk, the way others might to ensnare drunk drivers. I immediately nicknamed him "The Enforcer."

"One time he asked to see my fishing permit twice in the same day, on the same stretch of river," Levi said. "We will meet him."

Morning was perfect: bright skies and crystalline cold. Gun? Check. Bullets? Check. Extra set of long underpants? Check. Check, check, check. Check to make sure your headlamp is working and your binoculars are clean and the blaze-orange vest and hat are tucked securely in the duffel. Check to make sure you have enough contact lens solution. Because there were no convenience stores or handy supply depots where we were going.

I looked out the window of Smith Fork's horse trailer as it rolled down the dirt road toward the trailhead, kicking up clouds of dust. As we approached the gateway to the higher elevations, the players began to emerge. There was a battalion of trucks and a circus of ATVs, men in camo-and-orange-bedecked everything, tents with chimneys in them, women organizing provisions and tending fires and shaking out tarps. There were Winnebagos and dogs and mules, and horses being coaxed out of trailers. The whole place thrummed with the energy of a major sporting event. This was big, I thought to myself, watching the scene. This wasn't just fun in the woods or a way to obtain meat. This was something more.

Levi and Chuck ran their operation like a Swiss train, unloading four horses and five mules and then loading them up with boxes, duffels, packs, panniers, canteens, and coolers. As they saddled the animals they cracked jokes about nearby hunters whose horses were strewn with stuff, packs slipping off their tail ends. One horse had a pair of tennis shoes slung over its neck.

It was past noon by the time our convoy hit the trail, the Smith Fork River running alongside us. Levi, Chuck, and I were accompanied by the ranch chef, Nick, an artfully tattooed guy in his mid-20s. I was riding Ute, a smallish gelding with a scraggle of a mane. Ute did not have a winning personality. He was known for being off by himself in the barnyard, staring fixedly at one particular wall. As I had climbed into the saddle, he'd bowed his head low with resignation but at the same time pulled his ears back, foreshadowing trouble. It was clear from the start that Ute had the lightest load and the worst attitude.

All around us humans and horses picked their way across scree fields and catwalks, up to the high country. We wound our way up and up and up; thin white stands of aspens towered above us as though we were riding through a box of drinking straws. Along the way we encountered every kind of terrain imaginable: black, sucking mud, rivers of loose rock, logs and grass and heavy dirt, progressing to snow and ice. Throughout all of it Ute registered a lack of enthusiasm. His tactics swung between stopping cold for no reason, and speeding up to jam his head into the butt of the mule in front of him. The mule responded by issuing a staccato stream of farts.

As the hours went by—four and then five—the crowds thinned and we found ourselves alone. "Most people don't come up this high because of the work involved," Levi explained. The moment he said it, however, a large black horse ridden by a large bespectacled man appeared on the switchback above us. Both horse and rider had a purposeful air. Chuck steered our group to the side of the trail. Levi, riding behind me, said, "Get your permit out." We were being pulled over, in the unlikeliest of places, by the Enforcer.

In a beautiful way this was predictable. Above all, a lone guy patrolling a vast swath of mountainous terrain has to be crafty. He can't survey the entire area; he can only hope to be a threat and to catch the most egregious behavior. Offenses involved people affixing their tags to other people's animals, haplessly shooting a cow instead of a bull, or mistaking a spike yearling for a legal 4-pointer. Recently, someone claiming deeper confusion had even plugged a reintroduced moose.

The Enforcer, whose real name is Doug Homan, has been patrolling the region for nearly a quarter century and knows the land accordingly. Chuck greeted him and introduced me as a *Field & Stream* writer, whereupon he immediately asked to check my paperwork. As he unfolded the tag to check for t's properly crossed, i's dotted, I mentioned that this was my first hunt, as though that wasn't completely obvious.

"So you'll write about how you were checked," he said, handing the tag and the safety card back to me. "You're hunting Curecanti? They took some bulls out of there first season." He smiled, and the sun glinted off his glasses. "But there's probably a few left."

The high camp stood tucked in a snowy slash of pine, three white canvas tents and a matching outhouse. Though I had been told to expect snow at this altitude, the sight of the drift-covered tents was disconcerting. My legs shook from the long ride and Ute's shenanigans, but there was no time to think about it because less than an hour of daylight remained to scout our surroundings. A sharp bluff rose behind the tents, one that I hoped we wouldn't have to climb. Levi immediately charged up it. I followed; 10,000 feet and I could feel every one of them. At the top, the canyon rolled westward in the rich light, and on the far horizon we could see the mysterious edges of the Black Canyon of the Gunnison, America's deepest gorge.

Our vantage point was a small promontory from which you could look down on all of it, into the folds of mountains and hillsides and drainage cuts. Directly below us several game trails merged—a three-way elk intersection. "They'll run by here if they're driven higher by hunters below us," Levi said. It was a beautiful setup, made more so by the fact that less than 600 yards away three groups of elk stood foraging on the top of a rise, looking as peaceful as an Audubon painting. In the foreground, a 6-point bull grazed in profile. He was bigger than I'd expected, more Clydesdale than pony, and his pale buff coloring gave him an almost ghostly appearance. I kept my binoculars trained on him for every last drop of daylight, as the shadows dissolved and the coyote echoes began.

There is no sleeping in on an elk hunt, especially not on opening day. The wakeup call comes mercilessly in the frosty predawn, and when Levi rattled the side of my tent, it sounded like gunshots. All over the mountain, come sunrise, the game was on. Chuck was uncharacteristically silent during breakfast, eating his eggs and staring at the wall of the mess tent. Afterward, Levi and I headed to our promontory. "What's up with Chuck?" I asked.

"He's on a mission."

"What's that?"

"To find the horses."

I stared at him. During the night, apparently, the entire four-legged crew had made a break for it, one trampling down the fence, the others following. This wasn't good, nine elk-size animals running around the mountain on opening day without so much as an orange bandanna between them, and I instantly envisioned Ute as the ringleader.

"Will we get them back?" I asked.

"I think it's kind of an all-or-nothing deal."

Dawn was in full swing by the time Levi and I reached our spot, so there was enough light to see the spooked herd of elk cantering below us, white rumps flashing through the pines as they charged up a 45-degree pitch. Levi whipped out his binoculars, but in a second the animals were gone.

"Hmm, I don't think there were any bulls in that group." Looking in the direction of the vanished herd, he added, "Those elk were definitely spooked by something."

BOOM! The gunshot came from a ridge to our right. Silhouetted against the sky, a tiny orange-clad figure raised his rifle. BOOM! BOOM! BOOM! BOOM! Levi and I looked at each other. Someone was a very bad shot.

We hunkered down behind a pair of aspens, and I settled onto the frozen ground with the Dakota braced against my knee. We sat in that crusty patch of snow, sat and waited, sat and then sat some more, glassing the valley. Nothing seemed to be stirring, not birds or bugs or mice or any signs of life at all. By now the fleeing herd would be three valleys away and counting. Was that it? I wondered. Were they already gone, scared out of the canyon? It felt intensely frustrating; all we could do was sit and wait and hope that some hapless elk in this 176,000-acre wilderness blundered into our 300-yard shooting zone.

Before arriving here I'd read that the odds of success on a first elk hunt were approximately 16 percent. The statistic had seemed unduly pessimistic to me, especially since I'd been here less than 48 hours and had already seen a dozen of the animals. But when the bell went off and hunting season legally began, the woods seemed to have emptied out. Suddenly, it was easy to imagine an entire week going by without seeing so much as a single set of antlers.

"This seems heavily stacked in favor of the elk," I whispered to Levi.

"I was just thinking that."

Hours went by, body parts began to mutiny. By 11:30 my hands had become so cold that I couldn't hold my gun, let alone aim and shoot it, so we climbed back to camp for lunch.

The rest of the day was spent sitting on a damp log in a mossy grotto that lacked even a sliver of sunlight to warm things up. The light was muted, almost spooky, with pale shafts falling between dark spruce trunks. Three mule deer slipped through the shadows, giant ears swiveling around like satellite dishes before they pogoed into the gloom. So this was hunting. I'd learned to shoot but I hadn't learned about this, about the solitude and the sheer numbness of waiting, about the fast wash of adrenaline when any twitch of activity broke the stillness. It seemed to me now that the most familiar images of hunting—the gunshot, its aftermath—are the least representative. Hunting was a far more nuanced experience. It was about letting your rusty animal senses out for a romp. And even if that involved eight hours of sitting motionless in a bush, it was still the most seductive reminder that at the end of the day, we are unrepentant carnivores.

At the high camp, dinner was epic. Up here, the body's caloric requirements resemble those of a blast furnace, and so the evenings were devoted to chow; to working our way through a case of wine and kicking back, listening to one another's tales. I loved ducking into the mess tent at the end of the day, into its steamy halo of propane while Nick leaned over the stove, working his magic. After a single dinner I got it: Camp life is an integral part of hunting, perhaps the very crux of the sport. It's the bourbon late at night and the fact that anything tastes memorable when cooked on a smoky single-burner and earned by a day in the mountains. It's the stories and the kinship and the improbable shelter in nature's wilder spots, the juxtaposition of privation and privilege, each setting the other into high relief.

Chuck had returned with the AWOL animals in tow, and now they were grazing in the reinforced corral. After hearing a summary of the day's hunting from Levi, he seemed satisfied. "Aside from an utter lack of equine control, things are going pretty well," he said.

This wasn't always the case. Things could go very wrong up here, and did. There had been instances of less-than-stellar comportment under pressure: clients taking wild-eyed 1,000-yard shots, for instance, or chattering incessantly in the field. Chuck recalled one young man who'd managed to alienate the entire camp in short order: "There wasn't anything to him. It was just wind." Retribution, he said, came one night as the hunters rode in the dark, while the Chatterbox held forth, barely stopping for breath. "The guide pulled back a spruce branch and let it fly into his face." On occasion, people hiked with chambered rounds, or got drunk and picked fights. And then there was the time the liquor had mysteriously vanished. Someone had been filching both the clients' Scotch and the guides' beer, and after much dark suspicion in camp as to whom that might be, it was discovered that the cook spent her days nipping away at the supplies. "A very unpleasant woman," Chuck said. "Of course we weren't really in a position to fire her." He stood up and plucked a bug off the tent wall with a pair of needlenose pliers. "But we did find a better place to hide it."

Turning the subject to tomorrow's plans, he mentioned that while he was out capturing the horses, he'd stopped at a nearby deer camp and heard talk of a pair of big bulls that had been spotted in an area known as Lunch Creek. This was a bonanza of a tip, but daunting: meeting these animals on their home turf meant venturing into a steep cut that was one of the least welcoming spots in the canyon.

Hearing this, Levi nodded. "Wherever it takes the most energy to get to, the hardest possible place—that's where we'll find them."

Chuck leaned back in his chair. "There are a lot of hunters lingering around the edge of the drainage, but you two need to go right down into it." Noticing the pained look on my face he raised an eyebrow. "Elk are earned," he said.

Forging into Lunch Creek was easier said than done. As Levi and I moved closer to the bottom of the drainage, the hillside became steeper and the brush became a wall and any sort of viable passage became nonexistent. There was no getting down there. And furthermore, there was no way to get a 700-pound animal back out. "No wonder those bulls are big," Levi said, looking over a cliff at the jagged rocks below.

After scouting the neighboring surroundings we decided to head back to the promontory. We weren't the only ones who'd been there lately: all around our observation post the grass was tamped into elk-shaped depressions, and we stepped around mounds of fresh scat piled defiantly beside them. Levi examined several sets of hoofprints crisscrossing in the mud. "These were made sometime in the last hour," he said, shaking his head.

Though I'd expected a clever adversary, I was beginning to realize that an elk at the top of its game was nothing short of a phantom. Levi understood this; he had recently bagged his first bull. Though the elk had been taken on Saddle Mountain, only 3 miles from the ranch, the effort that had gone into the hunt had been anything but small.

"I scoped him out for a month," he said, describing how every morning he had observed the animal's habits through a telescope. "Then, one week before hunting season, I went up there and cut a trail." Saddle Mountain was avoided by hunters and favored by elk due to a head-high carpet of brush. Levi, who was willing to make a Herculean effort, bushwhacked his way to the money spot and waited. Sure enough, the bull returned and was promptly dropped with a double lung shot.

The elk had been traveling with half a dozen cows, and the animals ran in panicked circles as it lay on the ground. As he approached the downed bull, Levi noticed that one cow in particular just stood there and bawled. The memory of the distraught cow seemed to bother him. "I wasn't that excited," he said, frowning. "When I saw how big it was, I just wondered how the hell I was going to get it down."

He'd radioed Chuck, who came up with his sister, and the three of them field dressed and quartered the elk using a pair of axes. Then, they packed it out. The entire process took almost 12 hours from the time Levi had pulled the trigger.

But after that, all winter, mealtimes were a jubilee of elk. In the nearby town of Hotchkiss, a venison processor called Homestead Market rented out meat lockers. Levi got himself one and filled it. There were elk steaks and elk burgers and elk jerky, elk fajitas, elk tacos, elk in scrambled eggs, and elk meatballs sprinkled into spaghetti sauce. There was a bonanza of meat.

Elk hunting can be described in two simple words: up, down. When you aren't climbing, you're descending. When you're not standing up, hauling your gear, you're sitting down, looking up the mountain, down the valley, scanning the landscape for hints of motion. There are days when luck swoops down on you and days—weeks—of throwing up your hands in frustration. There is no comfort zone on an elk hunt, no middle ground, only extremes.

Levi and I began to frequent a small thicket below the promontory. This lookout held even more promise, he felt, because it offered a view of three hillsides within 300 yards. Should an elk appear on any of them, I'd have a shot. There was only one problem with the spot: to get there we had to make our way down a mile-long, 50-degree pitch of snow and ice, usually in the dark. It was a slow, arduous descent followed by a slow, painful climb out, but after one morning in this new location we'd seen several cows and come face-to-face with a massive mule deer buck that strolled within 10 yards of us before catching our scent and rocketing off.

The object of the hunt, however, remained elusive. In the last light of the third day, I watched a camprobber jay swan-diving from the top of a spruce tree while Levi dozed. I couldn't blame him. We'd whiffed entirely—again. But in the next instant, Levi suddenly snatched up his binoculars and tapped me frantically on the knee. "Look," he whispered, nodding at the easterly slope. I looked and saw nothing but a smattering of aspens. "Where? What?"

"A whole herd!"

And so there was. Four hundred yards away, the exact dun color of the hillside around them, eight elk grazed in the dusk.

All cows.

"There's got to be a bull with them somewhere," Levi said quietly, binoculars glued to his face. "Get ready to shoot."

The cows had no inkling of us and continued to forage, ambling closer and settling 300 yards away. Two spikes appeared in the mix, illegal yearlings with nubbin antlers. For 20 minutes I sighted them like arcade targets, practicing my aim. Where was the bull? Levi and I watched the sorority herd in frustration, until the curtain went down and their silhouettes melted into the hillside.

Waiting another 10 minutes to avoid spooking the group, we shouldered our packs and began the climb home. We didn't talk. The truth was harsh—we'd seen giant bucks and what seemed like every cow in Curecanti, while the deer hunters had numerous encounters with elk and the cow-tag holders sighed at the appearance of yet another pair of antlers. I was thinking about these ironies and listening to the sound of my boots punching through the snow when we heard it: a long and mournful bugle, echoing down from the ridgeline. We stopped and looked up. I'd been told that the noise that bulls make to call their cows was unique and that it made the hairs on the back of your neck stand at attention. No one, however, had been able to describe it to me, and now I understood why.

That night the temperature swooned and when I poked my face out of the sleeping bag at 4:30 a.m., the cold jolted me awake. A scrim of clouds blocked the quarter moon, and as I stepped outside all I could see was a salting of stars and a fresh dusting of snow. Levi was raring to go. "I want to get down there earlier," he said. "If possible, don't use your headlamp." I felt skeptical about this advice—it was one thing to navigate the icy elevator shaft with a bit of light, and another to climb down blind. "We'll just go very, very slowly," he said, but then took off at a fast clip, leaving me trudging behind.

At the top of the steepest pitch, I got scared and clicked on my headlamp, reasoning that I didn't want an elk badly enough to end up in a body cast, and when I caught up to Levi at the lookout, the dawn was coming. The sitting commenced. Levi clenched and unclenched his hands to stay warm, hawk eyes roaming the hillside. As the pale light bled skyward, the canyon awoke and was silent. Nothing moved through the naked stands of aspen. All morning we sat and watched the stillness, but the herd did not return. At 11:30, we called it.

The climb out of the canyon had become familiar now, a kind of dastardly commute that we loved to hate. Ahead of me, Levi dug into the snow staircase we'd gouged in the ravine. At the top he stopped abruptly and crouched to stare at something on the ground. Standing up, he exhaled sharply. "Look," he said.

I looked. Two sets of footprints stood out in the new snow—Levi's boots in front, followed by mine. But there was a third set too, pressed atop ours, dirt still in the tracks: four-pronged paw prints the size of coffee saucers. You didn't have to grow up tracking in the Kalahari to figure out what had gone on here.

Mountain lion paws trailed down the slope, through the untouched powder, taking a hard right at our trail and tracing my footsteps. Over the course of 30 yards, as the cat had crept behind me in the dark, the space between its tracks had tightened—in the way that house cats tend to shorten their strides right before they launch themselves at something. But then, at the spot where I'd stopped to turn on my headlamp, the tracks veered sideways, bounding across the facing snowbank and back into the forest.

Levi and I stood mute, our breath visible in small clouds. This makes sense, I thought, as a chill ran down my spine. I'd been slow and isolated this morning—perfect prey. Hunter, hunting, hunted: They all blurred together in a disconcerting way. Here I was, in full stalking mode, backed (supposedly) by millennia of innate animal instincts, and I'd had no sense of a 200-pound predator padding along only feet behind me. A few hours later, after the evidence had time to sink in, Levi would mention that turning on my headlamp had probably saved my life.

It seemed like a godsend, then, when Chuck announced that the last two days of the hunt would take place in the lower foothills surrounding the ranch, and that we would strike the High Camp immediately and head down. According to Chuck's wife, Kerry, Smith Fork's manager, hefty bulls had been sighted through the telescope every day this week. I packed enthusiastically.

And so, shortly, Levi and I found ourselves shoving our way up his old trail on Saddle Mountain. Though the foliage was almost impenetrable, down here the air was warm and the long underwear had been left behind. We settled in behind a scribble of chaparral and waited.

Almost immediately, 600 yards away, a large bull strolled out of a spruce glade. After days of bull-lessness, he looked almost mythical, this lone white animal standing in relief against the trees. He never came closer, and eventually vanished into the forest. I resolved to kill him the next day.

The heat beat down on Levi and me the next morning as we picked our way up Saddle Mountain once again, past bear and bobcat and deer tracks stamped in the mud. A trickle of sweat rolled down my leg; flies buzzed. Sharp brush lined the route at eye level. We reached the clearing below the spruce glade. There was nothing in the vicinity but more silence.

"Let's head around the other side," Levi said, after a time. We slipped our way up a muddy half-path, edging along the hillside, and it was here that we found them. A spindly-legged spike was mowing the grass less than 150 yards away, with a large cow beside him. Levi elbowed me, and we pressed ourselves against a rock. We were partly visible but downwind, and the animals didn't scent us. Slowly, I moved the rifle into position.

We didn't have to wait long. Three hundred yards away, visible through the trees, stood the bull we had been looking for. As he ripped up mouthfuls of sawgrass, everything seemed to move in slow motion. Levi spoke in a raspy whisper: "This is it. Wait until he moves out of the trees and then take him."

It was a clean shot, and just within range.

The bull came out of the trees and posed in perfect mug-shot profile. I steadied the Dakota on a crossed pair of hiking poles that Levi had brought, and for once my hands were not shaking. Everything felt calm. The air felt calm, I felt calm, the elk grazed calmly.

I put my eye to the scope and inhaled. At 4X magnification I could make out details—the bull was midsize and textbook perfect, with 12 lovely points on his antlers. I clicked the safety off. The spike, now less than 150 yards away from us, moved toward the line of fire.

It would take only an instant to squeeze the trigger. Then: a violent explosion, and we would assess the shot. The bull would be down or he would be running; the bullet would have done its mortal damage or it would have wounded him, and the tracking would begin. I would have set the process of killing in motion, and then I would have to finish it off. This is what I came here to do.

This is what I came here to do.

The bull raised his head and looked around. I imagined the impact of the bullet; the animal's body crumpling. Next to me, Levi tensed.

Another breath, another exhalation. Another minute adjustment to the scope magnification. The shot was there. But something wasn't right. Somewhere between my head, my heart, and my trigger finger, there was a blockage.

I lowered the gun.

Levi looked confused. "He's going to move farther out of the trees," he whispered. "He's moving."

Above us the sky was a seamless expanse of blue. For a week I had been searching and hoping for this shot, this animal, this moment. For months I had practiced so when it arrived, I wouldn't blow it. For years I had wondered what it would feel like to hunt. And here at the edge of the experience, I had lost my nerve. How had this happened? It was like climbing to the top of a diving platform and then slinking back down without even trying to jump. In the end, Dave Petzal had been wrong about one thing. I was not 105 pounds of inert matter. I was 105 pounds of warring emotions. This wasn't how I thought it would be.

I turned to Levi, and now I was shaking. "It's over."

"You're going to get a better shot," he said, his voice tight with adrenaline. But even as he said it, the bull turned uphill, dropped over the horizon, and vanished into the next valley.

"No, I'm done."

A gust of wind blew down the gulley, folding back the grass. The cow and the spike had turned away from us and were headed for the trees. Levi and I watched them go.

After a moment, he reached for the radio and hailed the ranch. Kerry answered.

"The hunt is over," Levi told her.

"We've been watching through the scope," she said. "We saw you; we saw the bull. But—did you take a shot?"

"Uh, negative," Levi said. There was a long silence on the other end. Chuck came on.

"Listen," he said as the radio crackled. "You did everything right. You were exactly where you were supposed to be."

"But I didn't shoot," I said.

"I know. But you had a hell of a hunt, and that's what matters."

I glanced at Levi, who looked dejected and a bit stunned and as though he didn't quite see the cause for celebration in this whole scene.

"I'm sorry," I said.

TRAILING
A DREAM

NATE MATTHEWS

Gasping, rifles across our backs, we scrambled up the hill with our hands in the dirt. I looked up into the sun, to where the blood trail crossed the ridge, and tried to blink the sting from my eyes. Sweat dripped off my forearms. We were moving fast. When you wound a kudu you must catch up to him quickly or he will vanish into the bush, and you will never see him again.

I was hunting in South Africa, on the East Cape, on a 10-day safari, with 10 animals to hunt. I had tags for warthog, wildebeest, bushbok, gemsbok, impala, duiker, two species of springbok, and blesbok. But the animal I had always dreamed about hunting was the last on the list: the kudu. Now I'd put a 180-grain bullet in one's chest, and I knew that if I didn't hustle I would never get a chance at another. In Africa you must pay for everything that bleeds when you shoot it, whether you find it dead or not. But money was not my concern.

On the slope above me, professional hunter Alan Shenck paused long enough to whisper, "Hurry up, I think you've hit him low." He pointed at some spatter on the rocks. Behind us our skinner, M'stele, held the leads restraining Shenck's two Jack Russell terriers, Muzzy and Fletch. Their panting matched my own.

We had spotted the bull an hour earlier; it had been standing on a ridge across the ravine from our setup on a cliff covered in baboon dung. We'd been glassing since sunrise.

Glassing for kudu requires great focus. You must memorize the shapes and shadows of bushes. Anthills will fool you. Stumps will make your heart jump. Your brain will tire and you'll lose patience, and then the animal will move and you will miss it. Missing movement is bad, because kudu do not move very often.

One way to maintain your concentration is to look for other wildlife, and when I saw this bull I'd been watching a shrike on an acacia. The kudu was behind the bush, and I saw him when his mane caught the light.

He was standing with a group of cows. The sun was rising over our shoulders, lighting his side of the ravine and leaving ours in shadow. To reach the bull we'd need to work down the cliff, through the brush at the bottom, across a dry gully, then up the other side to a small clearing from which Shenck thought we might get a shot.

Our first worry was that something would see us moving. There are many eyes on you in Africa. This includes baboons, which will bark like dogs when they startle. Then there are the ostriches, which peer at you over the brush like 7-foot turkeys. If one sees you, it will start running and spook every animal nearby.

When we reached the gully at the bottom of the valley, we took off our shoes so we could walk silently. M'stele stayed behind with the dogs while Shenck and I hiked toward a line of shrubs that ran up the ridge. Shenck figured the brush would conceal us as we moved within range of the kudu.

The bottom was dry sand, covered in loose rock and strewn with bones and branches. Roots punched out of the banks to twist in the shadows, and the brush overhead nearly closed out the sky. We stepped softly, hunched at the waist, Shenck in front. I focused on placing my feet in the same places he put his, and when he stopped suddenly I nearly knocked him over.

"Adder," he whispered, pointing.

Puff adders are the most dangerous snakes in Africa; they kill more people than any other serpent on the continent. Normally, a PH will kill any adder he sees, but we wanted to stay quiet, so we nudged this one with a stick from where it lay coiled in our path. It hissed, slithered into a tangle, then stopped there to glare at us. Shenck looked at my feet, looked at the snake, then looked back at me and raised an eyebrow. I shrugged; we kept moving. As we climbed out of the gully I tried to forget that I was walking in my socks.

We spent the rest of the stalk crawling on our bellies from bush to bush, closing to within range. The bull was still there, but he had moved into the open. It took half an hour to get into position. By the time I put a scope on him I had stickers in my elbows, thorns in my hips, scratches on my hands, and sore feet from stepping on rocks—none of which mattered when I finally saw his horns.

Kudu bulls are magnificent creatures with striped gray flanks, long necks, and full, regal beards. They move with an awkward elegance, like angels confined in the forms of goats. Their horns will make your hands shake.

This one was about 200 yards away, a long shot for a boy from the shotgun woods of upstate New York. But I was confident in my rifle, a .30/06, and had trained with it before leaving. I placed the crosshairs on his shoulder, let out my breath, and squeezed the trigger.

Through the scope I saw him buck. He kicked at his shoulder with a hind leg, dropped into a crouch, then vanished. Cow kudu flushed from the bushes. Shenck clapped me on the back. "Good shot!" he said. "You got him. You hit him good." He turned and whistled for M'stele, who arrived with our shoes and the dogs.

I was tying my laces when I caught movement out of the corner of my eye. I looked up to see the bull slip from cover and go limping over the ridge. My heart sank. Shenck swore. I grabbed my gun, M'stele grabbed the dogs, and we set off after him.

On the trail when we reached the top of the slope, all we could find were specks of blood. Shenck loosed Muzzy and Fletch, who bolted off toward the bottom of the next valley.

PHs like Jack Russells for three reasons. One is that the dogs move quickly through thick brush. Another is that if they find your kudu dead, they're not big enough to do much damage to its cape. The last is that if a bull runs after you hit it, a terrier does not look frightening enough to make it run faster.

The dogs reached the bull in a clearing 300 yards below us, down in the bottom. He wheeled to face them when they burst from the bushes. Blood was streaming from a hole low in his shoulder.

Fletch reached the bull first and began darting at his hooves, barking and dancing out of reach whenever the kudu made a move. Muzzy, the younger dog, took one look and retreated up the hill.

If a peaceful kudu is magnificent, a furious one is terrifying, rearing up, tucking his chin to his chest, then slamming his horns at whatever is irritating him.

"Shoot him!" Shenck said. "He's right on the dog!"

It is easier to be accurate when you don't have time to think; reflexes take over. I sat back on my right heel and put my left elbow forward so my tricep rested on my kneecap. Cheek down. Eyes open. Breathe out. Do not hesitate. I aimed at the top of his back and fired.

The kudu bucked and dove into the thicket. Fletch followed. When we reached the clearing we could see new blood in the grass, and I knew we would find him.

He had piled up deep in the thorns, the finger-long kind, as if to make even our last job difficult. We had to crawl to reach him. I did not know something so large could fit through brush so thick.

We gutted him there, then spent five hours winching him out of the thicket. My first shot had hit him where the heart would have been on a deer, which is too far back and too low on an African antelope. The second had quartered through his lungs and punched out his neck.

The stars were out by the time we reached the truck. Jackals were howling as I looked up and gazed at Orion. I looked down at my feet, at the beast I had killed, and thought that a kudu is not much like a whitetail.

THE
TOTEM BEAR

ANTHONY LICATA

The concept of an animal that is somehow uniquely connected to an individual hunter means different things to different folks. It might be a critter that brings you luck when you see it in the field. Or one whose grace, stamina, and cunning you admire. A totem animal might manifest itself in a single-minded devotion that creeps into your larger life—a big collection of canvasback paintings in your den, say, or a garage that can't hold a car because of all the whitetail antlers lying on the floor.

You might be obsessed with hunting your totem. Conversely, you might make a conscious decision not to hunt this animal. Or, as in my case, having a totem might entail a bit of both perspectives.

Hunting bears may be one of my favorite things, but like going to the circus or eating foie gras, it's not something I want to do often. Its very specialness demands moderation.

It also demands its own set of rules. Many people hunt bears over bait, and I'm not going to tell them that's the wrong way to do things. But it's the wrong way for me to do it. When I kill a bear, I want to spot it at a distance and then stalk close, and when it comes time to make the shot, I want to do it with a bow.

All of this sounds good in theory, but the hunting gods can laugh at this kind of high-minded stuff. I am superstitious and firmly believe that the right attitude brings good hunting, until you get too snooty or cocky about it and then all of a sudden it doesn't. I found myself in this territory on my last bear hunt, a fact I should've recognized as soon as my bow case came off the plane with a hole like a rifle shot punched through its gut. Next, I got to camp and promptly watched three consecutive arrows fly over, around, and below the target. By the time I figured out that the bow's cable guard had been snapped by the airline baggage goons, I had lost most of my arrows in the bush and my confidence was shattered as badly as the case. One hour into my hunt, my bow was unusable and the entire premise of my trip was blown.

Just because you plan for a totem animal doesn't mean everything goes according to plan.

My friend David Draper, communications specialist for Cabela's, and I had come to the rugged country around Prince George, British Columbia, because it's an ideal place to try and sneak into bow range of a lot of big black bears. It's an endless expanse of wild but actively logged forest with a few settlements scattered around the bush. The forests are a rolling patchwork of timber in different stages of growth. The clear-cuts and young regenerating stands are full of the green grasses and clovers that bears love to eat at this time of year. The massive blocks of dark, mature timber provide them with cover and other types of food. It's tough to think of habitat better suited to produce plenty of bears.

The way you hunt is to drive logging roads, or walk them when they're closed to traffic, and look for bears feeding in the openings. Once you spot one, it's a matter of working the wind, hiding, and creeping close enough for a shot. If it doesn't work out—and most likely it won't—no worries. There are so many bears that chances are you'll get to try another stalk before the day is out.

We were hunting with Opatcho Lake Outfitters, run by Ken and Crystal Watson. Have you ever heard the theory that some obsessed dog owners begin to resemble the breeds they own? Well, Ken Watson is proof of my theory that a guide can end up resembling his prey. Watson stands at least 6-foot-5 and is built, well, like a bear. Having spent several days following his wide back up and down the hills, I swear that the best word to describe his slow, rambling gait is ursine.

He might have seemed intimidating were it not for the fact that during our hunt, if he wasn't laughing, he was smiling. Ken and Crystal run an outfit that offers very serious hunting but in a way that is seriously fun. By the second day I felt as though I was hanging out with friends, not guides.

Crystal brought a welcome woman's touch to the place. She picked me up at the airport in a diesel VW Bug she got for the good gas mileage but also because "It looks pretty kewl!" Since the Watsons bought the camp four years ago (Ken was head guide there for 20 years before that), they've been tearing down the serviceable old cabins and replacing them with beautiful modern ones.

"I told Ken I want each cabin to be spiderproof so my sister and I can stay," Crystal said. Draper and I didn't see any spiders. The walls of our cabin and the main lodge certainly showed her influence too. Along with hanging trappers' pelts of bears and wolves were decorative signs that said things like Live Well, Love Often, Laugh Much. I had to laugh when I stepped into the outhouse and found it tastefully decorated in country-cottage style, complete with a bowl of colored potpourri sitting on the wide bench.

In another camp, I probably would not have survived my equipment meltdown, but it was hard to get too worked up here. Ken shrugged, smiled, and said in his laid-back Canadian lilt, "Oh well, man. You can just use my rifle and still get as close as you want. It works at 40 yards just as good as it works at 100, eh?" It was hard to argue with that. I'd be using a .300 Win. Mag., not a bow, but I'd still try to get as close as I could.

A big bear was feeding on dandelions along a logging road about 100 yards in front of us. Draper, bow in hand, took the lead, with Ken and me following behind. The wind was in our faces, and the bear had no idea we were there. Game on.

As we worked our way closer, the bear stepped behind a grassy hump. In about 30 steps, Draper would peek above the rise and be about 4 feet from the bear. I wasn't even sure he'd have to aim, but drawing a bow within literal spitting distance of a 350-pound predator should give you something to think about.

Black bears usually aren't looking for a fight, but there is no doubt: The rush that comes from creeping close to a beast that can rip you to shreds is one of the main things that make this hunt so special.

Watson gets the occasional client who views this not as some exciting yet respectful hunting experience, but as some kind of embarrassing test of manhood. These guys are never real hunters, usually just pompous fools with big bank accounts and bigger egos. And most of them are scared to death of bears. Watson told me he's had more than a few who would leave the truck only with a loaded rifle in hand. One such character from Spain really made an impression. He was petrified of bears, and Watson finally had to have it out with the guy after he started finding piles of feces, with toilet paper, on the camp lawn.

"He was afraid to go to the outhouse in the dark, man!" Ken recalled, still not quite able to believe it. "At night he'd walk 10 feet from the cabin and dump! He thought a bear was going to maul him on the way to the crapper."

Draper didn't hesitate to get right up on his quarry, but when he stepped over the rise ready to take the shot, the bear was gone. He had heard or smelled us on the final steps of the stalk and darted into the bush.

Seeing no bears where you expect them and seeing them when you don't was to be the theme of this hunt.

We spent our days driving and hiking logging roads, looking for bears feeding on the clover, and we saw a lot of them. We saw them at a distance, as black spots in openings far away. We came upon them suddenly, coming around the corner of a logging road only to have the bear at 60 yards see us and take off into the bush.

The biggest trick was that so many places looked and in fact were ideal for feeding bears, and there were so many bears, you tended to spend the entire hunt on edge, expecting at any moment to face one. After not finding a bear in a series of likely spots, your focus would flag and that's when one would appear. It was nerve-wracking.

One particular place we came across was typical. It was a perfect bear stalking spot, an abandoned logging road that circled up to a flat of a cut about 10 years old. All along the road were big black piles of fresh bear scat and tracks as big as pie plates. Working into the wind, we crept along the road until we came to a place that made my hair stand on end in anticipation. The regrowing trees were about head high, and the openings between them were full of thick, lush clover. You could see where the grass had been cropped close by feeding bears, and it was a challenge to walk through the area without stepping in fresh bear scat. Visibility was about 30 yards, and we'd slowly step, pause, look, look some more, and then step again, expecting to see a bear appear from behind a tree 10 yards away at any second. It took about an hour to cover the ridge completely—an hour when senses were heightened, time was suspended, and your nerves were on edge. At the end of the stalk we felt wrung out and exhausted, even though the walking was easy. That is the mark of a totem animal.

There was so much fresh sign around that for three days we refused to believe this cut wasn't where we were going to kill a bear. We must have worked it over half a dozen times before we finally realized we were surely burning it. In the end, although it was the locale of some of our most exciting stalks, we never saw a bear there.

After a couple of days, we'd seen about 15 bears and unsuccessfully stalked four. I thought we were doing pretty well, but Watson was not happy.

"We should be seeing more bears, man," he said. "I'm not sure what's going on, but we're going to a place that should be crawling with bears."

Ken's honey hole was a large farm that bordered the Fraser River and was surrounded by the bush. Bears would come out of the timber to feed just as in the clear-cuts, but here they were drawn to lush green alfalfa fields.

"We call the bears here Banguses, man," Watson said. "They're so big we think these farm bears are half bear, half Angus bull."

Draper and I hunted the farm a couple of times with both Ken and his guide Bill Dow. Dow, a firefighter, fit in perfectly with the camp vibe. He was tough as nails and a good hunter but with a laid-back, gentle demean-

or. Usually a moose guide, he had recently lost his wife to cancer, and Ken asked him to join our hunt to get him out of the house.

Going to the farm didn't seem to change our luck. Like everywhere else we'd been, it was covered in fresh bear sign. We kicked back and watched big alfalfa fields, waiting for the bears to show, but none did. We hiked the whole place, climbing ridges and looking into different fields and openings, but there were no Banguses.

But the tracks and scat made it hard to give up. On the second to last day of the hunt, Draper, Dow, and I headed back to the farm once more. We spent an hour or two watching a big, empty alfalfa field, then hiked a ridge into an opening that looked down into the next valley. We had covered this area three times already, and at first glance it appeared no different from the time before.

"There's a bear," Draper said flatly.

Coming out of the timber was a massive bear. Even at a distance of 700 yards, you could tell he was a brute. With his deep chest and the long grass, you couldn't really see him walking, and he looked like a massive black ship gliding across a sea of green.

"Big bear. Really, really big bear," Dow said.

The bear was sailing, and very quickly. If we wanted to catch up with him, we needed to do so quickly. Luckily we'd been over the ground enough that we knew exactly what to do.

We began running along a hedgerow parallel to the bear's course. Our only hope was to get to the end of the field first, and then drop down, using the terrain as cover to get close enough. I'd followed Draper on the last few stalks, so I was up.

We ran as hard as we could, reached the end of the field, wormed our way under a barbwire fence, and started down. Now we were ahead of the bear and could see him coming, but we still had to close about 600 yards between us. We ran in a crouch until the bear dropped below the curve of the field.

Halfway down, Dow locked up and pointed to the left. About 150 yards away was a sow with two cubs, staring at us. There wasn't much to do about that, so we kept on.

As we got close to the point of the hill, we slowed to a walk, got our breath back, and crept up, expecting to see the bear at any second. But as we moved forward, we could see the rest of the field, and the bear wasn't there. We stopped and glassed. The bear had beaten us to the timber.

We figured we'd work our way a little closer to the end of the point and have a seat. With any luck, the bear would come back out.

All of a sudden, Dow dropped to his knees, excitedly pointing. The field below was steeper than we'd thought, and hidden there, in the fold of the land, was the massive boar, feeding on the alfalfa. He was 60 yards away.

When I dropped to one knee, he was hidden again. I raised the rifle and shuffled forward. Inch by inch, the bear was revealed. His massive head was down and swinging back and forth, and I could hear him cropping the grass. He was directly facing me. His forelegs were huge and bowlegged as he moved closer to me and I inched closer to him.

When he was 40 yards away, he turned broadside and dropped at my shot.

In the end, I got a bear I would have been able to shoot with a bow, but as I lifted his massive head and felt the thick pelt, I couldn't have cared less what I was hunting with. And the next day, as Ken and I butchered him and packed the meat into a cooler for the trip to my freezer, I realized that no matter how you hunt for a totem, it's always special.

PERSISTENCE

DAVID E. PETZAL

Long, long ago I learned about the Code of the West, a hard and pitiless creed that governed the lives of cowboys, mountain men, trappers, and frontiersmen of all stripes. It stipulates among other things that you don't draw against a stranger, beat your horse excessively, or burst into tears and quit if things aren't going your way.

I subscribe wholeheartedly to the Code and got my chance to honor its precepts on an elk hunt that took place near Cody, Wyo., in the mid 1990s. Winchester sponsored the affair, transporting a gaggle of gun writers west to hunt antelope, mule deer, and elk. Of the dozen or so persons involved, however, I was one of only two to draw an elk tag, which placed a heavy obligation on me.

Having terminated the furtive existences of the mule deer and antelope, my guide and I traveled to either the Absaroka or the Big Horn Mountains (I can't remember which) to do the same to an elk. Said guide was a very young man named Steve Dube, son of a famous outfitter named Ron Dube. Steve was not only young; he was tough as a boiled owl.

My horse for the day was a chestnut gelding named Trooper, who distinguished himself that morning by farting nonstop most of the way up the mountain. It was a breathtaking exhibition of equine flatulence. The mountain itself was covered with loose volcanic rock of all sizes. This made for bad footing under normal circumstances, and on this day the ground was covered with snow, making things especially treacherous.

We were riding at the edge of a basin, and Steve warned me to kick my boots free of the stirrups, because if Trooper slipped, I was going to have to get clear of him fast. No sooner had I done this than Trooper's legs went out from under him. He flopped on his side, fighting to keep from taking the Big Slide, while I fought to keep clear of Trooper.

I was mostly successful, but at some point my face and one of his hooves tried to occupy the same space at the same time. My teeth were driven through my cheek under my lower lip, and I got the best bloody nose of my career. But I was lucky. I didn't have any teeth knocked out and my nose was unbroken, although it was pumping blood with great vigor.

Trooper and I stood up, and you could tell us apart because he had four legs and I had blood all over me. Now at this point you might expect Steve to say, "Are you all right?"

Instead, because he believed in the Code, he said: "You're gonna have to get back on him."

Because I subscribe to the Code, I said: "Don't worry, I'm not hiking up this goddamn mountain."

Trooper, perhaps out of sympathy, stopped farting.

And so up the mountain we rode.

When we got to the top, we found not even a trace of elk, and snow so deep and hard crusted that the horses simply quit on us—groaning and refusing to budge. So Steve and I dismounted and broke trail until we found a way down the mountain.

By the time we got back to the corral it was late afternoon. We unsaddled the horses, and the last time I saw Trooper he had his head shoved in the alfalfa, working up a fresh load of flatulence.

At this point we might have called it a day, but the Code of the West dictated otherwise, and Steve knew where there was a sagebrush flat where bull elk sometimes came out to view the sunset.

Off we went, by truck this time, and found the flat with perhaps five minutes of shooting time left. To get from the road to the flat, however, we would have to climb nearly straight up for 25 yards through a snowbank that was at least 5 feet deep. Steve volunteered to go first and take a look since I was older and busy leaking blood.

The snow was well above Steve's waist, but he made it, and then he leaned over the edge of the bank and looked down at me with an expression of pure joy. Come on, he semaphored, there's an elk out there.

Figuring this was as good a place as any to have a heart attack, I wallowed to the top through snow that seemed to come up under my chin, and there, far, far away under the failing light, was a bull elk.

I got in the prone position, held above the elk's back, and started shooting. The bull took a few tentative steps forward and collapsed. I used up 15 years' worth of hunting luck right then and there. Because the snow was so deep and we could not accurately count paces, there was no way to tell how far off he actually was—certainly over 400 yards. But in real-life elk hunting, if you get a chance you take it, because it's the only chance you're going to get.

Next day we went up and collected him. He was an average 5x5, but as the title of a story that ran in *Field & Stream* years ago said, "Any elk is a good elk."

Outside Cody, there is a reconstructed frontier town consisting of ancient shacks, shanties, and hovels scrounged from all over the state. In that town is the grave of Jonathan Johnson, the model for Jeremiah Johnson, and on his grave marker is the legend NO MORE TRAILS.

You and I will come to the place where there are no more trails, and before you do, I hope you have at least one hunt like this one, when everything looks hopeless and yet you succeed against the wildest odds. You can do it, even when it seems crazy to go on—provided you abide by the Code of the West.

JUST ONE MORE HUNT

PHILIP CAPUTO

When you've been glassing mountainsides for elk and there are none to be seen, your concentration falters and your mind wanders to places it shouldn't go, like, say, the suite you would like to share with a showgirl to find out if what happens in Vegas really does stay in Vegas. On this particular morning, however, my thoughts are as pure as the Rocky Mountain air as they follow a high literary trail to Joseph Conrad's "Youth," the tale of an old seaman, Marlow, reminiscing about his first voyage. I am musing on a passage in the story that goes like this: "And I remember my youth and the feeling that will never come back any more—the feeling that I could last for ever, outlast the sea, the earth, and all men . . . the heat of life in the handful of dust, the glow in the heart that with every year grows dim, grows cold, grows small, and expires—and expires, too soon—before life itself."

This is appropriate because my chances of spending a nanosecond in Las Vegas with a showgirl are less than my chances of becoming an Olympic pole vaulter; and after less than two days on foot and horseback, I fully empathize with that old sailor, yearning for "the feeling that will never come back any more."

Actually, what I yearn for is the absence of feeling, especially in my knees. Also, the arthritis in my left shoulder has flared, a saddle sore burns my rear end, and my feet throb. All this despite the fact that at my annual physical my doctor pronounced me quite fit for someone my age. That last phrase is key.

In my wallet is a kind of birthday card presented by the Social Security Administration three months ago when I reached a chronological milestone. The card has red, white, and blue stripes across the top, and in the white one are the words Medicare—Health Insurance. I may need it when I get out of here, here being Montana's Absaroka wilderness.

The night before I rode in (with five other hunters, a photographer, and three guides led by the outfitter, Duane Neal), I had dinner with writer Jim Harrison and his wife, Linda, at their house in the Paradise Valley. Their dining-room window framed the snow-rimmed Absarokas, which looked beautiful and formidable, prompting Jim to ask why, as a card-carrying geezer, I wanted to spend eight days in them looking for elk.

The obvious answer—because I wished to shoot one—wouldn't suffice. Although elk hunting is physically challenging under any circumstances, there are easier ways to go about it. I replied, "I seem to have a need to suffer," which might have been inculcated by my education in Roman Catholic schools, where I was taught that my sin-stained soul would be denied the joys of heaven if I failed to cleanse it through one form of self-flagellation or another. In other words, no pain, no gain.

This lesson was later reinforced by three years in the U.S. Marine Corps, an institution fully capable of transforming even a dedicated hedonist into a masochist.

I don't think Jim and Linda completely bought this argument, and upon reflection, I don't either. It has an element of truth but doesn't fully explain why a 65-year-old was going to subject himself to hardships that much younger men would find trying. There are other reasons, which I will get into in due course.

But suffering first. Elk hunting provides enough of it to gratify almost anyone with a martyr complex, but not as much as sheep hunting, which, if it weren't voluntary, would be classified as inhumane punishment. I had survived such a hunt in 2003 in Alaska's Brooks Range. Its rigors made me feel as if I had completed Navy SEALs boot camp. This achievement gave me a certain hubris. A wilderness elk hunt, I thought, would be a pleasant experience by comparison, a kind of trail ride with guns.

Our band of 11 men, six mules, and three packhorses left the Mill Creek trailhead on a cloudy September morning, bound for Duane Neal's Grizzly Creek camp, some 16 miles away, half of it uphill—very uphill, from roughly a mile in altitude to two. I was much encouraged to learn that I wasn't the only geriatric case in the crowd. Neal, who has operated Black Otter Guide Service for nearly 40 years, was 70; one of his guides, Dave Morton, was 66; and one of the hunters, John Nolander, was 64.

Perhaps an hour into the ride, we encountered a blowdown blocking the trail. We dismounted and took turns removing it with a double-bit axe and two-man saw. Farther up we hacked through another in the same way, then a third and a fourth. I can't speak for the others, but the chopping and sawing made me feel old-timey and rugged and ready for whatever the wilderness might dish out.

Snow is what it dished out, snow up to the horses' knees. The firs and lodgepole pines were flocked with the stuff, and clouds and mists veiled the rocky escarpments above. The trail grew steeper in a series of tight switchbacks, then leveled off and wrapped around the mountainside, the slope on our right falling a couple of hundred feet to the Mill Creek head-waters, the slope on the left almost sheer.

Approaching Wallace Pass, the trail became like a catwalk against the face of a tall building, and in this precarious position, the pack train stopped. I stood in the stirrups and was dismayed to see that the trail ahead had vanished under the snow. One of the guides, Gary Francis, was on foot, looking for it. He didn't appear to be having much success as he lunged through waist-deep drifts. Behind him, the mules and packhorses stood blowing steam. Without a trail to follow, the danger of a spectacular wreck had increased considerably; that is, if the lead mule took one wrong step and fell, he would pull the whole string down with him.

We shivered in our saddles. Neal passed the word to dismount and allow the horses to find their own way. That was when we knew we were, if not in trouble, then in an interesting situation. Getting off a horse on what amounted to the side of a cliff was a delicate operation. As I trudged behind mine, a pale gray gelding named Spirit, my sea-level lungs labored in the thin air, my heart thudded unnaturally fast, and my mind shot back to a story I'd heard about a 78-year-old man from Colorado who had accepted an invitation to go elk hunting despite his recent recovery from a triple bypass. When his wife objected, he replied, "I'd rather die on a snowy mountain than in a nursing home, watching TV, not knowing what's on."

Having undergone two cardiac operations in the previous year—a procedure to cure atrial fibrillation, then the insertion of a stent in a blocked coronary artery—I got to thinking about the septuagenarian's remark. I had come to terms with my mortality long ago in Vietnam, at an age when it is normal for you to think that you will never die. Now that I own far more shares of the past than I do of the future, my dread is not of nonexistence but the loss of physical and mental powers—the heat in the lump of dust that expires before life itself. No, I did not want to die on a snowy mountain, but given the choice between that and watching a TV in a nursing home not knowing what was on, there was no doubt which one I'd pick.

And therein I saw a better answer to Jim Harrison's question. I was on an elk hunt because I was capable of it, at the same time that I knew I might not be next year or the year after. I was greedy to do the kinds of things I love while I still could.

Wait, you say. Do you mean to say you love crawling up snow-filled mountains? Yes. Not for the sake of it, but for the rewards it brings. One of which was granted when, after some difficulty, we reached Wallace Pass. Below lay the Grizzly Creek and Knife Creek valleys, bounded by mountains that made a white-crested, jagged horizon, range upon range, some greened by dense pines, some blackened by the vast forest fires that had burned through the Absarokas only weeks earlier, but altogether a landscape that looked as wild and pristine as when the Crow and the Blackfeet and the mountain men had hunted and trapped there.

Some three hours later, we arrived at a broad meadow of copper-colored grass, through which Grizzly Creek meandered, cutthroat trout flashing in its pools. I was delighted to see smoke curling up from some hills overlooking the meadow. Camp consisted of several wall tents heated by woodburning stoves, a large mess tent, and a corral, where we were all glad to part with our horses, for the time being anyway.

We were served hot coffee by Terry and Elnora Neal, Duane's brother and sister-in-law, who do the cooking and manage the camp.

"Heard you had quite a time getting over the pass," Elnora said to me. "Duane said it was the worst crossing he's made coming in for nearly 40 years."

"Yup," drawled Duane, sitting nearby in the dining tent. "Hairiest I've ever seen it."

I was a little surprised to hear this. It hadn't seemed all that rough, but that, I now realized, had been due to my own ignorance of the situation. As the old saying goes, if you can keep your head while all those around you are losing theirs, you probably don't know what's going on.

After dinner, the hunters were assigned their guides. The two youngest, Rick and Tim, were given to Gary Francis, Duane's son-in-law (Black Otter Outfitters is very much a family enterprise). My tent mates, Bob and John, in their 40s, drew Delmer Cox, a well-traveled Canadian and licensed architect who, for reasons unknown, had become a hunting guide. Nolander and I, previously terrified that we would find ourselves trying to keep up with the comparatively youthful Cox or Francis, were pleased to be matched with our brother geezer, Dave Morton, a retired Forest Service ranger. Morton's head, innocent of hair except for a band of gray above his ears, and his—shall we say—less than killer abs were reassuring. We immediately dubbed ourselves "The Nursing Home Gang."

There are several disadvantages to camping out in the wilderness when you are of a certain age. Leaving a warm tent and sleeping bag to pee in the freezing dark in your socks and underwear is very disagreeable, but on my third trip outdoors since turning in, I tried to look on the bright side. The stars in those unsullied skies were as breathtaking as the 20-degree temperature. It was a view of the heavens that today's urbanites see only in photographs snapped by the Hubble Space Telescope.

In the light of the aforementioned stars, aided by flashlights and kerosene lamps, we mounted up at the old corral for the first day's hunt. Nolander, a retired air officer and now a defense contractor, works out regularly in a gym. Morton, of course, spends much of his time on horseback and hiking in the mountains, and I stay fit with a regimen of calisthenics, hiking, biking, riding, and kayaking. Nevertheless, each of us got into the saddle by slow, mechanical degrees, our movements reminiscent of the Tin Man in *The Wizard of Oz*.

The stars were out again when we returned after a perfectly fruitless day. We got out of our saddles even more slowly than we'd gotten into them and walked to the dining tent as if our legs were jointless blocks of wood. Elk hunting ain't for sissies. Neither is getting old.

There was some uneasiness around the campfire that night. No one had seen an elk nor sign of one; no one had heard a rutting bull's bugle.

Morton opined that wolves, reintroduced to the Yellowstone region in the 1990s, accounted for the scarcity. "Ten years ago, there were almost 20,000 animals in this herd. It's down to around 6,000 today."

Next morning we set off for the Red Rock plateau, some 6 or 7 miles away and 3,000 feet higher than the camp. Morning in the Rockies is a relative term; the high peaks retard the dawn by a good two hours, so we made half that ride in darkness, and the remainder in a prolonged twilight.

Morton halted us at a point where the trail went up at roughly the pitch of a gutter cleaner's extension ladder.

"We made it," he said.

"Made what?" I asked.

"This is the slide. If we didn't get here early enough, the ground would have thawed and the horses would have a helluva time climbing in mud. Kick 'em hard going up, and keep kicking, and if you feel them wanting to stop, kick harder. Otherwise they might fall backward."

Yeehaw! The Nursing Home Gang dug their heels into their horses' flanks, and up they went, lunging and snorting, plumes of breath blasting from their nostrils like steam from an antique locomotive. I have ridden my share of horses but have never been able to establish a meaningful relationship with a single one. A horse's main purpose in life is to dump its rider, and it will do so at the first opportunity, but I must admit that I acquired a semblance of affection for Spirit as he gallantly carried me up that incline.

I was certainly glad I didn't have to climb it myself.

After giving the animals a well-earned breather, we continued on and at last reached the plateau at 10,000-plus feet. Wide alpine meadows were broken by islands of lodgepole and whitebark pine, little knolls, and rocky, snow-dusted buttes. Looking southward, we could see the beginning of the Wind River range in Wyoming, 100 miles away. In the opposite direction, the Gallatins cut into a clear sky like a serrated knife, and the distant Beartooths rose picketed with pines until they turned to a solid white tinged rose by the new sun.

Morton thought the elk might have retreated here, to the high lonesome.

"Elk are really wild nowadays," he said. "It used to be that hunters were all they had to worry about for six weeks a year. Now, with wolves and mountain lions and grizzlies making a comeback, they've got something after them all the time."

I could not imagine a more magnificent place for them to seek refuge. As we rode on, the frost-covered trees on a ridgetop to the east, backlit by the rising sun, glistened like giant icicles turned upside down. The snow in the meadows sparkled as if strewn with countless bits of crystal.

As if to salute the grandeur, Morton blew his elk call, a curved horn that mimics a bull's bugle. It is a haunting sound, a cry of the wild, not really a trumpet-blast so much as a high, alto-sax note, somehow plaintive and challenging at the same time. We listened for an answer, heard none, and tethered the horses.

After giving me some directions, Morton sent me off on my own, while he and Nolander worked their way to a basin to the northeast.

It was no different from still-hunting deer: Cover your movements as best you can, walk slowly a few paces, stop, look, listen, test the wind (none to speak of that morning), move another few paces, sit down for 10 minutes or so, scanning the terrain, get up and move again. In this way, I covered perhaps half a mile in an hour, coming at last to the rim of the basin, opposite the side my two companions were hunting.

I sat on a shelf of caprock and swept my binoculars over the distant slopes, into pine stands where elk like to lie up, concealed by the shadows of the trees. Elk that do not learn to do this end up dead.

Suddenly, down in the basin and fairly close to me, no more than 200 yards away, a wolf pack started to howl. It is a sound at once doleful, thrilling, and a little scary. You hear it and in a twinkling, you're no longer *Homo sapiens* with a high-powered rifle, you're *Homo neanderthalensis,* clutching a spear. I couldn't see the wolves, nor was I expert enough in lupine vocalization to determine whether their yelps signaled a chase or something else.

Hope caused me to decide they were in hot pursuit of a bull elk with a rack like a tree. I slipped my left arm around the sling and got ready to shoot the Boone and Crockett record that was going to run past me at any moment. This fantasy went the way of the one about the Las Vegas showgirl (a great-uncle of mine, a high-ranking member of the Chicago mob in the 1950s, actually met and married one), and I got up and moved on.

A set of mule deer tracks, a day or two old, showed clearly in the snow, and as I had a muley tag, I followed them until they ran out in a jumble of rocks. Turning to hunt back to where the horses were tethered, I came across spanking-new grizzly bear tracks. The easiest way to tell a grizzly's print from a black bear's is by the length of the claw marks, and these were as long as my fingers.

As is always the case when you know His Lordship is in the immediate vicinity, I experienced a certain awakening of my senses, a wariness born of the knowledge that I, even with my .30/06, was basically a nobody, an irritation Sir G. could swipe out of existence in (choose one) a New York minute, a Detroit second, a heartbeat. Why this excited me is a mystery. Also—another mystery—it made me feel younger.

At any rate, I was glad to see that the bear's destination was not mine. I arrived at the meadow around noon, when it had grown balmy enough for shirtsleeves. Nolander and Morton had not returned, so I sat on a warm, flat rock, resting my tired back against the rocks atop it, and that was when the passage from the Conrad story flashed in my mind. The feeling that will never come back any more . . .

I thought about the matches I had fought on my high school boxing team, the contests I had won and lost on the Purdue University wrestling team. I thought about Marine Corps boot camp and officer's training at Quantico, where I had placed fourth (out of 175) in a grueling physical fitness test. And I thought about the time, way back in 1961, when a buddy and I had hiked into Michigan's Huron Mountains to go steelhead fishing.

That was before lightweight gear, freeze-dried food, and backpacks designed by NASA engineers had come into being. We carried our heavy sleeping bags, canvas tent, rubber waders, and tin cans of hash and beans in Duluth packs—some 75 pounds each—for 5 miles up and down steep hills, then waded wild rivers for a week from dawn to sunset, and hiked back out and got stupifyingly drunk on our false IDs in a north-woods bar and danced and partied all night with two women 10 years older than we.

I remembered other feats that seemed at the time to require not much more effort than getting out of bed, and asked myself: Had I, with my thinning hair, expanding waistline, fading vision, arthritic shoulder, stiff knees, and aching spine really done all that?

I had, but no more.

Oh, yes, Captain Marlow, the heat of life in the handful of dust, the glow in the heart that expires too soon . . .

Or does another sort of glow light the aging heart? I looked at the crystalline glitter of the meadow, at the great and still untamed mountains, at the grazing horses, and suddenly felt an acute joy. I had seen no elk and yet there it was: joy. I recalled a conversation I'd had years ago with a California winemaker. He'd told me that he produced an especially robust zinfandel by dry-farming. The vines were deprived of water until they were near the point of death. Reacting to the artificial drought, the vines poured their life essence into the grapes, giving them an intense flavor.

Something like that was happening to me up there on the Red Rock plateau. Painful awareness of my limitations granted a poignancy to the moment that the younger me would not have experienced. He would have been thinking about his quarry. He would have been frustrated, maybe even angry. He would have thought *I'll get one next season if I don't this season.*

But the older me, with the stent in his coronary artery, knew there might not be a next season. And even if that earlier edition of me did get his elk, he would have missed something utterly, utterly precious.

THE WIRE

DAVID E. PETZAL

We found the carcasses at 11 in the morning. The Zimbabwean sun had mummified them in the positions of agony in which they died. There were six, a young sable cow and five impala, spaced in a line 200 yards long. Their killer was the principal author of death and suffering among Africa's wildlife, the poacher's snare. They had been grabbed by the neck or the leg or the body and had perished from thirst and hunger and exhaustion. Whoever set the snares had never come back to collect the bodies while they were still usable as meat.

Clive Perkins, my PH, watched as our trackers collected the wire and said in a voice as filled with bitterness as any voice I have ever heard: "Welcome to Africa, David Petzal."

We were, however, to see worse.

Two days later I killed a dry Cape buffalo cow whose hoof had been ensnared at the hock. She had managed to break free, but the wire had dug so deeply that we could not dig it out with a knife, and the whole lower leg was grotesquely swollen. We heaved her into the truck and drove her back to camp, and on the way we saw another buffalo cow that had stepped in the wrong place. This one, however, had amputated her left foreleg halfway up.

Africa deals with the halt and the maimed in the form of lions and hyenas, which do not always bother with the formality of killing what they dine on, and though it would have been merciful to shoot the second cow then and there, we couldn't. She was only 75 yards away, but she was on another hunting concession, and woe betide the professional hunter who lets his clients trespass for whatever reason. The only thing we could do, said PH Wayne Van Den Bergh, was go back to camp, call the manager of the neighboring concession, and get permission. Then it would be a simple job to backtrack and shoot her.

"Of course," said the manager, so back we went, and she wasn't there. We didn't think she would move far because animals, particularly crippled ones, do not like to travel in the heat of an African high noon. We began to track her.

There were six of us: Clive Perkins; Wayne Van Den Bergh; PH Theo Bronkhorst, who ran our concession; Willard Ncube, who tracked for Wayne; Elias (he pronounced it EEL-ias) Mathe, who tracked for Clive; and me. When you trail game, the trackers normally go ahead of the people carrying rifles, but when you follow a wounded Cape buffalo, the people with rifles stay up front. I was carrying a Jarrett Professional Hunter in .416 caliber, topped with a Swarovski PV 1.5–6x42 scope—plenty enough gun, assuming I had the time to react. The trackers look for sign, and you keep your eyes forward, watching for a gray shape that will come hurtling at you with jackrabbit speed.

Her track led us out of the mopane woods where we began and into the open. She had gotten into a dry riverbed that was overgrown with waist-high grass. Elias shouted, and we got a glimpse of her head. She was cantering on three legs, moving much faster than we could, and there was no time to even snap a shot at her before she vanished into the grass.

We followed, and the grass changed to taller reeds, which soon were head-high. We were now trailing blind, and it was apparent that if we were tracking her, she was leading us. The reeds were so dense that if you thrust your arm into them you could not see your hand. Theo and Clive left the riverbed for the bank; if she came out of the reeds they would be able to see her and shoot her.

Within another few hundred yards the reeds were 12 feet high and we were reduced to crawling through tunnels left by buffalo that used this place as a refuge during the day. Sometimes our quarry left the tunnels and pushed her way through standing reeds, and we were forced to claw our way after her.

That she was going to charge eventually was a given, and there would be no warning, no time to aim. If we got a chance to shoot at all it would be point, pray, and pull the trigger. Wayne made his way back to me.

"Listen," he whispered, "if you have to shoot her off one of us, for Christ's sake shoot upward so you don't hit us."

Our own rifles were as much danger to us as they were to the buffalo. A trigger can snag, or a muzzle can cross a human back, and that is as good as a horn through the chest. A PH with whom I hunted years ago, as careful an individual as you would want, shot a colleague while trying to stop a leopard charge. The man he shot lived but will never really recover.

Theo and Clive yelled at us to come up on the bank. We lurched out of the reeds and into the shade. A water bottle was passed around and I took a couple of swallows, but it made no difference. It was like pouring water on a hot stove top.

There seemed to be nothing else to do, so the four of us prepared to wade back in.

"If she gets her head into you, grab her horns and twist," Theo said. "She can't stay on her feet with that missing leg."

I waited for him to smile and show he was kidding, but he was not.

Back we went. By now we had crowded her into the end of the reedbed. She had perhaps 2 acres in which to maneuver, but all she had to do was keep a few steps ahead of us and pick her time to charge.

She did. There was no warning at all. There was simply a crash of reeds and a massive gray shape blotted out the sun. Wayne fired at it from a crouch; I shot across my chest while falling backward. Then the shape vanished. I could almost have touched it with my rifle barrel. There was a patch of blood on the ground and Elias was smiling.

"Did we kill her?" I asked.

"No," he said, and I realized he was smiling because she had not killed him. I think the combination of nearly impassable reeds and the missing leg saved us. She could not keep her footing in that tangle, fell, scrambled up with possibly one or two bullets in her, and fled. If she had charged with four legs, she would have killed one of us.

We kept going, and after only a few yards Willard froze.

"Shoot," he said, pointing into the reeds.

I couldn't see beyond my rifle barrel, but I fired.

"Shoot again," he said, now pointing in a different direction, and I did.

"Reload," said Willard, but I was doing that.

We stumbled onward, and Wayne suddenly lurched back in agony. A reed stalk had speared him in his eye, and he was now down to one usable eye and one round of ammunition. Wayne, Willard, and Elias had a short talk in Ndebele, the sum of which was: "We're not going to get lucky twice. Let's get the hell out of here."

So we left the reeds, and Theo summed up our efforts perfectly: "Man, that was stupid."

There was only one thing left to try. Willard and Elias climbed an acacia tree while Theo and I stood on the roof of the truck. We would try to look down into the reeds and shoot from above. Clive blocked off the end of the reedbed, and Wayne, who has a wife and two children, borrowed ammunition from Clive and headed back into the riverbed.

We could see the reeds waving as the buffalo maneuvered, and Clive got a glimpse of her. He shot and was sure he had connected, but it was a standoff. She would not leave the reeds in daylight, and we could not go in after her. Theo called an end to it.

A few days later I asked Theo if he would ever know what happened to her, and he said no, something would drag her down and she would vanish. In fact, she was almost certainly dead as we spoke.

So be it. We failed. I would like to think that we got a few bullets into her and at least shortened her suffering if we could not end it outright.

There is one thing more. I would like to think that somewhere in one of the nastier neighborhoods in hell there is a wire loop waiting for the foot of the poacher who snared her.

ADVENTURES OF A DEER BUM

BILL HEAVEY

At the moment I am parked outside a strip-mall laundromat at 10 p.m. on a Tuesday night in Jackson, Ohio, a working-class town of 10,000. Most of the locals are in bed by this hour. Not me. Four days into my hunt, I'm as hyper as Paris Hilton on an unescorted visit to a boys' prep school. By the green glow of my Streamlight headlamp, I am shuffling through six adjoining topo quads spread out over the dashboard, scarfing down an 18-hour-old sausage biscuit and a 20-ounce Pabst (discovered while Dumpster diving in my own backseat), and madly scanning the radio for a weather fix.

Inside the establishment, my Scent-Lok is tumbling around in a dryer hot enough to cook pizza, and my other hunting duds are swishing through a final rinse of Sport-Wash. By forgoing a real dinner, I can do a total scent overhaul and still make it back to my motel for five hours of rack time. At 4:30 a.m., my nervous system will go off automatically, sending me afield again for a chance at an Ohio bighead.

Meanwhile, I'm poring over the dog-eared topos, pressing them for the secrets only they can impart. After hours of agony, I have whittled the Miss Stand Site contestants down to two finalists for tomorrow morning:

a shapely little ridge finger near Blue Hollow on the Pedro Quad and a perky bench along the stream in Pokepatch Hollow on the Gallia Quad. My whole world depends on the wind, and I'm endlessly scanning the radio for a weather report. But the night airwaves here have been seized by Bible study insurgents.

I note a faint odor of decay in the car and wonder if an unfinished sandwich from the recent past is out for revenge. A Jackson Township police cruiser rolls past, slowing to eyeball me. As always, any distraction from my quest fills me with indignation. Yes, I am sitting in a parked car at night wearing long underwear with a green light on my forehead. You got a problem with that? Evidently I look too whacked to be a real criminal, and the cruiser rolls on.

Searching for the source of the stench, I am drawn to my feet. I take off my shoes and socks and resist the impulse to scream aloud. I have a case of athlete's foot that would look at home in a leper colony. But there's no time to deal with that now. My immediate task is to figure out where I can put an arrow into a giant whitetail tomorrow in the Wayne National Forest.

I discovered the Wayne last year, when I was looking for a place to bow-hunt trophy bucks without having to pay a guide, an outfitter, or a lease fee. A review process including examination of QDMA maps of record-book deer and deer densities, state website inventories of public lands and hunting pressure, and the brain of every hunting buddy I could find soon had me leaning here: huge acreage, low pressure, and challenging terrain.

There be monsters here. Ohio is archery-only for most of November, so mature bucks enjoy high survival rates. On opening day of the 2005 season, Mike Rex killed a deer in nearby Athens County with antlers so big that he thought at first that he was looking at two bucks standing right behind each other. For the number Nazis: Think 6x5 main frame and 13-inch brow tines.

A convergence of conditions natural and man-made make this part of southeastern Ohio a heaven for bowhunters with big dreams and little wallets. Most of the wooded country in Ohio is leased up by guys with more money than you, especially in the northwestern Corn Belt. The standout exception is the southeastern quadrant, Ohio's hardscrabble Appalachian counties.

The glaciers that smoothed the rough edges of the land and dropped their load of rich topsoil during the last ice age never made it here. Geologically, it's part of the Unglaciated Allegheny Plateau, an elevated arc of shale, sandstone, and thin soils extending around southeastern Ohio into western Pennsylvania and the West Virginia panhandle. If you were a pioneer looking for prime farmland, you would probably have sifted the dirt through your fingers, said, "I didn't come all this way for this," and kept going. Deer, however, have always liked the rugged forests—oak, ash, hickory, and beech—just fine. The double bonus is that the three Wayne National Forest districts contain more than 237,000 acres of land—a lifetime's worth of country where a guy with a little grit can hunt until he either succeeds, has to go back to work and family, or loses his mind.

A bunch of guys from states near and far are already making the annual pilgrimage to this part of the Buckeye State. In the motel, I ran into Ricky Quaue, who comes up from Mississippi with friends to hunt. "I can drive up, go on a weeklong hunt, and have a chance of getting a monster for $500," he said. "Best so far this year is a 15-inch spread, but a boy from Hattiesburg killed a whopper." James Smith, from Tennessee, has been coming for years with five first cousins. "Big deer, nice folks, what's not to like?"

The hitch is that it's big-woods hunting. You know those neat little diagrams of imaginary hunting grounds in magazines (*Field & Stream* included) that show ambush points along fencelines, brush funnels, and powerline crossings? Forget 'em. This is subtler terrain. You will have to take your game to the next level to play here. The deer are more difficult, too, harder to pattern, seminomadic, and extremely wary. Spook one and he'll be gone for good before you ever lay eyes on him. And this year features a special wrinkle: a bumper crop of mast exceeding any in local memory, acorns and nuts two layers thick even in town parking lots. A deer can feed all day and scarcely have to turn its head. No matter. I am possessed of an attribute that surpasses all others: deranged perseverance.

By 5:22 the first morning, my car is parked at a trailhead, and I am climbing through the darkness along Blue Hollow to a ridgeline at 900 feet that broadens into a mini-plateau, ridge fingers running northwest to southeast. Acorns and nuts crunch under my boots at every step. I have picked my stand site too well and can hear deer running as I near the faint saddle in the ridge. I'm pleased at having my topo instincts verified and kicking myself for not trusting them enough to have set up farther off. The invisible bolting deer don't snort—a good sign—then bail off the ridge and out of earshot almost immediately. It's so steep that it's hard to say if they went 100 yards and stopped or are headed for the next county.

A climbable tree is silhouetted against the false dawn 50 yards downwind. I stalk it at glacial speed, set out some estrous scent, and settle in 25 feet up. As morning replants the last of the darkness into the ground, faint trails appear crisscrossing the leaves. All bear evidence of recent use, but none is a main route. Maybe there is no main route.

Just past 8 a.m., a 6-pointer with no brow tines pops over the notch from the opposite side, walking fast and purposefully. He passes 50 yards off, ignoring my scent wicks, grunt tube, even the bleat can. I wait five minutes and rattle lightly for 30 seconds—just casual sparring. Twenty minutes later the buck climbs back up, accompanied by a smaller 6, this one limping slightly. The two of them work the wicks' scent stream and pass 30 yards below my stand. I draw, but only for practice, and am pleased that they don't pick up the movement. They seem less pressured than deer around home. But I didn't come all this way for a 1½-year-old 6.

At noon, having seen only a couple of does feeding slowly along the hillside 70 yards below me, I descend and hike farther up the path, both to scout and to stop by the office of Dean State Forest (a pocket park surrounded by Wayne N.F. lands), seeking local intelligence. Here I run into Tim Boggs and two other equipment operators for the state Forestry Division. Boggs says he saw my car parked this morning, and I tell him about the 6-pointers.

"There are some pigs here all right. But they're tough deer. I rifle hunted three days a week in season for six years before I took my first buck as a kid." He and the other workers were all born within 400 yards of one another, not far from here. I'm expecting resentment at an out-of-stater horning in on hallowed local ground, but soon he's drawing on my topos, showing me the places he mowed recently, which often attract deer. Then he taps a spot where a creek he would prefer I not name runs through a deep hollow.

"They pull a couple of 150-class bucks out of there most years," he says. He writes down the name of a cousin who works just up the road for Wayne N.F. (who took a nice 10-pointer a few weeks earlier on public land). He even gives me the name of a retired farmer with land adjoining the secret creek and recommends I ask nicely for permission to hunt there, or at least to access the creek across his land. As if this isn't enough, he gives me a lift back to my car. I'm from the East, and anytime a stranger is this accommodating, I'm expecting to be assaulted, robbed, or carjacked. But he shakes my hand, wishes me well, and drives off. I stand there, wondering what the hell is wrong with the guy.

The cascade of inexplicable goodwill continues. Twenty minutes later, at the Wayne N.F. headquarters, Boggs' cousin shows me a picture of his buck, points out a few productive spots he has hunted over the years, and marks individual pear and persimmon trees on my maps that are worth scouting. An hour later, I'm buying meatball subs for the retired farmer, Coleman, and his friend, Pete, at a café in Oak Hill. Again, these are seriously ill men: friendly, content with their lives, and thoroughly decent.

Both are in their 80s and eat lunch together more days than not. When Pete excuses himself for a moment, Coleman confides, "Pete's wife died a couple years ago, and if I don't get him outta the house, he just sits there. I tell him, 'Pete, you're getting grouchy.'" When Coleman makes a trip to the men's room, it's Pete's turn. "Coleman's more like my brother than anything else. He's 87, but he won't tell you that. I worry about him. His brother died last year, and now his nephew owns half the farm." I ask what the nephew is like. "He's a butthead," says Pete.

Coleman returns. Soon they're finishing each other's sentences while telling me the one from 40 years ago when they were bringing a 60-inch moose home from Canada strapped onto the body of a '51 Cadillac. "Broke down with a vapor lock right in downtown Columbus," Coleman says. "Remember that, Pete? Jeez, we drew a crowd that day."

Coleman, naturally, gives permission to cross his land to get to the creek I want to hunt. I find a trail crossing three-quarters of the way up the hillside overlooking the creek, an area made almost impenetrable by trees felled in an ice storm two years back. It's noisy walking, and it's nearly 70 degrees. I sit for four hours. I sit until dark-dark, until even the bone-white sycamores are swallowed up in the blackness. Then, out of sheer cussedness, I sit some more. At last I hear the tentative sounds in the leaves—not crunching, more like a gentle sweeping—of deer. They pass somewhere below me toward the farmer's fields. They're here all right. They just don't much feel like getting killed.

My days fall into a kind of routinized frenzy, fueled by deer adrenaline and cans of Starbucks DoubleShot espresso. By dawn I am high in my trusty Lone Wolf sit-and-climb, which has yet to squeak in six years of use. From about 11 to 1:30, I'm a road warrior, speed scouting as many as six locations and making notes on the topos. From two until dark I'm back in the air, sometimes higher up than a lone guy should be in a place where cellphone reception is spotty at best.

I've yet to see the town of Jackson or the Comfort Inn where I'm staying by daylight. Totally consumed by the hunt, I am insatiable for the next new piece of ground, knowing that it's only a matter of time before a shower of antlered glory descends on my humble head. Daytime highs have been in the 70s for the past four days, well above the average of 50. It's not exactly a deer aphrodisiac. All I need is a drop in the temperature to pump up the rut or a hot doe to lure a buck past my stand. A tobacco farmer I run across while driving one afternoon confirms my fears. When I stop to ask if I might hunt his land, he answers the door still in camo from his own morning hunt. "They're just not moving till after dark. I hear them every morning underneath me. I just can't see them. I know they're chasing." I set up on a beaver dam deep in a heavily wooded bottom near his place along trails showing the hardest use I've seen so far. Three o'clock turns to four. Sunset turns to twilight; twilight fades until the brighter stars come out. Still I sit. Finally, there comes a gentle but regular sloshing in the water. I strain my eyes but can see nothing. For dumb animals, they sure are elusive.

Coming out, I get more than a little turned around. A creek I don't remember crossing blocks my way, and I fall off a log into the waist-deep water when a vine snags the stand on my back. Another step and I'm up to my chest. I claw my way across and up the bank and wait until the noise of an engine indicates the direction of the road. By the time I finally make the car, I'm sweating from more than exertion.

The fact is, revving this high for this long has begun to degrade my finely honed mental edge. Example: Unwilling to burn a moment of daylight to practice good shooting form, it has seemed like a good idea to shoot a single arrow each night in my room. Turning on the shower, TV, and radio for covering noise, I screw on a blunt tip, muffled with foam rubber and electrical tape, and take one point-blank shot at the Yellow Pages. The blunt penetrates all the way to page 358, Kitchen Cabinet—Refacing & Refinishing. Each day, the cleaning people replace the phone book.

I have taken to downing three or four Starbucks DoubleShot espressos before lunch and a couple more in the afternoon. Though tired, I have no desire to rest. Not while it's legal to be up in a tree with a bow.

One afternoon, bombing down State Route 141 in Gallia County after scouting a ridge studded with crab apples, their fruit spread on the ground in perfect drip lines around the trunks, I pass a cornfield where a combine is harvesting. Three or four men are leaning on the guardrail in the shade, watching.

A mile later, I come to my senses and pull a U-turn. "Any way a guy could bowhunt any of that corn?" I ask. A fellow about my age walks over and says that it's his land and he keeps the hunting on the farm itself for friends and family. "But there is a monstrous big buck running that ridge up behind you. He comes down just about every evening to get to it. You set up there long enough and you can kill him. I'll show you." He hops on a four-wheeler and leads the way, indicating with a flick of his hand where to park. "He's a pig, 250, 300 pounds," he whispers, pointing out a trail up to the saddle. "I've killed tons of deer right up there. I'd be hunting him myself 'cept I got cancer and had to do chemo." He lifts his hat to reveal a bald head. "Hell, I just thought you were good looking," I answer.

I see a basket 8-point, well inside the ears, waltzing carelessly down the trail half an hour before sunset. My heart leaps. The big guy can't be far behind. Except he is. It's the same old story. Half an hour after dark, I hear deer come sneaking down the ridge in ones and twos for the better part of an hour, maybe a dozen deer in all. In the morning, when it is still black dark, they do the same thing returning from the corn. They repeat the pattern the next evening and the next morning.

Time is running out, and the daytime highs are still hitting the 70s. As November 10—my last day—approaches, I find that my writer's luck is holding firm. The temperature is forecast to drop 25 degrees, and I can hunt the entire morning before I have to catch my flight home.

I decide to go back to the secret creek and its ice-storm blowdowns. In darkness I climb a poplar tree a quarter of the way down from the top of the ridge on a bench where several trails intersect. It is deliciously cold, in the 40s at dawn, with a light northerly breeze. The squirrels are out in force. I see a hawk hunting from a tremendous dead hickory that somehow is still upright. The hours pass with nary a hoofed quadruped to be seen.

At noon, I climb down with just enough time to haul ass to the airport. My disappointment is not as bitter as you might imagine. Bowhunting for whitetails is dicey under the best of circumstances. It is almost a relief to have the enforced deadline of a departing flight. Otherwise, I would keep at it until success or the calendar forced me to stop. I point the car west, pop a last can of double espresso, and feel a strange weight gradually lift from my body. I have no regrets. I hunted as hard as I could. I wasn't defeated, I just ran out of time. I would go again in a heartbeat.

Running dangerously late to the regional airport, I stop in front of the terminal, throw all my gear onto the sidewalk, and change out of my camo right there. Unbeknownst to me, the security guys have been observing the unshaven, distracted guy who just took all his clothes off out front. They wave me through the metal detector and immediately pull me over for a search. "How'd you do?" asks one, obviously a bowhunter himself. "No luck," I tell him. I sit and remove my shoes for inspection. My long-neglected athlete's foot makes him recoil as if hit with a stun gun. "Might want to see a doc about that," he says.

"I'm going to," I say. "Just as soon as rifle season ends."

PAIN

C.J. CHIVERS

Chris Ott knew the enraged grizzly was coming back to finish killing him. Knocked flat, half-scalped, blinded by his own blood rushing over his brow and down his face, he sifted facts from surprise. Seconds before, the big sow had exploded from undergrowth and hit him, slashing open his head and biting his face and neck as she forced him down. He had spotted her only seconds before she landed on him and her slobbering maw smacked his, transforming him from a fit 42-year-old man to wounded prey in the predator's grip. Now he was experiencing what sometimes happens to people as they die. It was mid-attack. Time seemed to slow. The momentum of the bear's lunge had carried her past. This was his stay—the time a grizzly requires to stop, spin, and pounce back on broken prey. It stood to be the rest of Chris's life.

He could hear the bear crashing across the few yards of thicket that separated them, her hot mouth reddened with his blood. He had time for a single word: "Bruce!"

The day in mid October had been set aside for the work that accompanies the end of a hunt. A two-week trek in northeastern British Columbia had run its course. Chris had taken an impressive stone sheep the day before, capping a 2007 season that had been carefully planned and well lived. He and his guide, Bruce Willis, had found a concentration of big rams in July, and had returned in fall to find the sheep down from the mountains to graze on willows, fattening up ahead of winter. Chris had never seen rams so low.

The previous morning, he and Bruce had left camp early, leaving behind their wrangler, Nick France. They walked about a mile and set up in a creek basin, to glass a hill overlooking the feeding grounds. There they spotted a fine ram, bedded down. When the animal rose, Bruce had already propped up a thick branch as a rest. Chris dropped the ram with a kneeling 250-yard shot from his .270 Weatherby Magnum. They dressed the animal and packed it back to the tents, where they agreed to load the nine horses in the morning for the walk out, which would take a full day.

Hunts can be hard to end. With this one a success, Nick asked for a few hours for himself in the morning while the other men broke the camp. He wanted to take a mountain goat. Chris lent Nick his rifle, and Nick walked out at dawn. Chris and Bruce would monitor the two-way radio and be ready to help. About two hours later, they heard gunshots. They stopped packing and headed for the creek bed to look up to where Nick had set up.

Their camp was in thick brush, crisscrossed with fallen logs. Even their short walk was slow going. Chris's peripheral vision picked up movement to his left. The movement assumed a shape: a grizzly cub, man-size, perhaps 3 years old and maybe 20 yards out.

"Bear!" Chris said. "Bruce, it's a bear!"

Neither man had a rifle; they were so close to camp that they had not thought they would need to defend themselves. Bruce reached down and picked up a large fallen branch. He began to wave it, projecting size and confidence. As Chris stepped backward, his feet caught on a downed log. He tripped, landing hard on his back. He had had run-ins with grizzlies before. He knew that body language signaling fear or vulnerability could trip a predator's switch. Falling down left him in about the worst position to be in. He had to get up.

It was too late. Scrambling for footing, Chris heard something heavy crashing through the thicket. He spun instinctively and faced the noise on one knee, looking directly at a charging grizzly. It was the mother bear. She was closing the distance without a snarl or roar, focused, intent to kill. Chris flinched and she was on him, hitting his head like a sprinting Labrador retriever comes down on a tennis ball. Her mouth closed on his face. Her claws raked the scalp beneath his hair. He smelled her putrid breath as their noses met. As she snapped her mouth closed, Chris's jaw shattered within hers, breaking like a coffee cup.

Then it ended. Somehow, she was past him.

In the inexplicable ways of violence, the bear had hit Chris almost as exactly as she needed to for an instant kill. And yet Chris was alive. Her teeth had closed on his face and neck but missed his carotid artery. The heavy swing of her mitt had not struck him squarely enough to break his spine or knock him out. And even as she had landed, the speed of her pounce had caused her to overshoot slightly. Whether this was fortuitous or cruel was a matter of perspective. It meant that Chris—sprawled on the cold ground, sightless, blood rushing out—would be both helpless and alert for the follow-up attack. He was a blunt and sometimes hard-edged investor who had conditioned hard so he could push deep into high-elevation wilderness. He ordinarily trusted his preparations and the methodical workings of his mind. He was outmatched.

As time slowed, he tried to decide what to do. Fight? Impossible. Flight? Not without eyes, and not this far into the attack. He saw one choice: Play dead, and hope the sow would lose interest.

"Bruce!" he shouted, as he covered up.

He heard a reply: "I'm coming!"

Chris rolled to his stomach, clasped his hands against the back of his neck, and locked his elbows together by his blood-soaked chin. He was offering his shoulders and arms to the bear, while protecting his neck. How long could he hold out if she began to shred?

The grizzly landed again, dropping her head like an anvil. This time she chose his back, biting through his canvas coat and wool shirt. He felt her canines sink into his meat.

With furious speed and in silence, she released him, then bit him again. Then a third time. Chris understood that she was trying to gut him, or to rip open his lungs. He heard a rifle shot. The bear released him, looked up—and froze. She had not been hit. She was recalculating. As quickly as she had been on him, she was off of him. Chris heard her rushing away. She was charging the camp.

There was a second shot, followed by silence. Chris remained belly down, feigning death. Was she eating Bruce now?

Bruce appeared in the thicket. Moving fast, he had made it to camp, retrieved his rifle, and fired a warning shot. This had prompted the bear to charge him. His second shot hit her neck and shoulder, breaking load-bearing bones. She collapsed among the terrified, tied-up horses. There she died.

It had all lasted only a minute or so, and stopped as quickly as it had begun. One more bite and Chris might have been dead—his head crushed, his spine snapped, his insides exposed. Instead, he was alive, though perhaps not for long. He sat up, felt wind rushing across his teeth through his exposed cheek. He reached for his face, part of which hung loosely, and moved it back into place. His hand filled with blood. Two cubs were bawling somewhere nearby, in the woods. They did not sound like a threat. Chris had no time for them. He was taking stock. He did not know how badly his back was wounded. But he had full mobility and motor skills. His airway was open. He was breathing clearly.

He began channeling thoughts. The bear was dead. His life now depended on him. If I panic, I die. If I let my heart rate climb, I pump out all of my blood.

His heart was pounding. Control. He needed self-control.

I have a family. I have two sons. I'm going to go home. I have to figure out how. Stay calm.

Pain crashed over Chris like a wave. As endorphins wore off, his body informed him of the damage. He felt intense burning in his back and across his head. He was being seared. He stood and staggered to camp, where Bruce gave him horse blankets to lie on. Chris knew he needed to stop the bleeding on his head. He asked for bandages. As he pressed the gauze to himself, he also knew he needed medical help but could not ride out on horseback to get it. There was no time.

He always traveled the wilderness with a satellite phone. He asked Bruce to retrieve it and get a helicopter moving. The weather was not bad. There was light. They could bring in an aircraft and take him out. Huddling for warmth, he realized that his bleeding was slowing. This fact provided information: The bear must not have opened an artery or torn a vital organ. Chris understood that he had a chance.

Nick, who had walked back to camp, was indignant as he arrived. No one had been answering radio calls. He saw the huge bear carcass, about 350 pounds, sprawled dead inside the camp. He saw Chris. It was perhaps 35 degrees. Nick quickly covered Chris up with more blankets, examined him, and changed the dressing on his mangled face.

The helicopter arrived in early afternoon and soon lifted the mauled man away. Chris Ott had a long recovery ahead, with extensive suturing, courses of intravenous antibiotics, and rounds of facial reconstruction. With time he would be fitted with a replacement titanium jaw. He knew nothing of this yet. But the aircraft was climbing and gathering speed. The wilderness was growing small beneath him. He was moving toward a hospital. From the mouth of a grizzly, with seconds to live, he had emerged. His life's duration and its prospects would not be determined by a grizzly's next bite. Chris Ott was alive, and headed home.

THE BADLANDS PACK

STEVEN RINELLA

I kept the first two reasons to myself out of consideration for Matt. Not only was he anxious about the well-being of the creatures he refers to as "pack princess" and "little buddy," but he was out here doing me a favor. He'd tagged out on a whitetail during the bow season and came along to lend a hand and an extra pair of binoculars. However, I did give him an earful about reason No. 3. I've been hunting mule deer for more than a decade and taken my share of bucks, but every year I hold out hope that I'm going to get the truly huge muley of my dreams. If you imagine this goal of mine as a rash, you can think of the AWOL llamas as a handful of poison ivy–infused steel wool rubbing against it.

Matt got his llamas, Timmy and Haggy, from a llama adoption agency in Idaho in order to increase the effective range of our backpack hunts. A llama can get into any place that you can reach, and it can pack out 50 or 60 pounds of meat. Perhaps more important, it can pack in 5 or 6 gallons of water. This means that two hunters with two llamas can hunt in dry country for a week without having to return to the truck.

Or that's how it's supposed to work. But on this day, the second of our trip, we were mired in bad luck. We'd left our camp before daybreak in order to work up a ridgeline while we glassed two parallel valleys. We blew a stalk on what might have been a decent buck, and we busted another small group by blundering through their bedding area at the head of a juniper-choked draw. The day was heating up when we dragged ourselves back to camp. We figured we would have a midday snack before packing the llamas into a fresh network of valleys a couple of miles to the north. We'd seen a nice buck in there the year before. If we were lucky, he'd be one year bigger and still hanging around.

I was still gnawing my first stick of mule deer jerky when the llamas' leads got tangled up on a hillside where we'd tethered them out to feed. Timmy and Haggy are 3-year-old siblings, and they fight like 3-year-old siblings. They started out by spitting on each other—Matt describes their spit as "kind of like vomit, or when you gut a deer improperly"—and then things escalated with some tugging and kicking. I walked down and untangled them, then returned my attention to the jerky for a couple of seconds. When I turned around I was greeted by a strange sight: There were zero llamas where there used to be two.

In southeastern Montana, the peak of the mule deer rut occurs around Nov. 18. It's hard to overestimate the importance of this date. To put it one way, you could spend the morning of Oct. 18 glassing from a peak in good country and see maybe one or two bucks. Go back to that same peak a month later and you might see 10 or more. I learned the significance of the rut the hard way—through experimentation and observation. Back in the mid '90s, when I was new to Montana, I spent a lot of time hunting in the wrong places at the wrong times. I focused my attention on the large tracts of ranchland that are made publicly accessible through Montana's wonderful Block Management Program. I was seduced by the easy thrill of seeing dozens of deer around the irrigated wheat and alfalfa fields of the Yellowstone, Missouri, Judith, and Powder Rivers. With all those deer around, I figured, there must be some dandy bucks in the mix. Because Block Management lands are often hunted quite heavily, I tried to hunt as close to the October opener as possible in order to get a crack at them before anyone else.

The problem was that I never saw the bucks I was after. I finally started to realize why after Matt moved to Miles City, Mont. I started to hang around there a lot, and now and then I'd run into the local taxidermist at a saloon. Whenever the subject of mule deer came up, Paul Faber, of Faber Taxidermy, would assure me: "Around here, right now is the good old days." Curious, I started to drop by his studio. Right off, I noticed that big mule deer only barely trickled in during the first couple of weeks after the October opener. But then, starting in mid November, huge bucks with rut-swollen necks flowed through his door like cattle to a Kansas slaughterhouse. It didn't take me long to realize that the peak of the mule deer calendar (the rut) was much more important than the high point of the hunter's calendar (the opener).

But that was just half my problem. The other half was location. Matt and I started to think that we weren't seeing big bucks because they weren't there, or because someone else was getting them before we came along. So we stopped thinking about high-pressure hunting spots where we could see scores of deer on opening day. Instead, we started thinking about low-pressure hunting spots where we might hunt during the rut and see just a few deer that no one else was bothering to look for. From then on, we began perusing topo maps with a whole new set of criteria. In essence, we were looking for the kind of country where you wouldn't want to lose your llamas.

Timmy eventually turned himself in. He's not as bold as Haggy, and he backtracked himself right to us. Catching Haggy was another story. We were hoping that she'd stop to feed, but that never happened. We followed her trail for a mile down a ridgeline with far more exposed rock than soil. Her route suggested that she was headed back toward the van (yes, Matt hauls his llamas in the back of a Dodge 12-seater), which was something that she'd never attempted on any of her previous unauthorized furloughs. So we kept going, trying to distinguish llama tracks from elk and deer tracks. Soon the idea of the vehicle destination was more than just a theory. Matt scaled a high outcropping of rock to have a look. I listened as his voice bellowed down from the heights.

"The van!" he yelled. "The van!"

About an hour later I was playing ring-around-the-van with Haggy. I ate dirt when I dove for her lead, but at least I put an end to her stint as a free woman.

We resumed our plan to push north into a hunter-free corridor formed by a barrier of outfitter-leased farmland to the west and some nearly inaccessible public land to the east. As we moved, we encountered a corrugated landscape. The larger valleys were covered in grass, but the small tributary canyons were shaded enough to support lush growths of chokecherry, green ash, and hawthorn. The ridgelines were wind-blasted sandstone dotted with mature ponderosa pines. While it is not uncommon to see gangs of 50 or 60 does bedded beneath irrigation pivots on the leased farmland to the west, in this country five or six is considered a big group of deer.

The next day, after slow, careful walking and glassing, we reached a ridge that offered some tremendous views of the surrounding country. We stashed our gear in a sheltered saddle, tethered the llamas, and split up with an agreement to meet after dark. I went west. Toward evening I glassed a pair of does and two fawns grazing on a distant hillside. They had a young buck circling around them like a moon around a planet. I watched as he performed the ritual of the rut; whenever one of the does let her guard down, he'd sneak in to bury his nose under her tail. The doe would swat him away as nonchalantly as if she were dealing with a horsefly. I marked the location of the group with nearby landmarks so I could check up on them later to see whether a more serious buck joined the action.

I've only seen living versions of the trophy mule deer I'm after twice: The first was in Estes Park, Colo., when I was 12. It was bedded down with a pair of does between a line of traffic and a tourist shop. You could have put wheels on its rack and used it for a shopping cart. The second buck was over a decade later on Wild Horse Island, a wildlife sanctuary surrounded by the moat of Montana's Flathead Lake. It was a towering nontypical, the kind of buck that would take all the work out of making an antler chandelier.

What I like about those two deer is how they stand out like bookends that accentuate and support the hundreds and hundreds of smaller bucks that I've glassed while hunting. It is their difference, the way they contrast with all those other deer, that makes them so special. This notion of contrast is important for trophy hunting. At its best, trophy hunting should come out of a deep and nuanced personal context with a species. I think of the way that some Great Plains American Indian tribes revered the hide of a white buffalo as the ultimate trophy, something far more valuable than personal wealth or accomplishments in war. The unusualness of the white buffalo made it an emblem of the way of life that is granted by the more typical and "normal" animals. To put it another way, looking for a trophy mule deer is, for me, a way of paying homage to the very essence of mule deer.

Trophy hunting can also be a good way of prolonging a hunt that might otherwise be over quickly. I was especially thankful for this extension of time once we were five days into our trip. It was a gorgeous morning and would be our best day of spotting deer. Before dawn, we were sitting on a high peak capped with rounded boulders of porous volcanic rock. We watched the stars fade above us, and started glassing as soon as there was enough light. Right off, we saw the first decent buck of the day. The 4x4 was silhouetted along with three does on the crest of a distant hill. Then we watched another good 4x4 streak between two patches of aspen just beneath us in the floor of a valley. A third was following a pair of does as they came off a high bench of land and descended toward a wedge-shaped growth of trees at a drainage head. There were a few smaller bucks, little forks and 3x3s, scattered here and there as well.

By the time the sun popped over the horizon, we were picking our way northward. We took it slowly—walk a little, glass a lot, walk a little, glass a lot. The loaded-down llamas were trailing behind us. They are actually quite helpful for locating deer, especially when you have to cut through heavy cover. The animals are extremely alert and often see deer before we can. First I'll notice one of the llamas staring intently with its ears cocked forward, and then I'll look in that direction and see the white rump of a deer off in the timber. The interest is not just one way. Mule deer are sometimes transfixed by the llamas. They'll often approach Timmy and Haggy, spooking only when they see that the llamas are accompanied by hominids. One time, Matt was bowhunting and watched a bull elk come out of nowhere at a fast trot. It covered 340 yards, right toward them. Matt hunkered down behind Timmy and nocked an arrow. The bull turned and spooked just outside of Matt's comfort zone at 60 yards.

We crawled up from the bottom of a creek bed in order to glass the opposite wall of the valley without anything seeing us. Matt caught the unmistakable glint of sunlight on polished antler.

"There's one that's worth looking at," Matt said.

Sure enough, there was a heavy-beamed buck with short brow tines. He was bedded on a point of land that jutted out from the slope. While we waited for him to turn his head and show off his rack, we picked out five does that were scattered around him. After a while a sixth doe rose to her feet. He turned his head to watch her and showed off a couple of nice deep forks on either side of his rack—a good 4x4 (or 5x5, depending on one's generosity when counting muley brow tines). I was now in a familiar mule deer hunting predicament: He wasn't exactly my dream muley, but he was far and away the best buck we'd run into in almost a week. And, who knew, he might still be the best buck we'd see even if we stayed another week. I thought about it for a few minutes and made a decision. I was going after him.

It was as if the buck read my mind, because his eyes turned back and settled right on our position.

"What did you just do?" I whispered.

"Nothing. What'd you do?"

"Nothing. I'm barely even breathing."

We looked back and the buck was definitely staring at us.

"I can't believe this," I said. "How'd he do that?"

Even before he'd spotted us, it was obvious that this buck would be tough. He was perched on an outcropping of land overlooking the open valley. A rear approach was out of the question because of the wind and the layout of the hills. If I came from the sides I'd never see him until I got really close, and by then I'd probably spook his does. What made the most sense was to do a belly crawl from below. Move slow, use lots of time, and employ the sage, rocks, and contours for concealment.

But with him staring at us, this plan was a bust. We sat back to lament our bad luck and then watched as the buck's eyes shifted toward our left. I realized what had happened. Haggy had undone her lead and had come out from behind the hillside where we'd hidden her. The buck was staring at her. I whispered back at her. "Nice work, Haggy!"

"If you're going to go," said Matt, "I'd go now."

It took me 45 minutes to approach a preselected destination that should have put me within 200 yards of the buck. I moved with excruciating slowness, only to reach the top and see that the deer were gone. Matt watched the whole thing and later explained what had happened: The buck got bored of Haggy and stood up to harass the does while I was crawling with my face down. The group then settled in another spot and watched as I approached their previous position. Once I was too close for comfort, they simply snuck over the next ridge.

Normally, Matt and I kick back in the middle of the day. There's little point in moving around and spooking deer that will be easier to spot once they're active again in the evening. But we decided to keep busy on our last full day, because the layout of the country that we were in was ideal for glassing. We were on a steep-sided ridge separating two valleys. On either side of the ridge, the slopes leading up from the valley were incised with brushy draws holding scatterings of ponderosa pine. It was perfect midday bedding habitat. From the ridgeline, you could look down into each draw without any serious risk of deer seeing you.

We played leapfrog along the ridgeline. Matt would stop to study a draw and I'd move up to the next one. Then he'd pass me by and go to the next. We checked a dozen draws like this, and spotted a few does and small bucks. I was out ahead of Matt when I stopped to glass a draw that formed a wide, bowl-shaped basin at its crest. The buckbrush in the upper right corner of the bowl was sprouting with six sets of mule deer ears. The deer were facing downhill, away from me. I studied the bowl for antlers without seeing any, though there were a lot of little pockets of brush that I couldn't see into. I thought of the buck from yesterday, and remembered the six does that he'd had with him.

I crawled down the opposite side of the ridge and doubled back to find Matt. I described what I'd seen up there. I then went back to the saddle and crept to the edge and positioned my rifle over my pack. Matt walked back a few draws and cut downhill until he was well below the elevation of the deer. He started walking toward the draw where I was staked out. Within 20 minutes, I saw the deer turn their ears in the direction that he was supposed to come from. Mule deer almost always spook in a general uphill direction, and these rose to their feet and did just that. I had picked a shooting lane and watched them pass over 200 yards out as they angled toward me. Doe, doe, doe . . . doe, doe, doe . . . buck. I knew immediately that he was the one from the day before.

The first shot hit a little lower than I would have liked, but the second shot came quickly and he dropped from view.

The most exhilarating moments when you're hunting big game in rough country come as you're climbing up or down toward a fallen animal. It feels like you could explode with tension and stress and anticipation. And sometimes you get to where the animal was supposed to be and you can't find it, and the sinking feeling almost makes you sick. But then you realize that you're in the wrong spot and you go uphill or downhill some more and there it is; you see horn or antler, fur or hair, and you realize that it's over. And all that tension falls away and you feel like you could just melt into the animal.

As Matt and I sat on either side of the buck, we ran our hands through the hair of his mane and patted his hams and tipped his rack back and forth. He was gorgeous, a 160-class buck with good, heavy bases. While Timmy and Haggy packed the meat and hide back out toward the vehicle, I thought about how a hunter's definition of the perfect animal will morph almost instantly to match whatever animal he's lucky enough to get. My deer wasn't a record-book buck by any stretch, but in that moment I caught myself being glad about that fact. If I killed the muley of my dreams, then what would I dream about?

STALKING
THE HIGHLANDS

BILL HEAVEY

I'm no stranger to unusual stalking situations, but this is definitely the first time I've had whortleberries in my pants. I am crawling down a 50-degree slope right behind my guide, Niall Rowantree. Right on my heels is gillie Steven Grant, 18, dragging the padded rifle case behind him. We are low-crawling through the heather or gorse or whatever the hell you call the wet, tundralike stuff covering the Scottish highlands, trying to keep from getting busted by the dozens of red deer scattered across this mountainside. I don't know about the others, but I'm doing more sliding than crawling. To stop, I have to stiffen my arms and shove them into the ground before me while flexing my toes to vertical and dragging them like anchors.

Meanwhile, the farther we travel in this manner, the more vegetation finds its way into my clothes. Every time Niall (pronounced "Neal") stops to assess our progress and the disposition of the surrounding deer, we rear-end one another with all the precision of the Three Stooges trying to burgle a house. I use these occasions to retrieve handfuls of herbage from my pants.

We are sneaking on a big red stag, an 8-pointer, lying on a bench several hundred yards below us. At least I think he's still below us. The weather was glorious this morning, when we were glassing the hills from the road below. Since then, curtains of mist and pattering rain have begun moving through from the southwest, reducing visibility to 80 yards.

I have come to Scotland on the advice of my dentist. He told me that for the price of an outfitted elk hunt, you could fly here, sleep in a clean bed each night, eat like a king, hunt the legendary highlands, and almost be guaranteed success on red stag. These deer, the largest land mammal native to the United Kingdom, are smaller cousins of the American elk.

For a long time, the beasts were reserved for royalty and landed gentry. Today, they attract English, German, and Scandinavian hunters, as well as an increasing number of Americans who, like my dentist, have discovered that red stag offer a challenging and satisfying hunt. I searched on Google, asked around, and eventually found Corrour (Ka-RAH-wer).

My first impression as I leave Glasgow and drive north into the highlands is one of disbelief. Given that the whole of the United Kingdom is a little smaller than Oregon, I figured the highlands would have the character of a good-size American theme park—you know, a few castles and golf courses, deep-fried Snickers bars (a national specialty, I've been told), and tacky little shops selling plaid T-shirts. Wrong. The "road" from the highway to the lodge and cottage where I'm staying, for instance, is 12 miles long and takes 45 minutes to navigate. One false move and you'd end up 400 feet below in a stream gushing along like a loose fire hose.

The estate itself is 52,000 acres and more isolated than you'd imagine was possible in Europe. Before the access road was finished in 1972, the only way to get here was by train via the tiny Corrour rail station, the highest and most remote in Britain.

It's not hard to see why. Big, stark, and strangely compelling, the countryside is nearly deserted, with a population density rivaling that of Papua New Guinea. This place zeroes in on your psyche and grabs hold. What I'm experiencing is not déjà vu, the sense of having been here before, so much as the feeling you get when you meet another person and intuitively sense that you already know each other's stories. Maybe it's ancestral.

This is, after all, the WASP Mesopotamia, the place from which my forebears and those of millions of other Americans were cast out or fled when the highland clans, the last vestiges of the feudal system in Europe, collapsed in the 18th century. Niall says that nobody lived here year-round in the old times. The winters are too brutal. It was only in 1899, when the wealthy classes created by the Industrial Revolution took up the gentlemanly sport of stag hunting, that a grand estate house was built, complete with four stalkers' cottages.

"The clans would send their cattle up here to graze each summer, tended by the women, children, and old men. Younger men farmed the glens below. The Road to the Isles, the route people from the Western Isles used for centuries to drive their cattle to market at Falkirk, runs right through the property. Almost every hill here has a legend or myth associated with it. It's all stinking with history."

In the morning, through Niall's ridiculous-looking collapsible telescope, we see at least three groups of deer from the road, including a nice buck feeding alone and into the wind below a rocky bowl. The telescope is just window dressing, I'm sure, something to complement the stereotypical image of the rustic highland guide. I say so. Niall shakes his head.

"Pure practicality. I loathe high-power spotting scopes. It's always windy here and you can't hold them still. And they weigh a ton. Twenty-power is all you really need in this country. Plus it fits in my pocket." He shows me how to steady it—right hand resting on the bones of my eye socket and cradling the eyepiece, left hand holding the objective lens, a car door or shooting stick as a brace. Suddenly I can count the tines on an animal half a mile away. I hand it back, impressed.

"Right," he says, collapsing the thing and tucking it in a pocket. "Feel like stalking him?" He doesn't have to ask twice.

To get in position, the three of us drive on down the road well past the deer, get the Argo eight-wheeler off the trailer, and ride it bucking and kicking up the mountain to get altitude and the wind in our favor. It takes several hours—and some rough walking. The ground is so uneven that I have to play the age card and commandeer Niall's ram-horn–handled walking stick or risk a fall.

"Hell, you do this every day," I growl, doing my best David E. Petzal. "Besides, you're barely 40." While I'm appropriately dressed in a Cabela's

Dry Plus rainsuit that performs admirably when vertical, we're not spending much time upright. When the mist lifts momentarily, we see stags and hinds not 150 yards distant. Red deer can spot a man a mile away, Niall says, and they know it's hunting season. Every move we make is careful and slow. When Niall freezes, Steven and I do, too.

All this crawling gets to be warm work after a while, and when a slight updraft hits, it wafts a mixture of my own familiar b.o. and the aromatic scents of the crushed flowers and plants inside my duds. I smell not unlike a wet mule sprayed with herbal bathroom freshener. It's a scent that might appeal to a certain kind of woman. But she would probably look like Petzal.

Niall has stressed from the outset that this kind of stalking requires close, careful travel. "The only animal that walks abreast is man. An alarmed red deer runs a long way. If we go single file, one that just gets a glimpse may take us for another deer." He should know. The Rowantrees have been in this part of the highlands for centuries, since the days of the warrior-clan subsistence farmers. A nearby crag even bears the Gaelic version of the family name.

He motions behind his back with two fingers for me to slide up even with him, then hands me the binocs. "He's facing us," he whispers. "About 160 meters. Get ready." It takes me a while to pick out the stag, but he's there, alone and bedded, the wind at his back. Steven uncases the Sako .308 with an 8X scope and a Reflex T8 suppressor at the muzzle. (The sound-reducing device is the law here, required to protect the eardrums of working guides. Niall says it also improves accuracy and reduces recoil without affecting range.)

I set up the rifle on its bipod at my feet and twist around to get the stag in the scope. "Don't shoot until he stands," Niall whispers. "You've got a so-so kill shot, and you'd chew up too much meat. Standing will give you a better angle on both counts. We'll wait. When you do this right, they never know what hit them." I can't help but respect the man. It's obvious that he loves to hunt. He could easily end his day's work now by allowing me to take a killing shot, but ethical shortcuts, however slight, don't appear to be part of the deal.

Downhill and feet-first is an awkward position to shoot from, not to mention a good way to put a hole in your foot. Also, my pants are steadily sliding up as the minutes pass, creating a massive whortleberry-scented wedgie. I'm wondering if it wasn't precisely this situation that led to the invention of the kilt, which suddenly sounds eminently practical.

The stag, it seems, has very few appointments today, for he stays bedded. While we wait, Niall breaks out sandwiches, and we pass around his thermos of hot tea. Somehow, he and Steven both manage the trick of wearing tweed knickers and matching Sherlock Holmes–style deerstalker hats without looking as if they've wandered off the set of *Queer Eye for the Straight Guy*. The fact that Niall is built like an oak might be part of it. Frankly, I don't know how Steven pulls it off. He's a quiet boy; it's his boss who tells me Steven was raised on a farm and is an expert sheep shearer and champion highland dancer. He passed up a good paying job on an Australian sheep farm to come here. One day he hopes to be a full-fledged stalker like Niall, and to count one of the four stalking areas—or "beats"—on Corrour as his personal kingdom.

The weather clears a bit, though the wind remains. To take my mind off how wet my butt is, I ask about the land's history. The Scottish Highlands, my guide explains, are, for all their beauty, a collapsed ecosystem. As late as 600 years ago, they were covered in Scots pine, aspen, juniper, and oak. Not so long ago, European brown bears, wolves, and lynx kept the deer populations in check. There were also beaver, hares, wild boar, and polecats. Over the years the forests were cut down and the predators disappeared.

After the English troops came and the clan system collapsed, the destruction escalated. The feudal commons became private land. Local small farmers were forcibly evicted and their homes burned down in the infamous "clearances" to make room for profitable sheep farms. The livestock quickly overgrazed what was left. The decayed vegetation became acidic peat, which supports only a narrow range of plant life.

The heyday of gentlemen's sporting lodges didn't arrive until the 1890s and was nearly over by the 1930s. During those glory days, wealthy European sportsmen arrived by private railcar, then boarded a steamboat and motored 3 miles down Lake Ossian to the lodge. Currently the estate is owned by a publicity-shy Swedish couple who did rather well designing and marketing cartons for milk and orange juice. They are interested in trying to balance continued hunting with restoring the biodiversity of the highlands.

Taking the welfare of the land itself into consideration is a relatively new concept here, a break with the long tradition of exploiting nature for immediate benefit and damn whoever comes next. It means not only harvesting larger numbers of deer but also reinvigorating the herds by taking animals other than the largest and healthiest, another break with the traditional trophy mentality. That idea has led the owners to build a state-of-the-art processing facility on the premises to market its own Taste of the Wild brand of gourmet venison. The idea is to capture more of the profits and jobs for the local economy.

Looking over this country, you can't help but wish them well. For all the indignities it has suffered, this remains a magnificent hunk of the earth. Wild brown trout, native pike up to 30 pounds, and otters swim in the lakes. The moors still hide red and black grouse, ptarmigan, kestrels, and golden eagles. There are still foxes and pine martens. Distilleries that produce some of the world's most sought after whiskies, Oban and Talisker, are nearby. I'm already hooked, wondering how I can come up with a way to stay longer than I planned.

"This country has always been good at raising three things: bards, poets, and warriors," Niall tells me. Both his father and grandfather were stalkers. His grandfather also served as a sniper in World War II in the famed Lovat Scouts, a force composed of highlanders. Circa 1900, the British Army thought it was taking a chance on accepting the rough Scotsmen into its sophisticated ranks. It soon discovered, however, that with generations of experience in fighting, stalking, and thriving in rough country, the men made superb soldiers. They gained a reputation as legendary warriors, scouts, spies, guides, and horsemen.

The Lovat Scouts were the forerunner of the elite British SAS. Niall's own father was sent into the Navy to learn a trade, "but he didn't like it, so he came back to the highlands to be a stalker." I ask what he did in the Navy. "Well, actually, he got a PhD in nuclear physics." When I look at him skeptically, he shrugs. "We're not a dumb people," he explains. "We just never had a lot of money." Niall works seven-day weeks for months on end as head guide and manager of the estate, and suffers more than the occasional fool client in the process. It's the only way he can stay on the land he grew from.

"It's not always easy, being a rich man's plaything," he'll confide over several wee drams of the Cragganmore single malt that I found out he likes from Jane, the office manager, before coming. (Always a good idea to keep your guide happy.) "But we highlanders have long been dispossessed in our own country."

My scope is still on the deer, but he's on stag time, happy to lie there and chew his cud. Niall doesn't want to try anything tricky like throwing a stone to get him to stand for the shot. He's a pro, and a pro knows how to wait when the situation calls for it. To pass the time, I ask when he knew he wanted to go into the family line of work.

"I've been obsessed with deer since I can remember," he says, ever since he saw his father bringing stags down out of the mountains after dark on specially bred hill ponies. Deer have been his life. He took whatever work he could find to stay around them, working as a forestry ranger and then as a contractor controlling deer populations for both private landowners and the state.

He tells me about the winter of 1989, when hundreds of deer died from starvation and exposure, the result of overgrazing, destruction of the forests where they sheltered, and populations spiraling ever upward. Ironically, to save the animal he loved, he killed an average of 1,000 of them a year for the next six years.

"It was sad, but it had to be done." His gun of choice was a .308 Mannlicher SSG, and he speaks admiringly of cartridges like the .300 WSM and .338 Lapua for long-range work.

"It was a bloody way to learn, but learn I did: how to tell what they're going to do next by what they're doing now and how they're doing it, how to identify the dominant stag or hind in a group at first glance, which way and in which order they'll run when alarmed, the best way to use the ground to your advantage, tricks about the wind . . . " His voice trails off, as if he's revisiting things he'd rather not see again.

Ninety minutes later, after my limbs have gone to sleep and come back several times, the stag finally stands, shakes itself dry, and then, as if offering himself, turns broadside. I squeeze the trigger, and when I recover my sight picture he's down. "Good shot," says Niall. I remove the magazine, clear the chamber, and hand the rifle back to Steven, who cases it and hustles off for the Argo.

Niall and I make our way down. We gut the animal, leaving the heart and liver in the carcass, which will be logged in and individually tagged at Corrour's processing plant. I admire the lyre-shaped antlers, smaller than an elk's, bigger than a whitetail's. He's handsome and hardy, with a belly round from fattening up for the coming rut. A stiff red fur ruff encircles the throat as if to protect that vulnerable area from the stag's primordial enemy, the wolf. Niall estimates he weighed about 220 pounds on the hoof.

Stroking the stag's side, I murmur my thanks and my apology for having stolen his life, and again admire the graceful antlers. My guide says this one is between 7 and 9 years old, a bit past his prime, a good candidate for the hunt.

As we wait for Steven to bring the Argo, I notice a tree trunk half-buried in the peat and gesture at it. "That's a Scots pine, probably a thousand years old, from the forest that was once here," Niall says. "The peat preserves things." He shows me a knob on the blackened trunk where stags, which were originally woodland animals but have adapted to the loss of the forests, have rubbed their antlers, revealing the reddish wood beneath. He looks up at the rim of the mountains above us and says something in Gaelic.

"It means Basin of the Bones," he says. "The story is that a fellow stole some cattle belonging to one of the clan chieftains. When he heard the chieftain was after him, he claimed he hadn't stolen them but knew who had, and would see they were punished and the cattle returned. He gave the cattle back, then murdered some people here and scattered their bones so it would look as if they'd been eaten by wolves. Hence the name." It's a grisly tale, and faithful enough to human nature to make you believe there's at least a germ of truth to it.

Steven shows up with the Argo, and we swing the stag aboard. Driving back toward the lodge, Niall makes a slight detour to show me Loch

Treag, a 9-mile-long lake bordering Corrour. "The water level is up, or you could see part of a crannog, a fortified island made from piling up stones, where people built their houses to be safe from attack. This one dates from the Bronze Age." He points across the lake to a somewhat sinister-looking saddle with nearly sheer walls rising on both sides.

"This road we're on is one of the old cattle droves, and it goes right through there. Place named Black Mouth in Gaelic." It fits. It's a dark, creepy little passage. Niall asks if I've ever heard the term blackmail. Of course, I say. "Well, you're looking at the place it comes from. There was a band of cutthroats who controlled this place. You paid a toll to go through or suffered the consequences."

We're bumping our way back to the lodge in the Land Rover to check in the stag when the sun, absent nearly all day, focuses a shaft of light atop a far mountain. Some kinds of beauty pierce your heart like a pain, and this moment is one. These ancient, stark hills may be the ruins of great forests, but they're lovely all the same.

The next morning, I'm around when Niall meets a just-arrived client, a wealthy man from the Netherlands and his son, who doesn't hunt but wants to accompany his father. The man is upset because the airline lost his rifle. It's his favorite, a double in some elephant-killing caliber, very old and expensive. Also, his son needs to return by 4 p.m. to take an important conference call. Niall tells him he'll do his best, and when the fellow leaves, he offers up a silent prayer that the rifle is not found anytime soon. It may be hard fitting it with the suppressor, and the rifle will likely either be unscoped or knocked off zero by now. Much better to use the lodge's .270.

By lunch they are back with a large-racked 10-pointer, one that was apparently just over the hill as breeding stock, riding in the back of the Argo. The man is beaming and very excited, clapping Niall on the shoulder.

"*Mein Gott!*" he exclaims. "He is a devil, this one! We approached downwind. Downwind! And when I shot, they ran toward us before mine fell."

Niall takes me aside and draws me a quick diagram. The stags were indeed upwind, but grazing in a high saddle about a kilometer away. But he noticed that they were grazing slowly toward one side of the saddle.

"So they were moving into the area where the peaks of the saddle cause the wind to swirl. And they don't like swirling wind, don't feel safe there. I was betting they'd keep on going in that direction until they got to a steadier breeze. And in any saddle, there's a place where the eddies create a current of air flowing against the prevailing wind direction. That's what I was banking on.

"But we had to move fast, because you could tell by the clouds that a front was coming in as we got closer to noon. And so we only had a half hour or so before everything changed. I wasn't sure he could move fast enough, but the adrenaline kicked in when he saw the stags.

"It was a bit of gamble, but not much, really. I knew the carry—the Scottish name for what the wind is doing in relation to you and the game. It was just a question of getting there quick enough, before noon. In Genesis, they refer to that as 'the windy part of the day.'"

He sees the slightly incredulous look on my face and says, "Oh, yeah. Dad was always a big Bible thumper."

Actually, it's a toss-up as to what I'm more amazed by: the Bible as hunting reference book or the fact that he is playing the stalking game at a level I can only hope to reach. I find myself blurting out that he has to come to the States. He has to try hunting whitetails. He has to try bowhunting.

"Can't," he says simply. "I'm afraid I might not come back." I look at him and suddenly get it. He's as crazy for hunting as I am, maybe more. And lives in a place where, by law, neither bow nor blackpowder firearms are used. If he got hooked on, say, ground-stalking whitetails with a bow, he might very well leave the whole package—family, job, and country—to chase his addiction. Ah, well. I tell him I'll smuggle a bow over next time and at least let him feel what it's like shooting a hunting compound.

"Officially, I couldn't allow it," he says loudly, then lowers his voice.

"Unofficially, how about next year?"

THE PERFECT ELK

RICK BASS

The best seasons are not necessarily the ones in which you are fortunate enough to find an animal early in the year, or even necessarily at all. When I was young it seemed that way, but the older I get the more pleased I am at the end of a day in which I simply see new country, and perhaps get close to an animal, but do not take one, for whatever reason. Even a stumble, a mistake with the wind, or the cracking of a twig that blows out the herd doesn't upset me anymore. That's just how it goes, sometimes. I've been fortunate to kill a lot of elk over the years, so more than ever it's the quality of the hunt that I anticipate, not the outcome.

I used to hear older hunters say this kind of thing all the time, and I didn't understand what they were talking about, and wasn't sure it was something I looked forward to: becoming such an old-timer myself, and losing my obsession and the uncomplicated way of measuring success—meat—that was so well defined. Because I loved that equation, and the way it pulled me over and through the mountains, I did not want to let go of it, and viewed its departure as a lessening.

It is not a lessening, though. It is a deepening and a widening. The pinpoint precision of the kill is no longer the focus, but everything else is still there, and richer.

All week I had been hunting new country, new ridges and basins, and had been finding fresh tracks, though not the animals. I kept bumping them late in the day, and rather than pushing them too hard, I had backed off and then returned the next day. At one point I found where the herd had bedded down in an old abandoned hunting camp, which would have made quite a Christmas card, if I had known the old-timers who had once briefly inhabited it. I envisioned snapping a photo of the elk arranged warm and cozy beneath the bare lodgepole frames of the tent spars, the bulls' sweeping antlers like the spars themselves, and sending the photo to the old boys in their rest home, with a caption, *Wish you were here*, or, *The neighborhood's not the same without you.*

When I go to bed each night after a hunt, knee-sprung and leg-hammered—groaning, I'm so tired and sore—that ache, that diminishment, is my gain. Someday soon I'll be like those old gone-by codgers, unable any longer to enter the territory I so love, and with the prey, always, ultimately victorious. These days, the longer I go without killing an animal, the richer my days are, for the thing I love does not end.

Still, when I cut new tracks in the fresh snow—when I come in behind them and have the wind in my favor and the elk are wandering through the woods just ahead of me—I want them as badly as I ever have.

Some nights when you go to bed you just have a certain feeling, a certain confidence, about the day to come. Part of it is an anticipation and excitement but part of it is a calm. The fact that new snow had fallen the night before deepened this feeling. It wasn't so much overconfidence as it was an awareness that all the conditions were right, and it was easy to imagine things falling in place as they had in the past. I knew there were elk on the mountain; there was new snow, I was rested, I had a good early predawn start, and the snow had stopped falling and the breeze was out of the north. I would go in from the south, walking quietly in that new snow. Best of all, the place where I was going was far enough from the road that I wasn't likely to encounter any other humans.

I drove and daydreamed, vaguely conscious of the idea that I was on one side of a dividing line—not having meat—and that at the end of the day, driving back, I might well be on the other side.

I turned up the old logging road, pleased to see no tire tracks in the new snow. The place I was going was steep and rocky and gnarly and the way there was difficult. Good choice, I thought, extending my goodwill to the 7 billion humans who had chosen not to climb this particular mountain before daylight on this particular morning. Stay in bed, sleep, be warm, read the paper. Enjoy your coffee.

Starting up through the forest, with every inch of new snow mine, I grinned like a kid, laughed out loud at how wonderful it—life—all is. I wish I could remember that every day of the year, but I confess to forgetting it sometimes.

I was surprised not to find them at first light in the basin where I had been seeing their sign. Maybe I had been a little overconfident after all. I had to decide whether to ascend to the ridge and work back downwind, back toward where I knew they sometimes bedded, or push farther on.

It was a joy, having the mountain to myself, and so much new snow. I decided to push farther on. The day was mine, so why not? No other animals were moving, not even the deer—I always choose, in my excitement over fresh new snow, to conveniently forget how in those first hours after a big snow, the elk, in particular, hunker down, knowing that they are vulnerable. No matter: The farther I went, the more it would increase my chances of cutting tracks. It was the logic of overconfidence. I didn't know where the elk were, but every step I took was bringing me a step closer to them.

Near noon, I climbed up out of the clouds and into the yellow sunlight. I was in a stunted high-elevation lodgepole forest, up on a plateau, when I found their tracks, looking as freshly laid in that deep new sunlit snow as they could possibly be. It seemed to me that the snow in the little craters of their hoofprints was still sliding down into the wells of their prints—that the elk must be right in front of me, close enough to touch, and that somehow I simply wasn't seeing them, was looking straight through them. I could smell them, and their wandering trail bespoke an attitude of extreme leisure.

In the old days, I would have surged ahead. Here in the new days however, I wanted to savor the moment—the butter-yellow sunlight on the new snow, the freshest tracks of the day, the blue sky with its frost crystals shimmering, the perfect stillness in the woods, the solitude, and the extreme good fortune of my having slipped in downwind just behind the elk, rather than coming across a skein of tracks just a smidge upwind. Though I was eager to see what lay ahead, and very much wanted, with the familiar old intensity, to shoot an elk, I also wanted to look around and think about things a bit.

It was a big transition, to have gone from so many hours of trudging on through deep silent snow without seeing so much as a squirrel, to suddenly being in the midst of the hunt, the midst of the moment. I wanted to retire all my previous daydreaming, and yet the daydreaming would not easily go away. It was a confusion of demeanors, a convergence of two entirely different rivers, and I sat on a fallen log and ate my lunch and waited for the elk to get a little farther out ahead of me. They weren't going anywhere. Where could they go? All the world was snow, and all the world was deep forest, and there had been no humans on this way-back mountain all season long.

They wandered in a braid, cows and calves and young bulls and surely at least one giant bull. Some of their tracks stepped over logs and branches and others went around them. The sunlight was beautiful; it seemed somehow like the light that might exist on another planet, with a shimmering sun dog when I looked at it, and the snow was so cold and dry and deep that I made no sound at all, accentuating the idea that I was living in a dream, or another world.

With the clock ever so slowly starting to wear down my body, I was hunting hard, intently, but savoring it. It was a perfect day: How many days are perfect? Maybe all of them, but some, I think, are more perfect than others.

They were moving so slowly: stopping to paw at the kinnikinnick far below the snow as if digging or mining for buried treasure. I had never encountered a more leisurely band of elk—eight, 10 animals, maybe—and I couldn't believe they weren't right in sight. Only the density of the forest prevented me from seeing that short distance ahead, into the future, and I hunted on, as carefully as I knew how, totally immersed in an intensity of awareness of sight and sound and cautious movement. I had the wind in my favor, and the level sun behind me as it trudged slowly from east to south toward west. The only thing less than perfect about the whole setup was how god-awfully far I was from the car, but so what? I had all year to pack out. I like packing out: not getting in a hurry, just humping one big pack load out after another, one a day, for days on end—a slow transition away from the dreamtime world of the hunt, and back into the routine workaday world of man.

There was lazy movement behind a tree right in front of me. A big dark animal with a nest of antlers was nibbling at something on the other side of the tree, not 10 yards in front of me, and calmly, I lifted the rifle and looked through the scope and saw that the antlers were those of a mule deer, and then the buck—a big one—stepped out into the open and looked at me, standing there so very close.

The woods were filled with calm. Sometimes there are just days and moments like that, and we move from one to the next, it seems to me, as if stepping from one stone to another while crossing a broad and shallow river.

The mule deer was still chewing. He looked at me for a long time—somehow he understood he was not in danger, as if knowing that my taking him now would end my elk hunt and possibly my elk season—and then, almost as if with resignation, he stotted off, his swagbelly swinging; the requisite escape, but maintaining his dignity at the same time.

The big bull's tracks separated from the herd. He had peeled off to the north to go bed in some thick timber, while the herd went to the left, and I was faced with a decision: meat or antlers? The herd would be bedded down in patches of sun in the old larch and pine forest just ahead of me, but the big bull was closer, and I wanted to see what he looked like. About the old assertion that big bulls are tough—which they sometimes are—I wasn't worried; I have found no bull so tough that 30 days of aging wouldn't tenderize and flavor the meat into the same exquisite taste of a younger animal.

It was like a lesson in behavior from an elk hunting textbook: The bull was high-stepping over logs and pushing through chest-high brush. Snow had spilled from the leaves and branches and needles as he sought to cover his backtrail in such a way that the approach of another would be audible.

When he jumped up off his bed in front of me, not 15 yards away, I thought he was a moose; he was so dark and tall. There was a clump of trees between him and me, and I simply didn't have a shot. He kept those trees perfectly between us and all I could see was an occasional wide ant-ler, or a patch of dark body, galloping up the hill.

I didn't think he'd seen me. I crouched and hid and watched the down-wind ridge, knowing he might circle around to take a look at what had so rudely interrupted his midday rest. I waited 15 minutes, then took off after his tracks, and found where indeed he had done that, and had peered down at me and seen or scented me without my seeing him, and then bolted. I fol-lowed his tracks down the slope to where he had come barreling through the midst of his herd, spooking them, and taking all of them down the back side of the mountain, into what for me was terra incognita.

The good news, I told myself, is I get to keep hunting.

The bull stayed with them for only a short distance, then must have seen or scented or heard me again, for his tracks bolted straight up the moun-tain, while the herd continued down.

I decided to save him for another year, and to follow the herd this time—in part because I knew an old bull like that would never let me get the drop on him, once he knew I was there, and in part because he was running ever farther from the car, while the herd was at least for now headed back in somewhat that general direction—south, rather than east, toward where I had parked, at least in roughly the same hemisphere.

I followed them all day. They went straight down, through cliffs and rock chimneys and into creeks, charging down slopes so steep I needed to hold on to lodgepole saplings to keep from sliding. I followed quietly, sidehilling, thinking they would calm down, but the line of their tracks was the pan-icked single-file exodus of fear.

It was a couple of hours before they began, ever so gradually, to ascend and spread back out, believing they had shaken me, and not even really knowing what I was, only something that had frightened the bull.

It was all new territory to me. I had a general idea of where I was, but every step was new, and I liked that. After an hour or more the tracks fi-nally began to unravel, spreading back out into a tentative wandering that soon enough grew more confident, though the elk had not stopped to feed again, but were instead still moving, passing through the same long slants of cold yellow sunlight that I was.

They led me to another plateau, more densely forested than the sidehill, and I knew they had to be getting tired, and looking for a safe afternoon bedding spot. I crept up over the edge of the hill and about 20 yards in front of me saw what looked like three vertical black bars hanging beneath a leaning lodgepole. The black was the exact color of the shins of an elk, though it puzzled me that I couldn't see the animal, just those three slender shins, and that there was not a fourth.

I raised the scope and peered at the shins through the dark forest but still could see nothing else. I crept a little closer for a better vantage, looked again—it's got to be an elk, I told myself—and still the shins had not moved. How odd, I thought; it must just be three trellises of moss hanging straight down. I crawled in a little closer.

The shins unfolded into a tangle of elk. Then there was a herd busting loose all around me, with some animals galloping south and others north; and once again, the chase resumed, the trailing through the deep snow, the never-ending saga of failure and desire.

Half an hour later I saw a young bull moving carefully through the lodgepoles and yellow light, his antlers like those of royalty—not huge, but what elk is not beautiful?—and when I fired, he dropped in the deep snow and—except for the gutting, packing out, butchering and wrapping—the year was over, and my gratitude for the luck of the day was no less than it had ever been, and all the more so, for having been led by the herd into new country.

As I was packing out at dusk, an immense mule deer buck—the largest I'd ever seen—blocked my path, coming up the game trail I was heading out on. It was blue twilight, still legal shooting light, and he wasn't 10 yards in front of me. For long moments we beheld each other. He clearly did not want to step aside to let me pass, and doubtless smelled only the bull I had just killed. I felt that I could have reached out and touched him with the end of the rifle. The woods were thick on either side of the trail.

Do you know what I mean if I say that his antlers were too large, the deer himself too large, and, in the blue dusk like that, too regal, and too easy, and that my day had been already almost too perfect?

All my life, I have heard older hunters speak of such moments—of letting trophy bucks pass—and now I was at that same place, as if at a threshold of something I didn't quite understand, but maybe didn't need to understand.

I would never see a bigger mule deer, but it just didn't feel right. I had all the meat I needed and then some, and I had been hunting elk, not deer. Part of it might have been my advancing middle age and part of it might have been the cultural pivot of history itself—the new post-recession austerity—but in the end a large part of it I think had to do with how beautiful the woods were that evening, and of how I did not want to break the quiet communion of the long pack out with the sound of a gunshot.

The giant deer took a leap to the downhill side, and then high-stepped around and past me, walking, not running, as if having known all along what decision I would make during this most perfect of days in one of the most perfect seasons, and situated perfectly and halfway between who I used to be and who I was on my way to becoming.

I suppose in theory every day is like that for each of us, but that particular cold starry evening, there on the new mountain, it felt very much that the buck had opened a gate for me, and I had made the right decision, and passed on through it, as had countless other hunters before me, in all the generations of mankind. It was a point where hunger yields to pleasure, and a point where enough is enough. A point when beauty matters more than ever before, and with the day's shadows, though slightly longer, ever more beautiful, ever more meaningful.

MOOSE MISERY

DAVID E. PETZAL

Having been narrowly missed by a peeing moose (no laughing matter; it's like a garden hose), I had for years harbored feelings of bitter resentment against the species, so when I got the invitation to go hunt them in Alaska I accepted like a shot, so to speak. Toward that end I went to Newark Airport, a vast and dismal place with an Alaska Airways counter stuck off in a corner. If you fly Alaska in the fall, you find yourself lined up with people who carry rod cases, coolers, and gun cases. They get their clothes from Cabela's and Bass Pro Shops, and they form a distinct subculture here in northern New Jersey.

Instead of the usual looks of suspicion and hostility that a camo backpack and gun case usually draw in a northeastern airport, people asked me what I was hunting, and when I said "Moose," I heard half a dozen "Good lucks." Even the TSA agent who checked my gun case wished me luck. Buoyed by this outpouring of goodwill, I went on into the bowels of the terminal for that combination of tedium and aggravation that is available only to the air traveler.

• • •

For this hunt, I was the guest of Charles and Jody Allen. Charles, a Texan, was a game biologist for most of his career, as well as being a hunting pal of *Field & Stream*'s former shooting editor, Bob Brister. Some years ago he started up a fishing lodge southeast of Cordova, Alaska, and also founded Knives of Alaska in case he ran out of things to do. Jody is the organizational half of the team and an experienced big-game hunter who has done some truly hair-raising stuff. Charles invited me moose hunting to pick my brains about knives and watch me suffer.

The Allens refuse to take out moose hunters for money. It's too much hard work, Charles says. The country where we hunted is dead flat, and if you view it from the air it seems innocuous enough. It is subarctic tundra and forms a pattern of greens interspersed by the tans of long grass, the yellows of alders, and the near-black greens of "islands" of fir trees that dot it. There is water everywhere: little rivers, streams, ponds, small lakes, and puddles.

In reality, this chunk of real estate is a nightmare where a man in good shape will work hard to cover half a mile in an hour. It sucks, it grabs, it slurps, it oozes. The only place where you can find firm footing is on the fir islands.

The tundra does not suck uniformly. There are places where you sink only to your ankles, and this is merely tiring and annoying. But then there are areas of Maximum Suck, where you go in up to your knees. If you pause, you will sink deeper. If you try to pull one leg out by putting weight on the other, the second leg will sink. If you stop for a moment to get your breath, you will sink. The only thing to do is to keep going, all the while remembering that dying on the tundra from a heart attack is better than dying in a hospital from a heart attack.

Your problems don't end with what's underfoot. The tundra is laced with alder hells, thickets of small trees (7 feet high or so) that are so dense as to be nearly impenetrable. The only way through them is to shove, and they in return lash back at your eyes and face, clutch at your legs and rifle and pack, and keep you from seeing for more than an arm's length ahead. Unless you have a good sense of direction or keep your compass in hand at all times, you can easily become lost in an alder hell.

In case you're undeterred by alder hells, there are willow thickets that offer an infuriating alternative. These invariably grow in deep water and muck, so you have that to worry about, and the willows are too stiff to push aside, so you twist, dodge, weave, bend, swivel, and duck to get through them.

And then, for the final refinement, you have Satan's Own Air Force, which takes the form of blackflies. There are the ones that bite and the ones that don't. The ones that don't bite swarm around your head and fly into your eyes, ears, nose, and mouth. It is a wonder to me how an insect that is smaller than a match head can feel like a red-hot 5-pound rock when it lands on your eye.

Blackflies that bite like to do so in awkward places such as the juncture of your cap and forehead, and under your shirt cuffs. You don't feel the little fiends at work, but they leave small blood blisters that itch like mad for a couple of days.

The giant cave bear is gone, as are the sabertooth tiger, mastodon, and mammoth, but the moose, which knew all of them personally, is still with us. Moose are the largest deer ever to walk the earth, and today they inhabit the northern forests in North America, Europe, and Russia. There are several subspecies, but the Alaska-Yukon variety (*Alces alces gigas*) is by far the largest.

An Alaska bull in good condition weighs 1,200 to 1,600 pounds, while a cow will scale 800 to 1,300 pounds. But weight and heft are only part of it. A big bull stands nearly 8 feet high at the shoulder, and when they are close to you (say, 10 yards, as one was), they loom like a locomotive. I've been in proximity to some very big animals, but for sheer physical presence I've never seen anything to equal one of these monsters.

Their eyesight is supposed to be poor (having run afoul of it, I have my doubts about this), their sense of smell is acute, and their hearing is positively supernatural. Charles Allen says a moose can hear a human voice, speaking at a conversational level, from a mile away.

Moose can live up to 30 years, but that is rare, and 16 is about average. They produce their best antlers when they are 10 to 12. The most common measurement for moose racks is from widest point to widest point. In Alaska, 50 inches is the legal minimum width; 60 is a super trophy, and 70 is about as wide as they go. However, antlers are also judged on palm size, heaviness, and number of points. You could shoot a spindly 70-incher that was wide but did not have much else to recommend it, whereas a heavy, massive-palmed rack in the mid or high 50s would actually be a much better trophy.

In mid September, moose go into rut and become territorial. They stop eating and concentrate on breeding as many cows as possible and on keeping other bulls away from their territory. Moose rely heavily on sound to conduct their business, and this leads us to the moose hunter's principal tactic.

The best way to dupe a moose is to use a combination of three sounds: crashing brush, the bull's challenge grunt, and the cow's call of passion. Of these, the last is the most spectacular, and this is how it is, as practiced by Charles Allen:

Charles cups both hands alongside his mouth, leans forward at the waist, bends to his right, and makes a loud (and I mean loud) moan that sounds like Aaaaaaaaaaaaaaaaaa-aaahhhhhhhhhhhhhhhhhhhhhhhhhhhhhh!

As he makes this horrible noise, he straightens up and bends his body from the right to the left, putting everything he has into it.

The call is a ghastly sound if taken in human terms. It is a moan full of rage and despair and pain. It goes on for a minute or more, and moose can hear it from a mile or farther if the wind is right.

If you take the call as moose do, however, all it means is *C'mere, lover boy.*

After Charles moaned a couple of times, he would take a sapling and beat hell out of the nearby brush, which is what bulls do with their antlers. Then he would cup his hands again and go UH . . . . . . UH . . . UH . . . . UH!

This is the challenge a bull moose issues, and it means *I've come here to kick ass and chew bubble gum, and I'm fresh out of gum.*

Charles carries a moose scapula and uses it to beat the brush (it makes the same sound as antlers) and will flash it at an approaching bull, who may mistake it for a rival's antler.

On one occasion, we called up what is known as a mulligan bull. (That's a moose with antlers so small that he's only good to shoot for a mulligan stew.) This critter was big-bodied, but his antlers were a joke; he was probably only 2 or 3 years old, a long way from being a player in the game of love.

•••

Before I get into this part of the story, I must introduce you to the third member of our hunting trio, the person who did all the heavy lifting. His name is James Minifie, 28, a game biologist who guides fishermen at Charles's lodge during summer and fall and goes on moose hunts when Charles wants to make someone suffer. He is a bit over 6 feet tall, 180 pounds, and possibly the toughest human being I have ever hunted with. Charles put the case succinctly in explaining James's ability to carry 60 pounds of moose meat over the tundra without even breathing hard:

"James," he said, "is an animal."

If we needed someone to climb 50 feet up a tree and perch for an hour looking for moose, James was our man. When we needed someone to leap out of a duck boat going against the current with two men and lots of gear in it and pull the thing free of a sandbar, we called on James. And he did these things all day long. Without breaking a sweat.

But back to the hunting.

Flying is a vital part of moose hunting. Because giant deer do not lurk in every alder hell, and because travel on the ground (or what passes for the ground) is so difficult, the only way you can find them is from the air, and so you go up in a plane, fly at 600 feet or less, and look for them.

You may not hunt on the same day you fly. If you do, the Alaska game wardens take your rifle and airplane, fine you heavily, and throw you in prison. So what you do is fly, take a GPS reading on where you see a moose from the air, and the next day travel by boat and foot to that spot and hope he hasn't moved.

Since we had done this and knew roughly where the moose was, our job was to get within a couple of hundred yards and call him in. So we got up in the dark, put on our chest waders (hip boots were not nearly tall enough for the stuff we had to slog through), and at 5:30 piled ourselves and our equipment into a rusted-out Jeep and drove over the sand dunes into the headwaters of the local river where Charles keeps a shallow-draft duck boat.

He parked the Jeep in the water, we loaded the boat, and off we went. (One morning we found a mink in the boat. The mink seemed pretty fond of it and was reluctant to leave.) Then we traveled across the broad, shallow headwaters until we found whichever feeder stream we were looking for and started up it.

Because this part of Alaska is brown bear country, you go armed all the time, cocked and locked. Charles carried a custom-made .416 Wildcat, and James a Marlin lever-action .45/70. I had a .340 Weatherby made by New Ultra Light Arms. You don't need a rifle this big to hunt moose, but since the bears were in the equation I thought it might help me come home alive. Last year, Charles had to kill a brown bear sow that came for him.

We sloshed and splashed until we came to a fir island. There, James would climb a tree and look and Charles would call, and we would all wait, and the blackflies would come and visit us. If you wait for two or three hours and no moose shows, you can assume that he's left the building, you've spooked him, or he's already with a cow and isn't interested in combat.

We called up two bulls the first day. One was legal but not much of a trophy. Charles said to hold off, that he could get a better one. The other was a mulligan moose. On the third day, in a dense fog, Charles called in two huge bulls. One was a veritable monster, high in the 60s and very heavy. But he hung up 90 yards from us, hidden behind alders, and I couldn't see to get a shot. He caught on to us and slipped away. The other bull departed as well.

After that, it was hard times. We could not get a shootable moose to come and be killed, and Charles was developing a haunted look.

Two days before the hunt was to be over, we spotted a bull and two cows on a knoll not far from the ocean. And so, on the next-to-last day, we left the boat at home and rode four-wheelers up the beach for 5 miles or so, parked, and plodded inland. This was a particularly bad slog, with a long stretch of Maximum Suck, and when we got to a fir island and called, nothing happened.

We hiked to a second fir island. Charles and James went up trees, and I lay upon the ground watching the blackflies swarm around my face net. Then, at 10:45 in the morning, Charles's leather glove sailed out of the tree and hit me in the head. This is universally understood in Alaska as a wordless way of saying *Pick up your rifle and get off your ass, there's a moose coming!*

Charles and I ran from the pine island for perhaps 20 yards, into an open spot. Charles grunted and beat the brush, and then, 60 yards away, a heavy pair of antlers appeared on the left, swinging back and forth, slashing at the alders. The bull had come in quickly from 400 yards out and was a very perturbed moose. He never saw us; he was looking for the rival who had the gall to invade his space.

As he drew parallel to me, I raised the rifle and shot him, aiming high in his lungs, and he fell on his side, breathing slowly, his life leaving him. I shot him again to end it. From the time Charles's glove had smacked me in the head until the moose drew his last breath, I doubt if three minutes had elapsed. I felt sorry for the moose who had, in a way, died for love. Charles was relieved, bordering on ecstatic. His haunted look had vanished. James smiled a huge smile; no more perching in trees and hauling boats off sandbars.

Dazed and joyful, we all shook hands. In two pulls of the trigger we had gone from the edge of despair to success. We would not have to look back on more than a week of backbreaking effort with nothing but blackfly bites to show for it. He was a good bull, 55 inches across, with heavy palms. And as we found when we started to skin him, he had almost no body fat. This fellow had been looking for love so hard that he had neglected to eat. Charles guessed his weight at 1,100 pounds, about 400 less than what he should have been going into the winter.

We started to work on the bull at 11 a.m. We had to butcher him, bone the meat, saw the antlers off the skull, and hoist everything into the trees so the bears wouldn't get it. We finished at 5:30 p.m. There were 10 bloodstained muslin bags hanging 15 feet from the ground like enormous, ghastly Christmas tree decorations, with the antlers tied separately in another tree.

The last walk out was the worst. We got into impossible willow thickets and an endless bog of the Maximum Suck variety. Usually in this country you can't see where a hike is going to end, but in this case we were marching toward the Gulf of Alaska, and I could see the beach—hard-packed sand, bless it—ahead of me. When we emerged from the bog, and onto the sand, I turned around and said, "Never again."

I had brought a pack frame with visions of carrying out some of the meat myself, but Charles put an end to that. He informed me that he and I would remain in camp the next day while the young fishing guides brought out the meat. They did.

And on that day it poured, and the wind howled, and I lay in my cabin unable to move, thankful beyond words that I was done with moose and bogs and blackflies, and that my pack frame was out there on someone else's back.

The best part of Alaska moose hunting is when you can say to yourself: I don't have to do this anymore.

THE LAND OF GIANTS

THOMAS MCINTYRE

In November in Saskatchewan, where temperatures may soar to a sultry 15 degrees, I went to find a whitetail that would give me chills. Over the years I'd squandered too many hunts (as much as any hunt is ever squandered) in too many places by turning down adequate bucks, waiting for something extraordinary. The result has been, of course, broad swatches of vacant walls for all the heads I never got, and extra room in the freezer for the venison not taken. In Saskatchewan there are whitetails that live and die without ever catching so much as a scent of a human being. And some are big enough that no hunter has ever had to have a second thought about them. That was the kind of whitetail I needed—the no-questions-asked kind.

To hunt in Saskatchewan, though, a nonresident is restricted to the northern half of the province, in what is designated "provincial forest." It is in actuality an interminable hell of poplar and spruce where a hunter will get irretrievably turned around in 10 yards. (The standard admonition guides give their hunters is never to go into the bush alone, not even on the trail of a wounded deer.) Still-hunting borders on physically unfeasible, and to attempt spot-and-stalk hunting would be like trying to find Waldo in a satellite photo of Calcutta. As for drives—considering that they only propel deer into some equally impenetrable sector of the bush—bailing a boat with a net would be more productive. So in the hope of seeing at least one no-questions buck in my life, and in my sights, I dressed in layer upon layer of poly, wool, and down, covered it with a white suit, pulled polar-expedition boots onto my feet and mitts on my hands, and sat in a ground blind watching a small clearing marked with fresh scrapes and rubs.

I sat all alone in the blind and waited quietly (no talking, no laughing—though after a while I was strangely tempted) from well before dawn till long after sunset. When you wait on whitetails in Saskatchewan, there are other things to see. On the rarest of occasions, a moose, elk, black bear, or wolf might wander by. Naïve ruffed grouse also strolled about, easy and tasty pickings for the locals who lamented nature's oversight in not creating the 250-pound economy size. At intervals during the iron-cold day, ravens caw-clucked overhead, flying so low the grunts that came from them with each wingbeat were audible. Mostly for me, though, surrounded by the poplars and spruces, there was only the silence of the limbs as the waiting developed into something resembling a state of terminal ennui. Luckily, deer appeared just often enough for total psychological collapse to be narrowly averted.

Almost always it was does that came. They materialized in the small clearing with wary gaits, heads bobbing apprehensively. The smaller does came first, to be driven off by larger ones that pressed back their ears and flailed with their front hooves. Even the largest does, though, were subjects of abuse, with magpies hopping onto their rumps. The deer wheeled in annoyance, flaring the black-and-white birds, which hopped right back on, until the does dematerialized, driven to distraction.

At the very start of the Monday that was the first day of the hunt, the does came and went. Then at 9:30 a.m. the first buck showed up, and he was only the biggest I had ever seen and could have legally killed.

He walked out like an inevitability, a 150-class 10-point, antlers burnished like the arms of an antique oak rocker. Seeing a buck like that, you begin to understand what a peculiar condition maleness is, especially during the rut. The buck wasn't drawn by any promise of food. He had come to find does, and if they weren't there, he might only lope through the clearing or hover tormentingly at the margin of the poplars before simply fading away.

He stood, though, in the open, right in front of me; and that should have been that. But once more, unable to help myself, I thought about it. It was less than two hours into legal shooting time on the first day. Couldn't something bigger possibly come along? My answer was to watch him walk away, even as a tiny voice in my head was bawling, What have you done?

No more bucks came out that day, and after dark the guide arrived to get me. He asked what I'd seen. I told him.

"Monday buck," he said with a shake of the head, meaning that more than one hunter had lived to regret not taking that first-day's deer.

Monday, Monday, can't trust that day; and after a full day Tuesday of sitting and seeing only one wee buck glide through the clearing, I was thinking that maybe I shouldn't be trusted, either, at least not when it came to making up my own mind.

On Wednesday there was a doe in the clearing under the moon before shooting time, then an 8-point in the first gray light. Even he would have approached a personal best, but after Monday I'd established a benchmark. There was no giving in, and if I had to sit out the rest of the days on stand and go home, babbling, without a deer, that's how it would be. As absurd as it might sound, having seen one real deer, I had to see one even more real before I could pull the trigger.

The day went on with ravens, does, and magpies and lunch from a sack. I fought sleep. Every hour or so I checked my watch to see how much time remained. It was 4 p.m. when he filled up the gaps between the poplars.

He was already standing there when I sensed him, feeling him in my spine as much as seeing him. Ten-point antlers heavy as an elk's rack crowned his broad head. This was without a doubt the deer I'd passed up all the others for over the years, and now my mouth was dry and I kept telling myself to move slowly as I pulled off my mitt and brought up the .300 Winchester Magnum. There was absolutely nothing to think about, except whether he would come out of the trees.

The buck went on standing, looking into the clearing. He took a step back. He took another and turned to his left, the trees shielding him. Now that I didn't have to make up my mind, he was going to take away the decision anyway. He walked forward, moving off, going. Then he began to circle in toward the glade. I almost jumped.

He came out from behind a tall pine an inch at a time, first his muzzle with the tips of the black, wide main beams extending past his nose. His head and neck appeared, but I waited, and then I could see his shoulder, and after that his side. I didn't wait anymore.

I thumbed off the safety, held behind his shoulder, and fired. He spun and was gone.

I left the blind and walked the 80 yards to where the buck had stood when I shot. I looked for blood and hair but could find none. I turned toward the poplars and spruces and remembered the guide's dire warnings. Still bundled in cold-weather gear, I stepped into the bush.

In the trees, a web of brown-leafed trails tangled through the snow. An hour of light was left. I looked back and made the tall pine my landmark and started down the first trail, pushing through the trees. After a few hundred feet I had cut nothing and turned back to try another trail. Twenty yards down the fourth I found one drop of blood, already frozen to a leaf. Ten feet farther was a second.

He lay big and yellow-brown 75 yards from the first blood. His almost perfectly symmetrical antlers were more like black walnut than oak, the flats of the beams wide as the palm of a hand, the eye guards long and thick. (Later, the antlers would green-score $163^2/_8$.) I was safe in imagining I was the first person ever to see this buck, certainly the first hunter. I risked going stir-crazy for that privilege, and what I saw was a deer beyond doubt, at last.

A HUNTER'S HEART

BILL HEAVEY

If you're looking for an unlikely pair, match the fresh-faced girl with two earrings in her right ear sitting with the cowpuncher with the droopy gray mustache, sweat-stained hat, and dusty jeans. He is leaning more than halfway over the coffee table in the windblown desert town of Rock Springs, Wyo., here in the lobby of the Best Western, and holding both her hands in his upright palms. He holds them like precious things he might break were he not careful, and behind a three-day stubble and his weathered features, he is smiling so hard as to be on the verge of tears. "I been looking forward to this more than any hunt I've booked all year," he tells her. "We're gonna get you a good deer, honey. I promise you that. You'll see hundreds of deer. They're moving down off the mountains now, coming down into their winter range. The big ones tend to move last. Oh, honey, I'm so glad you're finally here."

He turns and smiles at the girl's father, sitting next to her on the couch. "You have to hunt with me . . . forever. Every year. You and your dad. On me. Understand?" She blushes, glows, looks at her father, then back at the cowboy. He is serious. She hardly knows him, but he is, here and now, making a commitment that will last as long as either of them lives. The cowboy drops his eyes for a moment, giving her time to take it all in. But she doesn't need time. She neither flusters nor embarrasses nor flees to the safety of a polite protest that it is too great a gift. She smiles. He coughs, then continues in a different tone. "Now, it's O.K. to spend a little time with this fellow," he says, cocking his head in my direction but keeping his eyes on her. "Just remember," he says, slowly tapping his chest with a forefinger, "I'm your number one." His eyes are watering again. The gray mustache that obscures his mouth stays put while the silk bandanna around his throat rises and then settles back into its place.

Her eyes dance and change with the light, sometimes hazel, sometimes green. She is beautiful. Her metal crutches lean against the back of the sofa. She has been waiting for this moment forever, nearly 10 months, since last winter at a sporting show in Grand Rapids, when her two brothers wheeled her by the booth of the outfitter who had agreed to work with the Hunt of a Lifetime charity. That was when the man asked her and her father to be his guests for a mule deer hunt. Her name is Alyssa Iacoboni and she is 15 years old. Her head is smooth. Her eyebrows and eyelashes are gone. The chemo took them all (although she insists that a few eyelashes are already growing back). It is as if her head and face in their unashamed nakedness permit her beauty to shine stronger. She is unselfconscious about her appearance: her lack of hair, and the stump of leg that stops above where her left knee once was. She smiles and talks freely. Yet she holds within herself a world that is hers alone. Later, photographer Erika Larsen and I will discover that we both thought of Vermeer's famous painting, *Girl With a Pearl Earring*, upon first seeing Alyssa. In that picture a similarly luminous girl has just turned her gaze to the viewer, as if someone has just entered her room. Vermeer chose to portray his girl without hair, too, though hers by virtue of the blue and gold cloth that covers it completely. It is a trick the artist used to draw your eye to her expression. Both share that startling combination of openness and self-containment, present and vivid, yet reserving unto themselves a mystery.

Vermeer's picture, often dubbed "the *Mona Lisa* of the North" for its haunting beauty, was done more than 300 years ago. Alyssa Iacoboni (Yaka-Boni) is right here. And if she bears a wisdom beyond her years, she is also very much a 15-year-old girl. "I am so psyched to go on this hunt," she says. "My brothers are totally jealous." Just two weeks ago, she killed her first whitetail, a doe on 37 acres the family owns not far from home in Grand Rapids. Her father, Evan, says she is weary from the trip, from delays that caused them to arrive at 4 a.m., instead of 10 p.m.

The next morning, we caravan to the unit where the outfitter, Bruce Feri, who runs Canyon Creek Outfitters, has a special tag for Alyssa's buck. It's high desert country, about 7,500 feet, an endless undulating carpet of sage west of the never-ending spine of the Wind River Mountains. We load up in trucks and head up into the hills to glass for deer. Alyssa is being fitted for a hydraulic leg but is still on crutches at the moment. She hops nimbly into the cab and stows them beside her. I ask about the doe she took. "I'd taken my hunter safety even before I got sick, but didn't have a chance to hunt until this year. First I was nervous when I went out with my brothers. I was afraid I might not like hunting as much as they did. But when I saw that doe, I got so excited I could hear my own heart. It was so intense. And then I made a good shot with the .30/30 and I was even more excited. It was just really cool." She has been practicing with a .22 magnum, and her brothers helped her sight in the new .308 that Savage Arms donated to Hunt of a Lifetime.

There was already a foundation, Make-A-Wish, for young people facing life-threatening illnesses. In 1996, it granted a seriously ill Minnesota boy's wish to hunt Kodiak brown bear in Alaska, a gesture that enraged animal rights groups, prompting them to mount a national campaign against Make-A-Wish. Some members were threatened with bodily harm. When Tina Pattison, a school bus driver and mother of six in Erie County, Pa., told the group that her son Matthew, an 18-year-old with Hodgkin's disease, wanted more than anything to hunt moose in Canada, she was told the foundation could no longer grant such wishes. It simply wasn't safe. But Pattison was not the type to be intimidated. She and her husband, Chester, got mad. Then they got on the phone. In time, thanks to the hard work of his parents and the generosity of some outfitters, a lodge, a grocery store, and countless others, Matthew and his dad went on the hunting trip and bagged a 55-inch moose. The anticipation of the hunt kept him going through months of pain, Tina says. "He kept saying, 'I'll be all right because I'm going on that moose hunt.'" Matthew died in April 1999, at the age of 19. And Tina founded Hunt of a Lifetime to honor Matthew's memory and to grant the wishes of other youngsters who love hunting and the outdoors.

As we drive and glass muleys tucked away in the sagebrush, Bruce explains that this is the Sublette herd, the most migratory deer in the West. They travel up to 100 miles from the Salt River, Wyoming, Wind River, Gros Ventre, and Snake River ranges to winter in the desert of the Green River Basin. "They'll stay around here as long as the wind blows the snow off the vegetation. If the snow gets too heavy for that, they'll just keep heading south. Come spring, they'll follow the snow line back up into the mountains." The deer have a tough life, he says. "Sometimes it gets to 40, 50 below up here. That's without windchill. It doesn't stay that cold for long, but they can't stand it for long, either. Come spring, most of these deer are hanging on by their fingernails." The state recently pushed back the date that shed hunters can start walking in this area in the spring for fear of stressing the deer at a critical time. Alyssa doesn't say anything, but she has some experience of her own at the margins, the places where the distance between life and death is as thin as onion skin.

Bruce stops the truck and pulls out a spotting scope. It's a bright, windy day in the low 60s, warmer than usual, warmer than he'd like. There was a dusting of snow a few days ago. He points out four groups of muleys dotting the landscape, numbering nearly 50 in all. "Now let's see if we can find you a good buck." He glasses about six, all with does. It is just before the rut, the females not yet ready but tolerating the bucks, which merely jockey for position rather than fight. Bruce gives his 10-power Swarovski to Alyssa and shows her a bedded 4x4 nearly half a mile away. It takes her a while to see the gray deer hiding in plain sight. "I see him now," she says. Bruce clucks his tongue, thinking it over. "He's not bad, but we can do better." He shoves the truck back in gear.

• • •

Until she was sent the terrible blessing of cancer, Alyssa had been just another normal—if abnormally successful—schoolgirl. She was popular, the girl elected to represent her class at the homecoming dance, an athlete who played basketball and volleyball and ran track. She was the fastest kid in her junior high, just half a second off the school record in the 200 meters. High school coaches were already scouting her. She also did the long jump and shot put. I tell her that she looks too light to be a shot-putter. "Yeah, I know. Everybody thinks it's about upper body strength, but it's more about using your body the right way, momentum and leverage." Her brothers, Daniel and Justin—both jocks, both lifelong hunters, and both set on becoming sheriff's deputies—helped her learn that.

Then one day she came home from basketball camp complaining of pain in her left leg. At first the doctors just thought it was hyperextended and counseled rest. Eventually, they X-rayed it and saw the tumor in her knee, an aggressively cancerous mass in the bones. They scheduled her for an appointment with the oncologist for the next day and gave her a name for the disease: osteosarcoma, bone cancer. Two weeks later she was on her way to Detroit for her first surgery.

Another hour into the hunt, the sun high now, Bruce spots a better buck in the company of about 10 does. A subordinate buck lingers in the brush nearby, causing the big one to assert his dominance and move the ladies. The smaller male invariably shadows them. "Good and bad," Bruce says. "They're moving, but distracted enough that we might get close." He, Alyssa, and I aim for a rock that would give her a decent shot, but soon 12 pairs of eyes have us pinned. Then they take off running. "Don't worry," Bruce tells her as she swings her way back on the crutches. "We'll get you one. You feeling tired or anything?" She shakes her head. "I'm fine."

The diagnosis changed everything. It was as if a portal had opened into a parallel universe, a world invisible to those who live on the surface. All at once Alyssa could no longer measure joys and sorrows by a schoolgirl's standards: cute clothes and the coolest ringtones, popularity and which group you were going with to the football game. When the social worker assigned to her case asked if the idea of dying scared her, Alyssa confronted her parents. Were they keeping something from her? No, honey, they said. We'll never keep anything from you. They told her that her cancer was serious, possibly terminal, but that they would take things one day at a time. She understood that she was in a fight for her life. The possibility of death, someone wrote, tends to focus the mind rather intensely. Alyssa seemed to decide quickly that she still had the three things that mattered most to her: her family, her faith in God, and her belief in herself. That was not to say there weren't times she cried, times she lashed out at her parents, or times when she despaired. But for the most part she showed what many kids show, only more of it: an acceptance of the situation and its possible outcomes that an adult can only envy, and a resolve to fight. "I just realized it wouldn't do any good to be negative," she says. "It doesn't help, doesn't make you stronger. It's like when you're behind in a basketball game. You just focus on what you need to do to get back in it."

Her faith had always been important to her, and it became even more so now. Nearly every day she would recite her favorite verse, 29:11 from the book of Jeremiah: "For I know the plans I have for you," declares the Lord, "plans to prosper you and not to harm you, plans to give you hope and a future." She was in God's hands. Whatever happened, it was what He had chosen for her. She could live with that. If necessary, she could die with it.

We drive some more, stop and eat sandwiches, chew and look at the country. It's sparse and clean and pitiless. Alyssa seems at ease but doesn't say much, doesn't readily reveal herself. I will wonder about this so much that I will call her mom, Linda, after the trip. She will tell me her daughter's composure unnerved her as well. "At each new turn in her illness, she was like, O.K., let's fix this and keep going. She is incredibly competitive, I can tell you that. The coaches always had her run anchor for the 400- and 800-meter relays, both for her speed and because she absolutely refuses to lose." During Alyssa's last race, she tells me, the girl handing her the baton dropped it before the pass. "But it was still in the lane, so Alyssa picked it up. And I remember feeling the crowd's reaction, how they didn't think she could catch up. But she did. And she won. She has always been the kind of girl you don't want to say, 'I bet you can't' or 'I dare you' to. She's not insecure, but she has always lived her life like she's got something to prove."

The doctors eventually told her they needed to take the leg. She was offered "limb salvage," in which a combination of cadaver bone, metal rods, and bone grafts enable a patient to keep an arm or leg. But she wouldn't be able to run on such a leg, and there were other risks: increased chance of the cancer recurring and of infection, loosening of the implanted bone, and mechanical failure. On December 7, 2005, she let surgeons amputate her left leg above the knee. She also underwent intensive chemo, six rounds of three treatments each. Chemo, she tells me, is as much torture as it is therapy. The poisons kill the cancer cells, the fastest-growing ones in the body, but they kill everything else as well. The theory behind it is brutally simple: Inflict as much destruction upon the body as possible while still leaving the subject "viable." As soon as the patient has recovered from the last round to the point where she can be expected to survive more, more is administered.

Alyssa became so sick that her mother figures she attended school a total of 10 days during her ninth-grade year. She took drugs to flush the chemicals from her body between courses of chemo, drugs to cope with the excruciating "phantom pain" from the nonexistent leg. The human brain, perhaps perceiving that a limb has been chopped off, reflexively responds, activating the nerve cells in that area to register a traumatic event. Her immunity plummeted to nothing, leaving her defenseless against normally mundane maladies. A nosebleed might last for eight hours and require an emergency trip back to the hospital for a transfusion. Sores in her mouth and nasal passages became infected and required intravenous antibiotics and morphine. She seemed to live at the hospital. Her sense of smell and taste became abnormally acute. The odor of hospital food made her ill. Liz, a 17-year-old friend she had made in the hospital who had a more advanced form of the same cancer, died. "It was hard" is all she'll say. She doesn't dramatize the death, doesn't choke up about it for your benefit, doesn't use it to make some point about her own suffering. "It was hard when Liz died," she says. She reminds me of soldiers I've talked to who have survived extended combat. Such men tend to be low-key to the point of self-effacement. They have transcended any need for the approval—or even the attention—of others. Any questions about their identity, or worth, or place in life have already been settled. They know that each breath is a gift.

• • •

Bruce abruptly stops and brings his binocs up to his eyes. "Shooter buck," he tells me. He backs the truck slowly and angles it to get his window broadside so he can put the spotting scope on the buck. "That's the best one I've seen in a while," he says. Two bucks and two does are feeding about 500 yards away. Studying the lay of the land, however, we see there is no good approach. They are on a little ridge in the sagebrush, higher than everything around them. "Have to throw the dice," he says. Our only option is to drive a little closer before making a right that will take us into a fold in the land from which we could sneak up on them. "If we could get to that rock over there," he says, pointing to a boulder, "we might be close enough for a shot." He creeps forward and makes the right, then moves steadily onward. The deer do not take alarm. After a few more minutes, they all bed down: two does about 25 feet away from the bucks, the second of which is much smaller. We get out the .308 and a tripod to steady it on. Bruce asks Alyssa if she can crawl the last 50 yards to the rock or if she'd prefer to be carried. "I can crawl," she says.

"I'm gonna hustle up to that rock, make sure they're not spooked, and try to range 'em," says Bruce. Alyssa hops down from the cab and gets her crutches. I sling the gun across my back so I can crawl when we get close. We set off, Alyssa planting her foot, then swinging forward with her crutches. Each time she moves them, she swings them either around or between the crackly sage tufts to avoid unnecessary noise. I walk doubled over, staying as low as I can. We travel for about 100 yards this way toward Bruce, who is pressed to the rock, his hat on the ground behind him, rising as slow as a snake to peer over with his binocs. He drops back just as slowly, gives us a thumbs-up, and motions that we'll have to cover the rest of the distance prone. Alyssa balances on her foot as she places the crutches quietly on the ground. Then she lowers herself down to her two elbows and one knee and begins to pull herself over the ground.

At last we make it to Bruce and the rock, which is barely big enough to screen us even if we bunch up. Bruce whispers for the shooting tripod, but we have left it behind. I take off my parka and pass it forward. He folds it across the rock. I insert the clip, quietly chamber a round, check that the safety is on, and pass it forward. He helps Alyssa squirm into a shooting position, sitting on her folded knee. All four deer are bedded now, the two does to the right of the bucks. The little buck is bedded left of the bigger one and is easier to see. Bruce wants to make sure she is sighting on the bigger one. The sun is nearly in front of us, and she is having trouble seeing through the scope because of it. At last, she says, "Got him. Oh my gosh." Bruce claps her gently on the back. "We've got 'em where we want 'em, honey. That is a really nice buck. You just try to stay on him." He looks again through his glasses, then ranges the buck. "Two hundred yards," he says. He tells her to relax. We just have to wait now for the buck to get up and offer a good shot.

Minutes pass. Bruce is in an awkward position and needs to drop down and rest every so often. He tells Alyssa to stay on the buck, to wait until he rises and turns broadside, then to shoot just behind the front leg and midway up the body. I sneak a look and watch through the glasses as the big buck lays his head down so that just the four tines on his left side are showing, nothing more than tiny glints of sunlight 200 yards off. We sit some more. I'm lying on my side and it's getting wet, the last of the snowmelt still pooled on the ground. Just then, Alyssa says, "They're getting up!" She has had to shift slightly, causing the bill of her blaze orange cap to slide over her eyes. When she adjusts it, she can no longer find the buck. And the sun, lower now, is lined up almost directly behind the four standing deer. "I can't see them," she says, and her voice is plaintive and desperate. Bruce repositions her hat a second time to cut down on the glare and points in the direction of the deer, which he and I can see clearly. "I still don't have them," Alyssa moans. "Keep looking, honey," Bruce says soothingly. The barrel of the rifle is waggling. She is way off now. I'm worried. I'm worried that she'll acquire the wrong buck when she does get back on them because, once again, the smaller buck is standing in a more open spot. I'm worried that she'll rush the shot and miss or, worse, wound the buck and then we'll be in for a nighttime tracking job to find him before the coyotes do. Finally Alyssa says she can see the buck. I'm hoping it's the right one. I'm hoping he's standing broadside and still with his head down grazing so she doesn't get transfixed by the antlers. Bruce tells her to shoot now but she doesn't. I know she doesn't have a very solid platform, my coat and her shoulder, her body sitting atop her one folded-under knee, surely numb and cold by now. The longer she waits, the less confident I am that it will happen the way it ought to. After an eternity, during which I stay mum, prone, and praying, there comes the sharp, loud crack of the rifle. I had forgotten about the muzzle brake to reduce recoil on a girl's shoulder. Bruce explodes upward like a rocket. "You got him! You got him!" I rise in time to see the buck stagger and collapse. Bruce has lifted Alyssa and is hugging her. Then he hugs me. Then I hug Alyssa. Her dad and Erika, who've crept closer behind us, are shouting and coming up. "Run over there and make sure he's done," Bruce tells me. "I'll bring Alyssa." I take off, my own legs scarcely obeying me after being stuck so long in one position.

The buck is lying dead with his eyes open and a small hole in the middle of his body right behind the front leg. It is a perfect shot, the diagram any hunter has seen countless times of where to shoot a deer. The buck has a dark, forked 4x4 rack and is enormous, bigger than any whitetail I've ever seen, girthed up from months of feeding in anticipation of the rut. Alyssa swings her way over to pose for photos and get congratulatory first, second, and third hugs from everybody. The men, all three of us, are now looking away, drying the tears we would swear are just from the wind in our eyes. Bruce begins gutting the animal and has Alyssa take part, both their hands on his heavy knife as they slice up the belly. He removes the heart and hoists it for us to see. The top of it has been pulverized by the shot. "Can't shoot them any better'n this," he says. Alyssa strokes the flank of the buck quietly.

That night, after a celebratory dinner in Bruce's camper trailer, he prints out some of the shots he took on a digital printer. Everyone wants signed copies of Alyssa and Bruce together. She has her hands on the buck's antlers, striped in their own shadows by the slanting sun, the wind pushing both ends of Bruce's long mustache toward Alyssa. Alyssa signs all of hers with her name and "the deer slayer."

I tell her I can't get over the shot, that it is almost unbelievable. "Tell you something else," says Bruce. "It was actually 223 yards. I told her 200 because I didn't want her to overthink it or hold high or anything like that." I look at her and blurt, "You couldn't make that shot twice." I don't know why I say this, and even as the words come out of my mouth, I know they're stupid and just hope that she doesn't take offense. But the luminous girl with two earrings in her right ear and the Vermeer skin just regards me with that look, at once open and impenetrable, and says quietly, "I could make that shot again." She says this neither in irritation nor as a boast. It is just the truth, a thing that she knows. And she has never found there to be any great virtue in hiding the truth. It is at this moment that I see the steel beneath the beauty. Suddenly I understand. This is a girl who cannot be defeated, even if she should die in the fight. Of course she could make that same shot tomorrow. She could absolutely make that shot.

THE TRAIL

KEITH MCCAFFERTY

Back from elk hunting this weekend in the wolf country up in the Madison: My brother and I guided his son, Brandon, who is a varsity soccer player in college and can do 26 straight pull-ups, the hard ones with the palms facing forward. Which is to say Kevin and I had to stop a few times on uphills to admire the view while Brandon idled with his rifle on his shoulder, his pulse scarcely registering the altitude. It was the same rough country where I took a cow last season. This hunt would be no easier. It would prove to be one of my most instructive hunts in years, and anyone who has tracked elk or deer under similar circumstances should be able to relate to the ordeal we went through, and hopefully learn as much from our mistakes as from what we did right.

On the first day, we climbed up the south slope of the big timber knob where I shot the cow last winter. The snow was deep, midthigh on top with hard vanilla waves where it was exposed to wind, the kind of crusted snow that holds your weight for a pulse or two, then collapses. Postholing, we call it. This is snowshoe country, and as a result we always have it to ourselves. I have never understood why many hunters will gladly mortgage their homes for a hunting rig that will get them through the drifts into the backcountry but won't cough up $100 to put snowshoes on their boots so they could actually hike somewhere after turning off the motor.

I love it up here, floating along through the open forest. It's a magic kind of hunting—the soft creak of the shoes in the white silence, exhaled breath smoking in the crackling air—even better if there are elk. This first day there weren't any, just a few old trails. I made a couple of big swings while Kevin and Brandon posted at crossings. Drives like that have worked in the past. I managed to push three mule deer does past Brandon. After I'd joined them, a coal-colored moose sort of swam past us in a mist of pumping legs. Later, stalking downhill through a thicket, we put a bull elk out of his bed. But we had no tag for him and only a few seconds to shoot if we had. One of the problems when you're snowshoe hunting is setting up to shoot. Sitting is awkward. You can lie down in a twisted position to rest the rifle over your pack, but it's hard to get back up if the snow is deep. Kneeling on one knee and shooting over sticks works the best.

There was still an hour or two of light when we called it a day. Since we'd go at it hard tomorrow, we thought it best to drive back to my house and rest up.

We woke at four. As Brandon dozed in the backseat on the hour-and-a-half drive up the river, Kevin and I made plans. With this winter's snowpack, I thought we might find a few bands of elk fairly close to the road, on the escarpment overlooking the river. Wind can be a problem up there, can make a 10-degree day feel like 40 below, but this morning the grass tufts in the headlights weren't bent horizontal and the truck wasn't shuddering the way it does most days I've hunted this country, so the escarpment was an option.

About a half hour before shooting light, we started climbing: no stars, scattered zephyrs, about as pleasant as it gets in January. Through binoculars I spotted a small elk herd, 40 head or more silhouetted against the horizon on a hillock way off to the north. We knee-walked over the snow until we were out of their line of sight, then continued to climb. There was a decent chance another hunter might push those elk our way; if they came, we wanted to hold the high ground, where we could work down in position as they lined by. It was big open country, and the elk could choose any number of escape routes, so we were really just guessing. When you are guessing on an elk hunt, it's usually best to guess high.

Our snowshoes were strapped to our packs for the steep climb out of the valley. Progress was slow. Some places we could walk on top of the crust or pick out routes where the snow had blown thin, exposing sagebrush clumps; other places we'd sink up to our hips and have to elbow out, only to sink right back in. You have to have a sense of humor about it or you'd never go.

It was one of those Charlie Russell sunrises, violet and pink streaks on the peaks and heavier skies above. When we saw a second band of elk a quarter mile above us, disappearing into the high forest, their rumps glowed orange. Here the lower slopes were open, the ridgetops broad and holding big splashes of timber. We climbed up with little hope of catching those elk, but when I turned around to look back down the slope, here came more elk, maybe 300 yards away, a small band in single file, five calves trailing a yearling cow.

Brandon and Kevin plunged downhill to set up for a shot. I trailed behind, stopping well short of their ambush point. Through my binoculars, I watched as Kevin opened up the shooting sticks, and Brandon rested his rifle. Several moments of silence and mounting tension passed as the elk continued to angle toward them, then came the crack of the rifle. I watched for any sign that an elk was hit, but they continued on course without falter, circling out of sight behind a small knob topped by a solitary yellow pine. The shot looked to have been about 150 yards, with lots of time to aim and the targets walking slowly. Later, Kevin said that he was fumbling for his cow call, which he had on a thong around his neck, when Brandon fired. Experience has taught us that, had he called, there was a good chance those elk would have paused for a few seconds, long enough for a standing shot.

We held a brief council of war. Kevin would go down to look for blood, while Brandon and I hiked back up to cut off the band if they climbed toward the timber after circling the knob. Only if an elk was clearly faltering was he to shoot a second time.

The plan worked. The six elk passed us broadside across a deep ravine at 200 yards. One of the calves lagged a little behind, but only a yard or two, and it appeared unwounded. Our hearts fell as the elk disappeared above us. Exhausted, Brandon and I took off our packs under a tree to wait for Kevin. He came trudging up 20 minutes later.

"I've got blood," he said.

"How much?" I asked.

He shook his head, breathing hard. Not much, he said, a couple of soft-ball-size splotches 60 or 70 yards along the track, then just the odd drop as the elk circled and climbed the slope.

Was there any vegetable matter, dark blood or hair, any putrid smell?

No, the blood was clean, muscle-blood red, no indication of a gut shot. Plus none of the elk had hunched up, which gut-shot animals usually do. Brandon and I hadn't seen any of them favoring a leg. Maybe, I wondered aloud, it was just a grazing shot across the rump, or at the top of the withers? Maybe the elk would recover?

There was nothing to do but find out. First we ate lunch, killing an hour or so. It's better to let an animal bed down and stiffen up if a shot has found the body. Brandon felt bad and said little, though Kevin and I assured him he'd done nothing wrong. The setup had been pretty good and Kevin had told him to take the shot; he'd squeezed off a bullet that went shy of the mark was all. It can happen to any hunter. If anyone had made a mistake, Kevin said, it was him; he should have told Brandon to wait until he blew the cow call. Nothing to do about that now.

Strapping on our snowshoes, we followed the elk trails into the timber. They were going single file, one occasionally skirting a tree before joining up with the rest, making it impossible to follow any one set of tracks. There was no blood at all. Then, 30 yards inside the forest, a drop, and 30 yards farther, another—drops the diameter of a small pea or pencil eraser. We tried to isolate the track, lost it, and found it again 100 yards on. Then the band separated, two of the animals sidehilling to the right while the others continued straight up. Figuring the wounded elk would keep to the contour, we followed the two trails to the right for a couple of hundred yards. It was tough slogging in deep powder, even with the shoes. No blood, so we turned back to the other trail. Brandon found a smear of red the size of a playing card where the right hind leg had stepped in deep snow; another, a few yards farther along. Beyond this, the wounded elk had separated from the other three, making our job a lot easier.

We paused to examine the trail. The blood smears, as well as the isolated drops, perhaps 10 traces in all, had been in or near the pock made by the right rear hoof. Yet the elk had been below Brandon with its left side angling toward him at the shot. Had the bullet passed through the elk, so that the blood was coming from an exit wound? Or had it passed over the elk's back, grazing the off hindquarter, or somehow passed underneath the belly and clipped the far leg without breaking bone? If the shot had passed through the body, this elk, a calf, had never slowed or given any hint that it was hurt. The smears were telling: Because we saw them only where the snow was at least 2 feet deep, the wound was at least that high up on the animal.

Kevin and I thought about it out loud, arrived at no definite conclusion, and decided it didn't matter; we were going to follow the elk as long as we could anyway. I'd do the tracking, Brandon would stay a little ahead and to one side, ready to take a snap shot, and Kevin would search the forest with his eyes. This plan worked better in theory than in practice. I would lose the trail where it mixed with other fresh elk tracks, and Brandon had the sharper eyes and often found it again.

We had been on the track for 40 minutes or so—not quite two hours had passed since the shot—when the tracks topped out on the ridge. Here all the trees were bent over and stunted by the wind. Beyond the ridge, the country dipped for a couple of hundred feet before lifting in wide escarpments where we would have little chance of catching up with the elk. The calf seemed to have no more liking of this open country than we did, however. It turned along the ridge, staying just inside the treeline. In the last half mile it had left no more than a dozen drops of blood, none bigger than a ladybug, nor had it ever paused. Surely it would have bedded down by now if it were hard hit, and I didn't think we had pushed it to keep it from doing so.

Then, just as our hopes were fading, we found where it had bedded down in a clump of pine saplings. There were smears of blood on both sides of the bed, though it hadn't seeped into the snow very deeply. Kevin, who is a doctor, guessed a cup or two had leaked at most. The blood on both sides was encouraging, suggesting the bullet had passed through the body, but not conclusive. The elk could have changed its position in the bed.

Had our approach put the elk out of its bed? Almost certainly, though the tracks leading away betrayed a walking pace. Now I made a mistake. Guessing that the elk, spooked now, might go miles before stopping again, we quickly took up the trail, only to find that it had gone no more than 40 yards before pausing in dense forest to get a glimpse of its pursuers. Brandon, who was leading us by a few steps, jerked rigid. He turned, his face fallen.

"I just saw it," he said.

"Did it look hurt when it ran away?"

Brandon shook his head. He'd had a glimpse of hide, nothing more.

We took up the track again, Brandon ranging ahead. In the next half mile he saw the elk twice, each time bolting out in front of him and offering no chance of a shot. After the second encounter, he waited for us to catch up. I had been following the tracks carefully, just in case Brandon branched off onto the wrong trail, for several elk had crossed through the forest this morning and the calf was leaving only the odd drop of blood every 100 yards or so. Once, Kevin had pointed to a dollop of blood that was off to the side of the track and wondered if the elk had coughed it up. It was a doctor's diagnosis; I wouldn't have thought of that.

Where Brandon had last spooked the elk, the trail led up through thigh-deep snowdrifts, heading for the vast open country beyond. The elk had taken the drifts in giant bounds, smearing the snow with blood in several places.

"It's hit higher up than we thought," I said.

Kevin rubbed his hand on his jaw.

"I think we're going to get it," he said. "It's just staying a little ahead of us now."

"I hate to push it," I said.

"I know, it isn't pretty," he said. "You know, in the emergency room you usually have about an hour to save a life. After that, with a bad wound, the vital signs fade fast. By the third hour, it's over. We've been on the track now for more than two hours. I think this elk is on its last gasp."

"We could rest it awhile," I said. "Maybe it won't go as far before bedding down."

"I don't think it matters. We're going to get it either way."

Brandon was tracking ahead of us while we talked, and we hurried to catch up. He was 200 yards across the open escarpment when we caught sight of him.

Out there it was nothing but wind. Brandon shrugged when we reached him. He'd lost the trail. The snow was blown to a thin crust and there was a confusion of elk tracks.

"There's been one drop of blood since the trees," he said.

"Let's go back and take a look," I said.

He led us back about 50 yards. Sure enough, there was one blood drop mixed in with several tracks. A fresh calf track led south; the other tracks looked a little older and headed north. We turned on the calf track, lost it, got it again, then lost it for good on the thin crust. For the next 30 minutes we followed a shallow ravine in the general direction the elk had been heading, hoping it would follow its nose, keep to the contour. All wide open country, the wind the biggest thing in it: The elk could be anywhere. Brandon was extremely discouraged. He didn't want to leave a wounded animal, but the elk hadn't bled a drop in at least half a mile and even Kevin was beginning to doubt our chances. It looked like it was a muscle injury after all, with a decent chance the elk would recover.

Stopping for a breather—we'd been climbing through deep snow for nearly four hours—we talked things over and concluded that we'd followed this elk as far as we could and that Brandon should shoot another cow if the opportunity arose. But then, way off to the north and perhaps 500 yards away, I spotted an elk. I put my binoculars on it. It had the nose and short body of a calf, but no blood on the hide that I could see, nor any apparent infirmity. The elk did not seem to know which way to go. It would walk several yards in one direction, then the other. It was on the crest of a hill but reluctant to top over it. Twice I thought I saw it stumble, but I couldn't be sure. Then it went over the hill, gone from sight.

"That's your elk, Brandon," I said.

He and Kevin pushed ahead, all of us climbing as hard as we could to the top of the hill. The calf was lying down on the far side, bogged in deep snow, its head sticking above a sagebrush clump. It was 150 yards away.

Brandon rested his rifle over Kevin's pack and shot it through the neck.

• • •

It was our elk, all right. As we snowshoed over, I could see a big splotch of dried blood on its right flank, in front of the hip and slightly below the body's midpoint. Just above the splotch was the first bullet's exit, the tear in the hide about an inch and a half in diameter. Brandon had been shooting down at the elk. The outward curve of the animal's side could account for its not having bled from the small entrance wound, which we found high on the left side. Shot straight through the thickest part of its body with a 200-grain bullet from Brandon's .338/06, the calf had traveled 3 miles in three and a half hours before succumbing to the second bullet. It had climbed 600 vertical feet after being wounded, through snow that was often up to its belly. The snow was 4 feet deep where it had finally fallen. Kevin had recorded the trail in his GPS.

"It must have been very painful," Brandon said quietly.

"The important thing is that you got him," Kevin told him. "Not many hunters would have stayed on the track that long in this kind of snow."

Before dressing the elk we sat down, rested a few minutes, and dug out some food from our packs. God, we were tired, but if one part of this hunt was over, another was beginning. The hardest miles were still to come.

Once again I marveled at the strength and endurance of that small elk. There were just so many ways we could have lost it. If not for the snow, we might never even have known that it was hit. Had we not packed snowshoes, we could not have followed its trail. I also doubted we could have tracked it had Brandon been using a lighter rifle. Shot from the same angle with a bullet that did not fully penetrate and leave an exit wound, say a 130-grain .270, the elk might not have left any blood trail at all. With the confusion of trails in the timber, we wouldn't have been able to isolate its track.

Had we made mistakes? Certainly, starting with taking the shot when the elk was walking, when a bleat from the cow call might have caused it to freeze. The hour or so that passed before we took up the trail wasn't long enough. If we'd rested the track two hours or more, the calf would probably have bled out internally in its bed and been too stiff to bound away. We also might have waited an hour or so after bumping it from its bed, to give it time to lie down again and grow weaker. That might have meant a shorter blood trail.

I was surprised at how little the calf had bled externally with an exit hole the size of a silver dollar in its side. How many hunters would have concluded that the animal was lightly wounded and dropped the track? This stressed to me the importance of perseverance, as well as of being equipped to follow tracks where they lead. With our packs and snowshoes, we could have trailed the elk until dark without regard to depth of snow or worry about our safety. Without the proper gear, we would have had to turn back much earlier.

Also, while it may be helpful to cast a critical eye on a blood drop or pattern of behavior and make an educated guess about shot placement, it is dangerous to draw conclusions. This elk did not exhibit the typical reactions of a gut-shot animal. It did not hunch up; there were no blood splotches in the first 50 yards with vegetable matter in them before the blood trail disappeared. Rather, the initial splashes of crimson, the diminishing blood trail, and the long distance traveled without bedding were hallmarks of a muscle wound from which an animal is likely to recover. Hunters are not above telling themselves stories they want to hear, especially when the trail is long and the day cold, and sometimes it takes a hunt like this one to remind us of our responsibility to follow until the final truth is revealed.

This wasn't an adventure, nor was a trophy animal involved. There were no guides, no human peril, no celebrity of any stamp. Instead, this is a story about an honest hunt, a misplaced shot, and the lessons of the hours afterward. It could have happened to any of us, and perhaps someone who reads the tale may recall it when he grows discouraged. Perhaps he will be compelled to press on and collect an animal that otherwise would have languished beyond the reach of mercy, dying slowly in a forgotten part of the forest.

But our hunt was not yet complete. We were sitting on the rim of the world, with a long march through deep snow to the valley below. I thought I was in great shape when the elk fell, but after dressing it out and cutting it in half, I discovered that the quarters don't weigh any less as the years pass. Brandon put us to shame, I have to admit—he dragged out the hindquarters by himself. Kevin and I struggled together with the lighter front half. Five hours later we stumbled down to the road. The car was still a mile away, and while Kevin set off with the keys, Brandon and I took seats on the elk, the moon hanging pale and the mountain once more arranging itself in silhouettes of stone and silence.

SEVENTEEN GUYS, ONE OLD SCHOOL BUS, AND MORE GUNS THAN WE CAN COUNT

BILL HEAVEY

As Roger Tolbert and I are getting dressed one morning in his trailer to head out for the hunt, he carefully loads four knives into his rubber boots: a short, stout, double-edged saw and a big Kershaw pigsticker in one, and two smaller fixed-blades in the other. He doesn't necessarily expect to use the smaller ones, but it's good to have some sharp backup. "Roger," I say, resolving never again to argue with any man wearing boots, "you must really like knives." Roger smiles broadly and shakes his head. "Naw, what I really like is guns."

He isn't kidding. When he invited me to go "redneck hunting" in Alabama, he offered to lend me a rifle to save me the trouble of toting one through the airport. "What caliber you like for deer?" he'd asked during that call. I asked what he had. "In deer? Let's see: couple .270s, couple 7mm mags, a .308, a .30/30, whole bunch of .30/06s, a .300 mag, a .338 . . . Wait, we're getting out of deer now. The .338's my Alaska gun." He suggested a 7mm mag. "That's my go-to deer round. Ever shot that Browning Lightning Bolt? They only made it from '78 to '84. First five-lug bolt, I b'lieve, strongest mechanism around at the time. Liked that sucker so much I got it in three calibers. Jimmy down at the club makes up a handload for it. With a 200-yard zero, you can hold on the top of a big buck's back at 400 yards and hit him in the heart."

Well, I thought, maybe you can. I asked Roger how many guns he owns, and after a pause, he admitted, "I really don't know." This reminded me of a story about oil-man J.P. Morgan, who once observed that any man who knew precisely how much money he had probably didn't have that much.

Tolbert has worked in the same Birmingham steel mill since the week he completed high school nearly 30 years ago. He supervises a crew of 42, loading large-diameter industrial pipe onto railcars. It's dangerous work. He says he has "planted" four men he knows who died on the job, watched another lose his leg above the knee, another lose four fingers. "I pray before each shift that I get off it in one piece. Railcars and pipe are dangerous enough by themselves. Mix 'em, and you got to be real particular about every move you make." During the year, he banks leave for deer season. He and 16 other guys have a 2,500-acre lease down on the edge of Alabama's famed Black Belt region, about three hours away.

As the date approaches, his calls become more frequent. He wants to double-check my arrival time and gear choices, and to say once again that he hopes I understand that this is redneck hunting, nothing fancy. Finally, I ask why he keeps telling me this. "Hell, Bill, you're the first real celebrity we've ever had at the lease," he says. I explain that if I'm his idea of a celebrity, his first worry ought to be about getting a life. This seems to calm him down. Three weeks later, Tolbert and I have left Interstate 20/59 and are bombing down the back roads south of Tuscaloosa, headlights illuminating gnarled old trees in the night, the roads getting ever narrower and less traveled. "I don't know what kind of camps you're used to," he says. "But I've got an old trailer about 8 miles from the lease. It's got electric but no running water. My buddy Slowpoke, he sleeps in an old school bus he's rigged up with a shower and commode if you want. Anyway, you'll sleep dry, and you sure as hell won't go hungry."

• • •

The lease is in Choctaw County, one of the poorest in a poor state, and right on the edge of the famous Black Belt, the crescent-shaped region about 300 miles long and up to 25 miles wide that extends from southwest Tennessee to east-central Mississippi and then east through Alabama to the Georgia state line. The inland sea that covered this land about 75 million years ago left a layer of marl known as Selma chalk on top of which a rich, black topsoil formed. By the 1830s, that dirt attracted an influx of planters, many of whom made fortunes growing cotton tended by slaves. In the 1960s, the area was at the forefront of civil rights activity, including the Selma-Montgomery march led by Martin Luther King Jr.

It also has a worldwide reputation for producing big bucks. After the decline of cotton, the Black Belt was widely planted in corn, soybeans, and other favored deer foods. From the 1950s through the 1980s, the area cranked out a disproportionate share of the state's record bucks and became a destination for deer hunters. Part of the reason was the big heads, part was that the rut here occurs in mid to late January—a second chance for those who could make the trip. In recent decades, however, pine trees have become the dominant crop, resulting in a predictable decline in megabucks. Although the area no longer dominates Alabama's tally of big racks, these woods still yield some extremely respectable deer: two 160-class bucks in the 2002–03 season and a bow-killed 22-pointer grossing 227 and change from Lowndes County in 2004. Just up the road from the lease is Bent Creek Lodge, where hunters pay $550 a day to hunt, and an extra $750 if they shoot a trophy. Tolbert tells me a 6½-year-old grossing 161 was killed on his lease in November. I could be content with that kind of "consolation" buck.

At last we turn onto Camp Road in the town of Whitfield, a collection of sagging houses and tar paper shacks, where we bump off the last of the pavement and pull up in front of a big oval trailer that probably looked futuristic 40 years ago but now features heavy plywood nailed over the windows and back door. "Welcome to the Goose," announces my host. "Put five layers of ply in for the floor and she's sound as a dollar. That's Slowpoke's bus, Rat Chonder." I nod, standard procedure when I have no idea what someone is talking about, and get out in search of a place to pee.

Rat Chonder? I'm sizing up Slowpoke's cabin, a derelict school bus with an 8-foot addition that looks like some hunk of aluminum that was frozen in the act of attempting to mount the school bus, when I have a flash of insight. "Rat Chonder" isn't a name; it's a directional indicator: "right yonder." Welcome to the Deep South.

The next morning, we hop into the "lease trucks" that, like most club members, both Tolbert and Slowpoke keep down here to spare their good rides. Tolbert's is a Jeep Gladiator 4WD of early 1970s vintage that he calls Armageddon. "She's got a heavy-duty back end, a 360 V-8, and there's not a whole lot of things on the road that pass her." He starts it up and even standing still it bellows and roars like its namesake. Slowpoke is driving a '78 Chevy that emits sounds I've never heard from any vehicle: hydraulic sighs that seem to come from some personal tragedy it refuses to discuss, sudden moans that hint at a deep inner emotional life. Slowpoke calls it the Meat Wagon.

Half an hour later I'm tucked into a shooting house, quite a change from the tree stands I'm used to. Not only can I fidget and scratch freely; I've got a roof and walls protecting me from the wind and the occasional burst of rain. The house commands a large swath of real estate: a clear-cut to the left, woods out front, a propane pipeline on the right. The pipeline is green with winter wheat and ryegrass. The clear-cut is shades of black and gray, with more than enough scrub for a deer to bed undetected. I glass constantly but spot only a few birds flitting around in the cut. I can see at least 600 yards down the pipeline and more than that in parts of the clear-cut—a lot farther than I'm comfortable shooting.

After an hour, during which the only movement is the occasional pinwheel of a hawk's wing as it swoops down on something in the woods, a deer shape emerges far down the pipeline. Through 10X glasses I can just make it out as a long-tined spike. It feeds for no more than a few seconds, then melts into the woods. Over the next hour four more deer show, all does, and all distant enough to be in the next zip code. Finally, tired of being cooped up, I still-hunt out the back door and into the woods to my right. I move deliberately, taking an hour to cover 50 yards. No deer, but I run into the strangest rodent I've ever seen: a critter the size of a big squirrel with golden fur and a big splotch of white on its nose like some Kabuki actor. It looks at me like I'm the weirdo, then continues about its business.

"That's 'at fox squirrel lives down that way," Roger tells me when I describe my encounter at lunch. "Been there for years. You don't have 'em up north?" Lunch is preceded by grilled homemade sausage—regular, jalapeño, and jalapeño with cheese—dished up hot and dripping. It's followed by deep-fried fillets of spot and bass, as well as fried venison medallions. We eat standing around a smoky oil-drum fire for warmth while Jimmy Baxter, a truck mechanic and the club's reloading guru, mans the grill. I don't need all 5,000 calories, but it's mighty tasty, and soon I'm on thirds. Every so often, another truck rolls up and other members report on the morning's sightings and load up on meat. Nobody has fired a shot. What's more, nobody seems the least bothered by this.

"Alabama bucks may not be the biggest, but they're smarter than any I've ever hunted, and I've done some traveling, too," drawls Slowpoke. "It's on account of rifle opens the Saturday before Thanksgiving and goes until the end of January. Pretty soon, the wary bucks are the only ones left." Freddy Jowers, the fellow who shot the 161, shows me photos of that buck. "We don't see many that big down here," he admits. "Other hand, we've got lots of places too thick to hunt where a buck like that could die of old age."

"We're almost more a shooting club than serious deer hunters," Roger tells me. "All the guys like to shoot. We're not all that serious about trying to grow super deer. As you get older, it's more about getting away and seeing your friends than about horns. Heck, I'd 'most rather shoot a coyote than a deer. They're harder to fool, I'll tell you that."

The longer I hang around these guys, the more I'm struck by the current of goodwill humming along just beneath the surface. It's an interesting contradiction. These are fairly rough guys, men with dangerous jobs in whose veins still runs that uniquely Southern strain of Scots-Irish blood that is never happier than when marching toward a fight. And yet there is an undercurrent of something approaching tenderness in the way they treat one another. I've been a member or guest in a good many hunting clubs, and almost invariably there is some kind of testosterone contest under the surface noise. It can be a clash to secure a favored stand, a dispute about late dues, or tension about who bent the rules by bringing his brother's kid to camp during the rut. These guys seem to be the opposite. They take more pleasure in what they can give to one another than in what they can get. Every time I catch one alone to ask him about somebody else, at some point I hear the words " . . . and he'd do anything in the world for you." Take Jimmy, for instance, who presses his wonderful sausage on everybody and asks what handloads he can make up for them. Or Roger, who's going around behind my back canvassing the members as to where is the best place for me to get a shot at a buck. Or Slowpoke, a.k.a. Ken Wilson, who has been scouting for a buck this morning rather than hunting, but it's not for him. His nephew is coming up this weekend and he'd dearly love for the boy to get a good one.

Tolbert tells me I need to return for the annual end-of-season barbecue. "We come down on Friday and cook, clean up for the winter, have a big ole time. Everybody brings their favorite pistols and puts 'em on a table with ammo. And the rule is that anybody gets to shoot any gun they want: .22s up to, Lord, whatever you can handle."

I ask how Slowpoke, a gentle but self-contained fellow, got his moniker. Roger says the two of them shared a house for a couple of years and that he was the one to bestow the nickname. "That boy just does everything at the same speed," he says. "But you don't want to shoot pistols against him, I'll say that." Slowpoke himself has already volunteered that there was a time when he began his day by taking a large slug of vodka, throwing up, and downing another. He leveled out the juice with marijuana. "Then one day, he up and quit," says Tolbert. "No meetings, no nothing. Just did it himself. Now he carries a thermos of coffee everywhere he goes and smokes cigarettes like he gets paid for it. But he's the nicest guy you'll ever meet, and you got to admire somebody can do that."

I do. Slowpoke reminds me of men I've encountered over the years, most of them Southerners, who seem ill suited to 21st-century life. He drives a pallet loader in a grocery warehouse near Birmingham and lives in his parents' house. Slowpoke doesn't knock down a lot of money, doesn't cut a wide swath through the world, feels no need to call attention to himself. And yet I find him one of the most interesting people I've met in a long time. He's special precisely because he doesn't think he's special, because there is nothing puffed-up or fake about him. And a truly humble, honest, and gentle man treading the earth these days is a rarity.

You get the feeling that he's pretty much a loner, somebody more comfortable in the woods than anyplace else. "I used to come down here for the whole month of January," he tells me. "Roger would leave Sunday and come back the next Friday and look at me and say, 'You haven't even gone to town yet, have you?' And I wouldn't have. I'd hunt, and walk the woods, and sleep. Don't get me wrong: I enjoy company. I'm glad to see everybody when they come on Friday. But I'm just as glad to see 'em go on Monday." Slowpoke can tell you that he caught 752 fish last year—mostly largemouth and spotted bass—and let all but 50 of them go. He has seen 82 deer so far this year on the lease, 19 of which were small bucks. He says he hasn't been able to get out as much this year because of his father's health. He also jokes that as he gets older he's "just not as mad at the deer as I used to be, you know?" He recognizes that the club ought to shoot more does if they want to grow bigger bucks. But he can only eat three deer in the course of a year. What is unspoken in all this is a deeper truth: As you get older, hunting is less and less about the act of killing and more and more about being there, being swallowed up in the telltale sounds and great silences of the woods, about rubbing shoulders with men who like you fine just the way you are, and getting back to a place where the only digits that matter are the five on each hand. "I just like seeing the animals," Slowpoke says. "If I can go out and see a deer, just get to watch one, I'm happy. That's a good day."

Tolbert motions his head toward Harry Rogers, an older man warming himself by the oil-drum fire—stoop-shouldered and soft looking, with white hair and a voice sanded down soft so you have to lean in to catch his words. I can overhear just enough to know he's saying what a good time he had squirrel hunting in Missouri last year and how he's planning to go back again with his grandson. "He was a helicopter door gunner and weapons expert in Nam," Roger whispers. "One of those guys we sent on missions into the places we didn't send guys, if you know what I mean. He doesn't

184

talk about it much, but when he got a medal it was President Johnson himself who gave it to him. You especially don't want to shoot against Harry."

On my last morning, Roger has decided my best chance is stand No. 9, a particularly well situated shooting house along the gas pipeline and 300 yards from a well-used stream crossing. I stalk in by the glow of a tiny penlight and set up so the Browning is already pointing toward where the deer can be expected. "You need to be ready," he told me. "They may not know what a shooting house is, but they know a green field ain't a healthy place to be for long." I sit and try to memorize the pattern of the distant disturbances in the green of the pipeline right-of-way, because each of them—bare spots, downed timber, or brush—looks like a buck to the naked eye. Around 10:30, while glassing idly, I discover an extra bush on the pipeline, one with four legs and a tail. The only thing moving is her head as she turns it to nip and chew. Soon another doe materializes, then two more, then three more. They are grazing on the near side of the creek and drifting my way, which concerns me. I haven't bathed in three days and the winds are light and variable. But they stop 140 yards away and, after eyeballing the shooting house collectively for the better part of two minutes, return to the business of browsing. Then, one by one, they filter into the woods and are gone.

Well, I'm thinking, trying to make the best of things, you got to see some deer. As Slowpoke says, that's a good day. Ten minutes later, the buck shows, following the same path. He's no monster, but he's the biggest I've seen: a 7-pointer with 3- or 4-inch brow tines. I guess him to be a 2-year-old, but my heart cranks up just as hard as always. I put my scope on him as he sniffs at where the does have fed, judging if any of the girls is feeling frisky. He's broadside now, 180 yards out, and the gun is anchored and steady. He's legal by state and club standards, but I suddenly know I won't shoot. For one thing, I've got meat in the freezer at home and don't need to be paying the airlines extra to bring home what I don't have room for in the first place. For another, I've been on a one-man campaign to let 2-year-olds walk so that we may all take bigger bucks one day. And there's another thought in the back of my mind: The season ends in a week, and this guy has made it this far. If anybody is going to take him this year, it ought to be a boy. Like Slowpoke's nephew.

When Roger and I meet up, he's disappointed at my news. "Hell, I wanted you to kill something," he says, feeling as if he has somehow failed in his duties as host.

"Hell, Roger, I did kill him," I say. "Put the crosshairs right on his shoulder. Just decided not to pull the trigger. I hear those things are awful messy to clean."

GHOSTS OF SHEEP RIVER

STEVEN RINELLA

As far as I can see, there is no top and no bottom to this central Alaskan mountainside. The clouds are low and solid, and the blowing sleet is almost horizontal. My field of view is about as expansive as it would be inside a living room. This is terrain where you could walk off a cliff in the dark. But the mountain's 60-degree pitch, and a heavy backpack loaded with a rifle and 10 days' worth of food and gear, has me moving slowly and carefully.

The hood of my rain jacket is pulled down to shield my eyes. I lift it a bit to check on my hunting partners. My brother Danny, an ecologist with the University of Alaska, is behind me. To my right, I can make out the shape of Chris Flowers, a buddy who flies 737s for Alaska Airlines. When Flowers isn't working in airplanes, he plays in them. He and his Piper Super Cub live in a private airstrip community in Anchorage. (Imagine a golf-course community except there's only one fairway, and it's 100 feet wide and 1,300 feet long.) Two days ago, Flowers shuttled us to a gravel bar along a glacial river about 40 miles into the northern end of the Alaska Range.

We've been walking since. The first day we waded through spruce bogs and alder thickets while downpours flooded the game trails with calf-deep water. On the second day the rain let up, but the brush got nastier: The spruce gave way at higher elevations to willow and dwarf birch so thick we had to pry it apart and walk through sideways. Now that we've entered the alpine tundra, we're climbing into clouds and snow.

Finding a Dall ram in this weather is tough. I don't care how good your eyes are; it's difficult to spot a white critter against a snowy background in the middle of a whiteout. We could spook sheep without even seeing them, so we agree to hole up. Before long we arrive at a shoulder of flat land on an otherwise steeply rising ridge. We scrape away enough of the slush to pitch a tent. Later, during a break in the snow, I open the flap and stick my head out. We're camped on a narrow saddle between two cirques. Within 10 feet on either side of us is land too steep to stand on. It occurs to me that a ram's survival strategy relies on its willingness to go places where you won't. It's sort of like a game of chicken, but I can't decide if the game is played against the sheep, the land, or your own mind.

Dall sheep are creatures of the cold. Their genetic ancestors first crossed from Siberia to the New World during the Pleistocene Ice Ages, following routes along the now-vanished Bering land bridge. For millennia after their arrival, there was probably just one species of sheep ranging from Siberia's Kamchatka Peninsula down into what is now the Lower 48. Eventually, the population diverged into three distinct species: the snow sheep of Siberia; the Rocky Mountain bighorn sheep (including the desert bighorn subspecies) of the western United States and southern Canadian Rockies; and the Dall sheep (including the stone sheep subspecies) of Alaska, northern British Columbia, and southern Yukon.

Hunting Dall sheep is more complicated than simply locating them. The real trick is finding a legal-size ram. In most of Alaska's hunting districts, a legal ram must meet at least one of three requirements: (1) Both horns are "broomed," or broken; (2) one of the horns shows at least eight annuli, or annual growth rings; or (3) one of the horns is full curl, describing a 360-degree circle when viewed from the side. These requirements describe only about 3 to 8 percent of the sheep population across the seven Alaskan mountain ranges where they live. Many guided sheep hunters obsess over additional attributes, such as extra length or mass, which might signify a trophy-size ram. Most do-it-yourself hunters operating on a limited budget, however, will agree that any legal ram is a trophy.

To reliably find rams, you need access to a lot of land containing a lot of sheep. If you know of such a place, it's not the sort of thing you advertise to strangers. In fact, Danny was tipped off to our current hunting area when he overheard a snippet of conversation between a bush pilot and an outfitter. They were talking about a valley—I'll call it Sheep River—with a good supply of rams and an absence of hunting pressure. A year later, Danny happened to fly over said valley. He was impressed by the terrain, but most exciting was the absence of landing strips. There was only one way to get into the area: land in a neighboring valley and bushwhack through a couple of thousand vertical feet of nasty terrain. We began making our plans.

In the evening, just when our ridgeline campsite is beginning to feel like a prison cell, the snow lets up and the lower clouds break apart. Soon it's possible to get a few minutes of visibility between each passing mass. We scramble uphill toward the eastern crest of the Sheep River drainage. On the leeward side of the ridge, we wade through a small cornice of snow, then emerge on a windblown plateau. It's the highest piece of land within miles. If not for the foggy conditions, we'd be looking westward over Sheep River and eastward into a series of creeks that drain into another large valley. Only a fraction of that is actually visible, but we do the best we can do with our binoculars and a spotting scope.

I notice a faint trail in the snow on a parallel ridge toward the east. Scanning leftward I see that the trail disappears over the top of the ridge. I scan rightward and notice that the trail terminates in a sheep's body. I direct the guys to what I'm looking at. With the color of the animal locked in our minds—they're just a touch yellower than fresh snow—we begin to see that the slope is peppered with at least a dozen sheep feeding above and below the first one. It's impossible to see horns in the hazy conditions, but about a third of the sheep are much smaller and spindlier than the rest. It's a group of lambs and ewes.

A few snow squalls blow through as we watch the sheep. Soon the sun sets, and we pick our way back toward the saddle where we pitched camp. A hundred yards from the tent we cut two fresh sets of caribou tracks. I'm reminded of the caribou permit I brought along in case we encountered a bull within a reasonable distance of the landing strip. I had that distance fixed at 3 or 4 miles, but the sight of these tracks tempts me to stretch that number outward.

Throughout the night we have to knock frozen sleet off the walls of the tent every hour, but by midmorning the skies are clearing up. By noon it's downright brilliant, and the sun is coming off the melting snow as bright as a welder's arc. We're back up on the north-south drainage divide high above Sheep River. I'm glassing a band of five Dall rams that are about 2 miles ahead of us. The sheep are out on a westward-jutting spur of this same ridgeline. They're lower in elevation, bedded in a shadow of the mountain below the snow line. One of the rams looks good.

Danny takes a long look through the scope. "He is big," he says. "But we're just too far out to say for sure."

Sheep have amazing eyesight—about the equivalent of a human using a pair of 8X binoculars. To stay out of view and make a stealthy approach, we figure that we'll have to surrender our hard-fought elevation and climb back down into the bed of Sheep River. From there, we can use the channel and the brush as camouflage while we ascend the valley to a point even with the bedded rams.

It takes about four hours for us to get into the vicinity of the sheep. We sneak a look at them and mark their position in relation to a prominent outcropping of rock. Then we head higher up the valley in order to put a mountain between us and them. Once we're completely shielded from view, we leave the valley floor and start trudging back uphill.

By the time we approach their elevation, we haven't laid eyes on the rams for more than an hour. It's likely that they'll be up and feeding in the cool of the evening. For now we have to trust that they're in the same place. Tomorrow Flowers has to start walking out to his plane, so this is his only chance. We agree that he'll take the stalk.

The wind seems O.K. Flowers just has to work his way around the mountain until he comes to the shoulder of rock. When he crawls around that, he should be in sight of the rams but still a couple of hundred yards away. Hopefully he'll have plenty of time to check out the larger ram and, if it looks good, take a shot.

Danny and I stay well behind. As Flowers nears the shoulder of rock, he freezes in one of those "you got me!" positions and then slowly collapses his body onto the ground. He peers around to us and points in an unexpected direction—essentially straight up the mountain from us. I lift my head a few inches and stare into the faces of four rams that are very concerned about having company. I could throw a rock to them. I hear a clattering of hooves and see that the fifth and largest ram is already skittering up the mountain. Without pausing he vanishes over an impossible wall of rock. The other four follow in his path at a leisurely pace. Within a few seconds they're so far gone that they might as well be on Mars.

Danny sits down, takes off his hat, and scratches his head: "That was a legal ram."

The best piece of sheep hunting advice I've heard came from a bush pilot out of Wasilla, Alaska. "Find the one you want," he said, "and stay with it." At the time I had little idea how important this was, but since then my faith in the tactic has been fortified by a number of experiences. I've been involved in three Dall sheep kills that began with one or more failed stalks and played out over miles of terrain. Danny's taken part in even more, including the pursuit of a ram that lasted a few days.

We wake in the morning with the idea that we'll do it again. Flowers says goodbye and begins the long hike to his plane. Danny and I figure that we'll continue northward by following Sheep River upstream. We'll glass as much of the country as possible from down low, and hopefully get a fresh fix on the rams before committing to a new climb.

The valley floor narrows as we get higher. Soon it's a quarter-mile-wide passage covered in nothing but ankle-high tundra and the gnawed skeletal remains of caribou. The grizzly and wolf scat we're seeing is mostly packed hair and shattered bone. The same craggy peaks occupy the skyline throughout the morning, and the warming air causes the snow to retreat farther up the mountains. We continue to get fresh glimpses into tributaries and basins where the slopes are gentle enough to allow the growth of grasses and sedges that support sheep. We turn up several small herds of cow caribou and a distant band of bedded Dall ewes and lambs, but there's no trace of the five rams. Once we've covered a few miles it's possible to see all the way to the head of the drainage. There's no doubt that the rams have left the valley.

We discuss a few travel routes. For me, logic says to climb eastward, up to the drainage divide that we spotted the sheep from yesterday. For Danny, curiosity says to climb westward, in order to get a glance into a new valley that we haven't seen yet.

"You know that we'll get all the way up there and see the rams on the east side, don't you?" I ask.

"Yes, probably," he said.

"But you still want to go west?"

"Yup."

We reach the crest at dusk and lay out our camp in a low spot amid some boulders. At daybreak I'm surprised to see that there's a group of 17 ewes and lambs feeding just up the ridge from us. The animals look faint and ghostlike in the low light of dawn, and they don't appear to be going anywhere. Although it's highly unlikely to see a mature ram with a gang of ewes during the fall months, we're reluctant to spook the sheep out of a simple reverence for animals that aren't spooked. As the morning heats up, the ewes begin feeding downslope. Soon we can scoot past them by dropping down along the opposite side of the crest.

It's slow going throughout the day. There's a lot of land to look at. We glass a pair of three-quarter-curl rams bedded on a knife's-edge ridge and several more groups of ewes and cow caribou. But we don't see anything promising until the afternoon. We're sitting on a peak while I look through the spotting scope. I comment to Danny that it's possible to see all the way across the valley to where we'd spooked the five rams two days earlier. I crank up the scope's magnification.

"You've got to be kidding me!" I say. "There are five white dots up above that same spot."

Danny takes a look through the scope. "That's got to be them," he says. "We must have passed them by. Or maybe they came back."

Neither of us says anything, but we both know what the other is thinking: We've got to climb down this mountain, wade across Sheep River, backtrack down the valley through the alders, then climb back up the other side.

At first it goes pretty well. A two-hour hike puts us on a flat tableland above Sheep River. We continue toward the creek, and a moving set of caribou antlers catches my eye. They belong to a mature bull headed our way. I go prone and rest the barrel of my rifle over my backpack. The bull enters the bed of a tributary stream and then climbs out 75 yards away. He cuts sharply leftward and exposes his right side. I lead him just a couple of inches into the shoulder, and the Ruger .300 mag. puts a clean hole in the rib cage midway up the body. The bull takes a few more steps and tips over.

"I don't want to be a downer," Danny says. "But this trip just turned into a hell of a lot of work."

The rams are gone in the morning. We take a good look around, then start heading back up Sheep River. Soon we're stumbling across our own boot prints from two days earlier. We travel about 2 miles and stop to glass a short, steep basin carved into the mountainside to the east. The basin is shaped like a giant soup bowl. A wedge of the bowl is missing where two small streams come together and spill out of the basin toward Sheep River. The two stream branches are separated by a narrow dividing ridge that rises from the basin floor and climbs toward the crest of the wall. The ridge is carpeted in grass and has a well-worn sheep trail running up its spine. As I study the ridge, I see a shoe-size piece of white amid some boulders. There are no other rocks that color, and there's something about the way that it reflects light.

"I've been looking at that, too," says Danny. "But it hasn't moved."

"Uh-oh!" I almost shout. "There it did. You see that?"

We're looking at the muzzle of a sheep. To get a look at the rest of the head, we sneak over and climb the wall of the basin that is opposite the muzzle. It belongs to a three-quarter-curl ram. Sure enough, he's with the other four. Two of them are grazing just downslope. The largest of the group, the legal ram, is bedded down.

Getting to them seems like a laughable notion. They have a commanding view in every direction and would be gone in a wink if they saw us. But there's got to be a way, I tell myself. I look carefully at the small stream in the basin floor. The stream channel is cut deeply into the gravel in places, and the left fork runs perpendicular to the sheep's line of sight. It wouldn't be much fun, but if a guy was desperate enough he could belly-crawl right up the stream channel for a few hundred yards. If he kept low in the water, really low, the sheep would be looking right over his back. Then, when he got to the toe of the ridge, he'd be shielded from view by the curvature of the hill. A long belly-crawl up the trail on the ridge's spine would deliver him into range.

We retreat toward the mouth of the basin and stash most of our gear. Then we start crawling up the streambed. After 15 minutes my hands and knees are numb from the cold rocks and water. My legs and back are cramped. But we continue along, dragging ourselves across the ground like worms. Now and then I peek up behind a jumble of rocks to see a tuft or two of white on top of the ridge. The sheep haven't budged. It takes 45 minutes of crawling to get close to the ridge and beneath the sheep's line of sight. I stand up and walk off the arthritic ache in my knees. I bagged the caribou, so we decide Danny will lead the stalk, and then we commence another long, rocky crawl.

There are many ways to blow a stalk, and most of them end in the same manner: You arrive at the place where the animals are supposed to be, but they're not there. On this stalk, it takes us a while to realize that this has happened. At least half a dozen times I watch Danny approach small rises along the ridgeline. Each time, he prepares himself for a shot before crawling ahead. And each time, I see the tension fall away from his shoulders as he realizes that there must be one more rise separating him from his quarry. Soon the remainder of the ridge comes into view and there aren't many more places to hide a group of rams. Danny turns back to look at me. His face says it all. We blew it.

There's a temptation to stand up and curse, but we keep cool and move slowly ahead. On the right side of the ridge, the slope drops away quickly enough that it's impossible to see what's directly below. Maybe they fed their way down. Danny tells me to wait behind, and he creeps ahead to take a look over the ledge. He then backs up a few feet and gives me a series of hand signals: The rams are there. He sees two of them, but not the big one. I should stay put and wait.

He slinks from view, and I hang tight. An hour goes by, and the sun drops. The temperature plummets. I'm wet and shivering. I start to hope that Danny will come back up the hill. But that would mean that he couldn't find the ram, so instead I hope for the sound of a rifle shot. When it finally comes, the shot sounds crisp and distant. I choke back a yip of excitement, and I'm on my feet. I trot over the lip of the ridge and come to a nearly vertical cliff. I can't see Danny, but I do see four rams scurrying up the wall of the basin across from me. I throw up my binoculars. The larger ram is not with them. I almost let out a whoop but choke the cry back as well.

With my rifle slung over my shoulders, I climb backward down the rocky cliff face and come to a spot where I have to jump down from a chest-high ledge. I almost land on Danny's boot. He's tucked into a little crevice with his rifle shouldered and propped over a wadded jacket. It's aimed almost directly downhill and following a moving object. I look forward and see the sheep rolling like a runaway piece of firewood down the mountain. The carcass is still when it stops just above the creek we were crawling through a few hours earlier. In a flash I can see the upcoming days with perfect clarity. Two trips back and forth to the airstrip: one with a sheep and one with a caribou. In other words, about 40 miles of walking with packs ranging from 75 to 100 pounds. There will be sore knees, blisters, and vows of never hunting in the mountains again. But I quickly force those thoughts out of my mind. Instead, I turn my attention to that yip of joy that I've been holding in. It feels good to let it out.

FOWL
TERRITORY

T. EDWARD NICKENS

We are soaked to the skin and shivering. An hour earlier, my buddy Scott Wood blew a boot seam in his chest waders, and I went overboard to the shoulders when I lost my footing on a third shot at high overhead birds. Now a cold North Dakota prairie pothole sloshes to my thighs, and my teeth chatter through the call. Thankfully, the ducks couldn't care less. Cattails tower overhead as the birds strafe the marsh. I grab a handful of reeds and pull them close as more ducks light 20 feet away. We pick out mallards from gangs of gadwall—flocks by the tens, scores, and hundreds— and pull triggers only on the greenheads. The birds are in our face, orange feet stuck out kickboxer-style, homing in on Wood's soft hen quack like it's a piece of prairie catnip.

After months of planning, the world is made of ducks. "This is what we came for," I whisper to Wood.

"This," he says, "but a touch drier."

Now is the time to freelance North Dakota. On the one hand, 2011's epic floods ravaged the state's northern tier. But all that prairie water pushed duck populations to 35 percent above the long-term average. For at least the next year or two, the best place in North America for a figure-it-out,

D.I.Y. duck hunting adventure will be tucked up against the Canada border, in North Dakota's freelance-friendly prairie-pothole region.

We've landed in Bismarck lightly laden for a couple of hunters. Earlier we'd shipped out chest waders, two dozen decoys, and a cooler packed with pots, pans, and a stove. We rent an SUV and lock up a bunkroom with a full kitchen at the shop of a local plumbing contractor. We're anxious to see what a couple of Eastern swamp hunters can scare up on our own, but first, we've lined up a pair of locals to give us a three-day crash course.

Our first pothole professor is Erik Myre, a Minot-area cabinetmaker (and 2011 Heroes of Conservation finalist) who'd rather watch a quarter-acre pothole suck ducks out of the sky than shoot geese flocked up by the thousands. We barely say howdy on Myre's front porch before he herds us into his truck and heads for open farm country. "Here, duck hunting means duck scouting," he says. "Ninety percent of the hunters are chasing geese and will ignore a mallard flight bombing into a slough the next section over. Few locals have figured out how much fun the potholes can be."

The amount of water here is astounding, and a big part of the fun is simply finding the ducks. Prairie potholes are shallow, marshy wetlands created when receding glaciers gouged the Pleistocene plains. There are tens of thousands spread across the Great Plains, and while the duck hunting can be as straightforward as hunkering behind giant bur reed until the sky turns dark with ducks, so much water also gives the birds plenty of places to hide. Even here, nothing's a given.

Our first morning hunt unfolds in a pothole that was skimmed over with mallards just a few days earlier. We never touch a trigger. Undaunted, Myre corrals us back in the truck. Just after lunch we pull up to a soaring ridgetop that overlooks a sweep of prairie, corn stubble, and cattail, sunlight glinting off distant windmills and silos. A mile and a half away, a trickle of ducks drops behind another gentle ridge. I dig through maps, and Wood keeps a tally on the birds. "More," he says. "More. More. More." Myre hits the gas.

Thirty minutes later, Myre drops us off at a fringe of cattails. High water from the wet spring laps at our wader tops, but as we wade through a jungle of reeds, it's clear why there were no ducks in our morning pothole: Every duck in America wants to be right here.

It's here where I take a swim and where Wood's waders spring a leak. And it's here where we pick up our first lesson of prairie-pothole gunning: Stay at it. Scout every waking hour. Follow the ducks. Don't give up, and the memory of one morning hunt's empty skies might just vanish into feathered air.

The potholes around Minot are mostly wader-shallow and small enough that a Modified choke will reach from shore to shore. There are bigger waters around, however. And they hold a different sort of duck.

"You can have a conversation with a mallard and try to talk him to you," says John Devney one morning as he works a gangline of unmallard-like decoys. "But a diving duck is either gonna come in or he isn't, so you've got to make it easy on him."

Which isn't always easy. By a huge margin, North Dakota duck hunters are here for mallards, pintails, and wigeon. It's rare to pull together a big-water diving duck hunt in the midst of such puddler pickings, but we have found just the guy. Devney lives and breathes prairie-pothole ducks as Delta Waterfowl's senior vice president, but the Minnesota native has never lost his taste for chasing big fowl like bluebills and canvasbacks. "I have friends who are big prairie duck hunters and they don't own a boat, much less chest waders," Devney says. "That's just crazy."

This morning, Devney aims to school us on the finer points of picking a single trophy canvasback from the tight, swift squadrons of birds that dive-bomb our decoys. We're at a sprawling lake—its shores fringed with wild rice and coves armored with rock. When the sun rose, parts of the lakeshore were frosted with hundreds of tundra swans, chortling a constant chorus. Other than one threesome manning a midchannel island, we're alone on a lake that could easily host a dozen parties.

And we seem to be invisible to the flights of divers that come skidding around our point. Our backs against an 8-foot bluff of rock and rich prairie earth, we play a game of chicken with crazy numbers of ducks. Flights of canvasbacks rocket across the decoys, most at 20 yards. With a one-canvasback limit, we're looking for the biggest ducks, and I allow two good bulls to skirt the decoys unscathed. I find the next drake, crossing right-to-left, but a pair of shot sprays exploding the water behind its feet are like visual peals of taunting laughter. "The mallard has guile," Devney says. "For a bird like a bluebill or canvasback, though, speed is the only survival tool."

Speed—and a bit of luck that we can shoot only a single trophy canvasback apiece. Eventually we put No. 2 shot where it needs to be, and with a pair stretched out on the boat deck, we pass up hundreds of birds silhouetted in the sun. Back home we'd never give so many ducks a hall pass, but here we're being prairie-pothole picky—trying to pick out drakes and pick around the pair of canvasbacks already in the bag. I pull up on a big redhead drake, its gorgeous noggin flashing in the sun, as three canvasbacks suddenly join the flight. I lower my gun. I can't take the chance.

It is exhilarating and frustrating, and curiously, it's a classic way to gun the potholes. "Shooting prairie divers has a lot more heritage than you might think," Devney says. From the end of the Depression through the '60s, hunters flocked to well-known passes—strips of land connecting large pothole lakes—such as Chase Lake Pass and Buffalo Lake Pass. "Guys would come from all over to sit in a half pit and shoot canvasbacks and redheads boiling over a pass." That might, in fact, explain the origins of the term pass shooting.

There's no question that the spectacle in front of us validates the attraction. As we pull up the decoys, canvasbacks and bluebills continue to swarm the cove. Devney's grin is ear to ear. "We've seen more canvasbacks this morning than most hunters will see their entire lives," he says. "I'll cheat and go mallard on ya every now and then, because they're so much easier to hunt. But it's hard to beat what we've just experienced."

We nod in agreement. But we have five more days to try.

"You getting enough protein?" Wood asks. I'm munching on a grilled goose breast, thanks to a honker that made the mistake of hanging around with mallards one morning. It's the latest delight in our daily regimen of eating through the birds we've put on the ground. So far down the hatch: duck cacciatore, duck stir-fry, duck with cream sauce, duck pasta, duck sandwiches, duck fried rice with livers and gizzards, and goose on bagels.

By now we've figured out what it takes to hunt here: gas and glass. We shoot the mornings, then hammer down all afternoon, looking for a good place to greet the dawn. It is stunning country. From ridgetops, we glass sprawling mosaics of farmfields ribboned with marsh and timber. There are state-designated waterfowl production areas and waterfowl resting areas, and private lands registered with the state for hunting access. Mixed in is perhaps the biggest draw: All private, unposted land is open to hunting. Yet sometimes these birds still hold all the good cards.

This morning's hunt is a prime example. We're winging it in a wheat stubble field, an alien experience. Instead of layout blinds, we use Devney's oversize Canada goose shells. Lying on the ground, I cover my lower legs with one shell, my belly with another, and heap grass and stubble over my torso. Chest waders serve as a pillow. We want to pull this off on our own, with a mix-and-match of local knowledge and our own duck smarts. But I'll be honest: Snuggling under a couple of magnum honkers makes me feel like an idiot.

The ducks seem to share the sentiment. In the muddled dawn light, dribs and drabs of birds course over the field, ignoring the goose lumps until it's too late. Once the sun is up, however, the raised goose shells throw garishly long shadows across the field. Suddenly, 150 mallards and pintails swoop in, a gigantic flock with 300 eyeballs, circling the field and chattering to themselves: What are those guys doing to the geese down there?

We're being made right and left, but we can't beat ourselves up too much; an hour after shooting light we have five mallards. "Think about it," Wood says as we stack the shells in the truck, headed for a late breakfast. "We are killing ducks in a field in North Dakota. Given how little we know about what we're doing, I feel pretty good about myself."

He's right. We've shown up with little more than credit cards and time to burn. We have to find the water, find the birds, figure out access, and put two and No. 2 together before we pull the trigger. It could be easier, but I'm not sure it could be any more fun.

Two afternoons later, we're in a place we've been before: empty-handed. For five hours we pound the gravel. Then, just as the sun slips below the horizon, we spot a black river of ducks pouring into a field. As we glass, marveling at the open spigot of feathers, something else catches our eye:

white squares of paper staked around the field. Our last-ditch honey hole is ringed with posted signs.

We've been told that most farmers post to keep deer and pheasant hunters at bay, and often will grant duck hunters access. We want this field badly. We are relatively young and somewhat clean, with expertly honed Southern manners. We start knocking on doors.

It takes an hour to find the right house. Now it's dark, and I'm uneasy stepping up to the porch of a red farmhouse set back from the road. We'd never consider this back home.

But we're not in North Carolina anymore. Answering the door is the Nicest Lady in the World. Marilyn Bromley is hardly fazed by a couple of out-of-towners on her brightly lit porch. She waves us in. Her son is at the kitchen table, homework papers everywhere. A younger daughter waves shyly from the kitchen. We shuffle our feet, call her ma'am, and apologize for our muddy boots. "Look around, guys," she says. "This is a farm."

Bromley's husband is still in the fields. She has dinner to fix, homework to oversee, but she listens to our carefully crafted plea. Her son maps out the firm spots in the field so our truck won't bog down. We chat in the kitchen for a bit—marveling at how friendly folks have been, while she can't believe we've flown 1,500 miles to shoot birds. "They don't have ducks in North Carolina?" She shakes her head, grinning. "It's funny, hunters show up from all over everywhere to shoot the ducks we get sick and tired of!"

We walk out with permission to hunt her farm, warmed by this kind of prairie-pothole hospitality. We trudge out of the Bromley field 14 hours later, our arms groaning with mallards, a pair of lesser Canadas, and a single greater Canada goose. I can't say what did the trick—the goose decoys, the duck decoys, the duck flags, the roboduck, the duck calling, or just the fact that we're in the duckiest place in North America. But this much we know: This is a special place, and we'll be doing this again tomorrow, and the next day, and the next day.

We couldn't have dreamed up our last-day setup. The evening before, we scouted a shallow seep that drained a vast field of wheat stubble just as the last light ebbed from the sky. Ducks streamed in and out of the meager pothole. Glassing the scene from a timbered ridge a few hundred yards away, we could see the challenge: For a hundred yards in every direction, there was nothing taller than a 5-inch stalk of wheat. "You couldn't hide a pencil out there," I say. But Wood is thinking deeper: But you could hide a hunter.

When dawn breaks we are as camouflaged as I've ever been. We hiked to the water two hours before sunrise and dug a pair of coffin-size trenches 10 yards from the edge of the pothole. Covered with mud and armfuls of wheat stubble, we lie like a pair of crocodiles in the muck, shotguns across our chests. When the ducks come we burst from the ground in eruptions of straw and wet dirt, our hands grabbing as much wheat straw as pistol grip, pulling triggers with stubble in the trigger guards and mud in our eyes as ducks scramble skyward, as shocked to see us as we are that our ruse is working so well.

Fifty minutes into the hunt, we have two limits of mallards and three odd ducks down, so we set our hearts on a pintail sprig or nothing at all. Flights of three and 15 and 40 ducks whirl across the wheatfield, cutting tight circles overhead as we try to spot a pintail in a flock of tightly packed mallards. It's Wood's turn to shoot, so when I spot a scythe of narrow, pointed wings mixed in with all the greenheads, I fix my eyes on the duck. "Pintail," I say. "Third from the left. See him?"

"Yep."

I call out the pintail's coordinates to Wood. Five times the flock circles, but my eyes never leave the sprig. Finally the flock makes a wide turn, setting up for their final descent, and the pintail slips past a half dozen other ducks like a stock car on a banked track.

"He's on the outside now," I say. "Far right on the lead triple. See him? Scott? Far right?"

Seconds later Wood rises like some prairie zombie, slinging dirt and steel shot. The far-right bird tumbles to the ground, and we war-whoop like banshees, dancing with aboriginal glee around a pair of rude holes. It's not what we'd imagined a prairie-pothole duck shoot to be, but that's just fine. It is so much better.

TROUBLE

MIKE TOTH

This was 25 years ago, when I'd moved to Georgia for a new job. By co-incidence, a guy I knew who hunted land bordering the Pennsylvania property I hunted had moved there about a year earlier. When a couple of Yankee hunters find each other deep in Dixie, they become friends quickly, as Tom and I did.

Tom worked at the big Lockheed plant outside of Atlanta and had met a few hunters there. One of them, a guy named Brad, lived out near the Alabama border, an hour-plus drive southwest of the city. Rural Georgia.

Brad told Tom that his family had property with a lot of turkeys on it, and we could hunt it if we wanted to. So one afternoon in March, Tom and I drive out to scout it.

We have a handwritten map and directions from Brad to a stretch of woods along a two-lane road. We park, go in, and immediately find turkey sign. Tracks, droppings, and feathers are everywhere. We even hear some birds. We don't want to spook any, so we quickly mark a place near a roost tree to set up for opening morning and get out of there.

Boy, are we pumped. Georgia gobblers! On private land!

Tom picks me up at 3:30 a.m. on the opener a week later, and we get to the property way before sunup. We walk in, get settled, and start calling in the predawn. For about an hour we have a flock around us, but nothing comes close. We decide to walk back to the truck for coffee and to plan the rest of the morning.

We're heading up the slope to the road when I see a thin man wearing a pressed khaki uniform taking a leak at the edge of the woods. "Warden," I tell Tom. We stop, look at each other, shrug, and walk toward him. After all, we're not doing anything wrong.

If only I had known.

"Licenses," the warden says as he leads us back to the truck. Tom and I open our wallets and hand them over. He's agitated and I can't figure out why. He gives the licenses back to us and says, "You're on private property!"

"We know," says Tom. "We have permission." He tells the warden about Brad.

"This isn't his property!" the warden says.

"Yes it is," says Tom. He goes to the truck—which, I realize uneasily, still has a Pennsylvania license plate on it—and gets the directions. "See? Brad said—"

"It's not his land!" the warden says, hotly.

"So whose land is it?"

"It's my land!"

The three of us get into a heated discussion about why we thought we were on the correct property, the state's posting laws, and the lack of posted signs on the land, but at the end we say O.K., if we made a mistake, we'll leave.

The warden has other ideas. He writes out tickets and says we can settle right there by paying him the fines, which come to more than $200. Tom and I have about $17.

"Get in your truck and follow me," says the warden. Ten minutes later we're at what appears to be a large police station. We follow the warden inside, where he has a quiet conversation with two officers.

One of the cops walks up to us and says, "Empty your pockets. Take your belts off. Turn around, feet apart, hands against the wall." Shocked, we do so. We get patted down and are led to a jail cell. A thick metal door slams shut on us.

We're in jail. In the deep South. With our broad, nasal northern accents and our truck with the name of a faraway state on the tag.

And no one knows we're here.

"I can't believe this!" says Tom, pacing back and forth in front of the stainless-steel, seatless toilet. "This is bulls--t! How long can they keep us here? How do we get out?"

"I don't know," I say. I look through the tiny window where an officer is sitting at a desk. I pound the door. "Phone call! We're allowed one phone call!" He ignores me.

Half an hour later the cell door opens and an elderly man in an orange jumpsuit passes us foam boxes containing beans and a very red hot dog. A smiley face and the words Have a Nice Day are embossed on the lid.

Soon after that an officer opens the door. "Follow me," he says. Soon we're getting our front and profile photos taken. I still have camo paint on my face. I feel ridiculous.

The officer eventually lets us use the phone, but we can't reach anyone in Atlanta. In desperation I tell the officer I'll give him my ATM card and tell him my PIN if he'll go get cash. "I can't do that," he says.

"So what can we do?"

"Well, there's a bail bondsman in town. Here's his number."

I get on the phone with the bondsman, explain our situation, and tell him how much cash we have on hand, which isn't even enough to cover his fee. "Sounds like you boys are in a bit of a bind," he says.

"How about our guns?" I ask him. "Can you take them as collateral?"

"What kind are they?"

"A Winchester 1200 and—hey Tom! What do you shoot?—and a Remington 870."

The bondsman, an elderly white-haired man, arrives an hour later. I watch as he jokes with one of the officers. Our cell door opens. We get our personal effects and walk out. The bondsman puts his arm around my shoulders and says, "Here's my card. If you ever find yourself in a bind in Atlanta, call me."

I'm insulted at first, but then I see myself from his perspective: the type of guy who gets into trouble.

Months later, Tom and I pay our fines, pay the bondsman, and get our guns back. We found out that the warden was a member of a club that hunted that property. The members were voluntarily not hunting turkeys in order to let the flock propagate. We also discovered that Brad and the warden knew each other—and didn't care for one another. Brad became scarce, so I never learned why he'd sent us there.

I carry my own up-to-date, well-marked maps now whenever I hunt. Along with some extra cash in my wallet. Just in case.

BEAR
DOWN

STEVEN RINELLA

Ronny and I were drifting in a Lund skiff 200 yards offshore along the coast of Southeast Alaska's Prince of Wales Island, about 8 miles from my hunting and fishing shack. To my surprise, he'd just announced that it was no longer necessary for him to share in the duty of glassing for black bears.

"How do you figure that?" I asked.

He was kicked back on the bench seat, smoking a cigar. "Because I can tell without even looking that there are no bears within sight right now," he said.

"How can you tell that?"

"Because if there was, you'd have said, 'Uh-oh, there's a bear!'"

There were limits to how far I could pursue this argument. Ronny's a contractor, and I'm indebted to him for employing me all through college with higher-than-normal wages and lower-than-normal hours. So rather than pressing my case, I returned to my preferred position for observing bears: feet over the engine's tiller, back against the gunwale, eyes on my binoculars. Ronny tried to return to his preferred position, but first he had to adjust his makeshift pillow of flotation jackets. As I scanned the shoreline, I noticed a black object emerging on a patch of sedges that grew along the seam where the coastal rain forest ended and the tidal zone began.

"Uh-oh," I said. "There's a bear!"

"See? I told you."

The bear had a swayback, a potbelly, and a block-shaped head with ears that seemed short and rounded rather than tall and pointed. In other words, it looked like a good-size boar. But before we could form a plan, the bear fed its way back into the timber. I lifted the outboard out of the water and used an electric trolling motor to silently approach a point of land that would shield us from the bear's last location. We beached the boat beneath a large cedar that had tipped into the water. A long stretch of shoreline reached away from us, and we watched it to see if the bear would reappear. If it did, the wind would be perfect for Ronny to climb out of the boat and make a stalk. (It's illegal to shoot a bear from a boat on Prince of Wales Island.)

Maybe 15 minutes passed without anything happening. I assumed that the bear had either headed off into the forest or turned back the other way. I had a Knight & Hale predator call around my neck. I got to wondering if the plaintive bleats of a deer fawn might inspire the bear to come out and have a look. I cut loose on the call without mentioning my plan to Ronny, as I figured whatever happened would happen very far away. Instead I was answered by the sudden and close sound of claw on rock. Ronny and I both whirled our heads around to see a large male bear coming toward us like a pit bull crossing its yard to meet an uninvited intruder at the gate. If it had been a fish, we could have cast to it with a cane pole. I yelled at Ronny to jump out of the boat and shoot.

He glanced over the gunwale and gave a frantic announcement. "The water's over my boots!"

"Your boots?" I yelled. "Who cares about your damn boots?"

By then the bear had realized that he was not approaching a wounded fawn after all. He spun around and vanished back into the timber. Without saying a word, Ronny and I started laughing so hard that it eventually became painful. It was his third close encounter with a boar in as many days.

•••

While smart-asses do not generally make the best hunting partners, Ronny turns this generalization on its head. He's an ambitious and dedicated grouse hunter, the kind who can turn a one-flush day into a one-bird day. He's also a reliable friend who's willing to make sacrifices for his buddies. One time, when I was down on my luck, he traded me a perfectly good Ford for a not-so-good chain saw. Though he didn't realize it, I'd taken him on this bear hunt for reasons that went beyond my appreciation of his company. Years before, Ronny had been on a guided bear hunt in Canada that had left him with a bad, long-lasting impression. He'd gone up there as the guest of a business associate who'd arranged the trip. Their outfitter didn't like to do anything in the morning. His clients would just sit around eating bacon and drinking coffee. In the afternoon he'd drive the hunters out to their stands, which were positioned near bait barrels along logging roads. The barrels had been filled with liquefied hard candy at a factory. Bears came in as though they were under a spell, like kids visiting their Halloween baskets the day after trick-or-treating. Later, Ronny remarked that the only thing he'd learned about bear biology or ecology was that bears behave in unusual ways when presented with a blend of refined sugar, corn syrup, artificial flavors and colors, emulsifiers, suspension agents, and preservatives. When Ronny killed a bear and inquired about the guide's method of packaging meat, the guide behaved as though he'd never heard of something as outlandish as eating a bear.

Hearing this story put me into the position of being a bear hunting ambassador. I felt obligated to show Ronny another side of bear hunting—a side where bears go about their natural business in a region that forces you to develop an appreciation for the land you're on and the species you're after. As it happened, I had the perfect setup for such a task: a shack on the southern end of Alaska's Prince of Wales Island.

That I own the place is thanks to the fact that my two brothers and I, back in 2004, simultaneously entered that brief period of life when you have money but no spouse to tell you how to spend it. Along with a buddy, we made the largely impulsive decision to buy the lopsided and shoebox-shaped structure that sits on tilted pilings over the tideline of a remote cove. The cove is surrounded largely by Tongass National Forest, and is accessible only by plane or boat. It is completely off the grid. We get our water from a gravity-fed hose dunked into the creek that comes off the mountain behind the house and flows beneath the front right corner of the deck. For the most part, phones do not get a signal. Electricity is from a Honda generator. Our hot tub is a Rubbermaid livestock watering tank that we shipped up on a boat from Seattle; the water is heated by a woodburning stove. Instead of a flush toilet there's a hole in the ground and a bucket of lime. Mink drag their catch into the workshop and leave the bones and scales where they fall. Old-growth spruce and hemlock lean menacingly over everything we own—including the three chain saws, three outboard engines, one skiff, and dozens of rusted oil drums and hundreds of even rustier tools that the previous owner abandoned when he walked away from the place and never returned.

Whenever I'm justifying my purchase of the shack to my wife, I remind her that Prince of Wales Island has one of the—or perhaps the—densest black bear populations on earth. The animals inhabit a crazily shaped island with a third less landmass than the island of Hawaii but over three times as much coastline. Since it's difficult for a bear to get more than a few miles away from the shore, you tend to see a lot of them hanging out along the water's edge. This is especially true during the salmon runs of mid to late summer, when it's common to encounter a gang of three or four mature bears milling around a stream mouth. As easy as it is to find bears during the salmon season, it's not a good time to hunt them. Alaska tourism brochures love to show bears eating chrome-colored salmon dragged fresh from the water, but it's just as common for them to eat dead and rotten salmon that they dig out of the mud at low tide. This leaves their flesh tasting like . . . well, dead and rotten salmon.

Some hunters will happily kill these salmon-gorged bears, but that makes as much sense to me as raising a tomato garden and then collecting the fruit after it falls to the ground and turns moldy. Rather, the best time to kill bears is within the first couple of weeks after their emergence from hibernation. Their salmon-flavored fat has burned off, and they're eating little besides the grass found along the tidal flats and stream mouths. This gives their meat a beefy goodness.

On Prince of Wales Island, bears can emerge as early as early April or as late as late May, depending on myriad factors such as snow depth, air temperature, fat reserves, and even the gender and size of the bear. Typically, though, you'll start seeing mature males consistently during the first week of May, and that's when Ronny and I landed in Ketchikan. The weather was typical for that time of year: low 40s to mid 50s, plenty of rain. The next morning we hopped a small floatplane that landed us at the cove. It took us a day to get ready: We cleaned up after the mink that had scattered a hundred dollars' worth of freeze-dried food all over the place. We hauled in some firewood and split kindling. We wiped away the new layer of mold that had grown over most of the shack's interior surfaces since my last visit. And we waited for a high tide so we could launch the skiff. We started hunting early the next morning.

Prince of Wales Island is surrounded by an intercoastal maze, where small islands are scattered across the ocean as thick as black pepper sprinkled on a fried egg. To find bears in such an area, you want to look at either a lot of shoreline very quickly or a small amount of shoreline very carefully. I tend toward the small and careful end of the spectrum, though to make this work you need to make sure that the small area is the right area. Bears are looking for grass when they come out of hibernation. It grows best where there are accumulations of soil without the towering stands of timber that block out the sun. These conditions are generally provided where streams come roaring down from the mountains to meet the ocean. The annual flood cycle prevents the growth of trees, and the streams' sediments collect as wedge-shaped deltas and low-lying floodplains just inland from the tideline. These are known as grass flats in bear hunting lingo, and you're doing the right thing if you can cut your boat engine and drift on the current through a place where it's possible to see two or three of these grass flats all at once. That's what Ronny and I had been doing when our argument about glassing etiquette was interrupted by the bear that gave us the slip, thanks to Ronny's momentary fear of wet socks.

We tried a different tactic the next day, mainly so I could avoid any nagging feeling that I'm a complacent hunter who's stuck in his ways. Instead of glassing likely areas from the boat, I figured that we ought to split up and try some still-hunting. I dropped Ronny near a large grass flat in the late afternoon and then motored to a network of meadows formed where a shallow, braided river flowed into the head of a fjord. The tide was all the way out when I got there. I tied an anchor line to the bow of the skiff and carried the anchor across a couple of hundred yards of mud and busted clamshells. I figured I had a couple of hours until the water came up that high.

I moved slowly as I entered the first meadow, paying special attention to the shadowy edges where the grass ended and the timber began. Maybe just a half hour later I got a glimpse of a bear—or at least a bear's rump. It was about 200 yards away, ambling away from me along the edge of a meadow. It vanished before I could tell if it was a male or female.

Figuring that I might see the bear again if I moved forward a bit, I continued carefully in an upstream direction. As I eased along, I caught another glimpse of the bear, a little farther away. Again it was just the rump, and again it disappeared. I crept forward until I reached a large uprooted stump where I could see the entire meadow. I looked around for several minutes, but there was no bear to be found.

I gave a few bleats on my predator call, half expecting a bear to come busting out of the trees. Instead, a blacktail doe crashed out of the timber and headed right toward me. I thought that the deer had nothing but an expanse of flat ground to cross, and I was curious to see how far she'd come before she realized what I was. But all of a sudden she mysteriously dropped from view. Apparently there was a dip in the topography that was big enough to conceal a deer, so I crawled in that direction until I came into view of an agitated female deer staring at a completely unconcerned male black bear. Both were hidden in a large, soggy depression. All I could see of the bear was the upper third of its body, but I could tell it was a mature male. I hunkered back down, checked the wind again, and crawled forward. The next time I popped up, the bear was only 40 yards away. I was shooting a Carolina Custom Rifle in 7mm Rem. Mag. and put a round through both of its lungs. The bear entered the woods along a heavily used trail covered in moss and bear droppings. I followed for about 30 yards and found a dark shape lying in the middle of the trail. I watched the shape for any twitches or movement. It was dead still.

By now I was worried about my boat. It was fixed to a light mushroom anchor and I had visions of it drifting away. I gutted the bear quickly, doing a careful job not to spill any fluids on the exposed meat inside the chest cavity. With the guts out, the animal was light enough for me to move it a little bit. I dragged it out to the meadow and sprawled it out, belly side down, with the pelvis split open. It would cool quickly in the evening air. I put my jacket over the carcass to add a touch of human odor that might deter other bears. Then I went back into the woods and dragged the gut pile off in another direction. Any bear that came along would go for the guts first—they can eat soft tissues in a hurry, wolfing them down before a larger bear has a chance to come along and steal them.

With that taken care of, I raced down to my boat. When I got within sight of the inlet I was relieved to see that the boat was still anchored in place, though it was now floating in deep water. I waded out up to my chest, feeling around for the anchor with my feet. Just when I was thinking that I'd have to swim for the boat, my ankle hung up on the anchor line. I pulled the boat in and then picked up Ronny in the early moments of darkness. He hadn't seen a thing.

Ronny's bad luck continued. One day, for instance, we spotted a boar from the boat and hatched an initial plot to land on a small island just across the water from where the bear was feeding. After a short stalk, Ronny would be able to reach the bear by shooting across an expanse of water. But after we studied the layout of the island from a distance, we decided that the shot would be too far away. So, instead, we planned a convoluted stalk coming from down the beach and over a house-size outcropping of rock that jutted into the water—a stalk that somehow ended with me falling into a crevice in the rock and cutting my lip and biting my tongue and scratching my face. The bear was long gone by the time we got to where it had been. From there, though, we could see that the small island was actually only 200 yards away. It would have been easy pickings.

My concern about Ronny's impression of bear hunting was quickly being replaced by a more worrisome concern that he'd come up empty-handed after a week of very hard and honest hunting. Those feelings were amplified even more when the last full day of our trip rolled around. We spent that morning still-hunting meadows along river mouths, and the rest of the day watching grass flats from the skiff. Toward dusk I announced that we were out of time, and we began the long trip back to the shack as the evening faded toward darkness. Ronny was at the tiller and I was up front, giving myself motion sickness by looking through binoculars as we cruised over the low swells. At one point I got a particularly long-ranging view down the length of the fjord, and I began a careful study of various blackish and roundish objects that littered the beaches far out ahead. Within seconds I blurted out the now familiar words.

"Uh-oh! There's a bear!"

Killing a bear requires that a lot of things come together all at once, and this time the initial components all fell in place. The wind was right; the bear stayed on the shoreline and kept coming along; we found an out-of-sight place to land the boat where the stalk wouldn't be interrupted by insurmountable outcroppings. Ronny climbed from the boat and made a careful upwind approach. He moved when the bear was occupied with feeding, and he held tight whenever the bear checked its surroundings. At 200 yards Ronny stopped behind a boulder to wait. From my vantage I could see that the bear was a solid boar. It moved another 30 yards toward Ronny and gave him a broadside shot. The bear went down hard and fast.

It was well past dark by the time we had the animal gutted and loaded into the skiff. Another hour would pass before we picked our way back to the shack through the dark and hazard-filled waters; another five hours would pass before we had both of our bears skinned and the boned-out meat packed for shipment. Toward dawn, as it started to drizzle, I watched Ronny kneel on the floor of the shop and run his hands through the thick and iridescent fur of his bear. He looked exhausted and relieved and rewarded, like a guy who'd just taken possession of something that he'd earned through hard work.

THE LONG STALK

RICK BASS

Blessed with an elk early in the year, I have been able to afford the luxury of passing up bucks, on the occasions that I am fortunate enough to see any, and it is halfway in my mind that I would like to wait until my younger brother B.J.—visiting from Texas—is with me, before possibly taking an animal. It certainly does not work that way—the hunter never does all of the choosing, and is never capable of determining in advance on which date, if any, an animal might be taken—but still, it's in my mind that if it works out that way, it would be nice for B.J. to participate in a good backcountry hunt. In order to not yet kill the one mule deer allowed to me each year, I've been passing up shots, but with the season winding down, this makes me a little uneasy knowing that each little buck I see might very well be my last opportunity—only seven days left in the season, and then six, and then five.

The plan calls for B.J. to fly up from his home in Austin to Spokane, arriving the night before Thanksgiving, and to then wait six hours in Spokane before catching an Amtrak train after midnight that will travel east to Libby, arriving about 5:30 a.m. I'll drive over the summit and pick him up, and since he can only stay two days, we'll go hunting straight from the station on Thanksgiving morning.

I pack our lunches the night before and gather up gear for both of us. I go to bed excited and wake up at 3:30 the next morning and drive up and over the snowy summit, my excitement building—it's perfect tracking weather—and sure enough, B.J. gets off the train, and it's great to see him.

In the train station, he stares blearily down at my hunting boots and gaiters, and tries to rally. He goes into the restroom and splashes water on his face, comes back out, looks out the dark window at the snowstorm, and tries to summon the desire for a dawn hunt. But it's not there, and I feel like a crazy person, an Elmer Fudd kind of fanatic, for having even dreamed that it might be.

It's just that I'm so anxious to get him into the winter backcountry, and we have so little time.

"Do you think we could go out later this afternoon?" he asks.

"Absolutely," I tell him. And driving back up and over the summit, driving through the night while he sleeps, finally sleeps, in the front seat, I know we've made the right choice, and I'm just thrilled that he's come all this way. There's nothing like having family here for Thanksgiving. When we get back to the house, he sleeps some more. We'll hunt later.

As B.J. naps, the house smells incredible. A fire is going in the wood-stove, and there is the fragrance of pies and rolls baking, fresh coffee, and citrus peels being zested for the evening recipe, spiced tea, and roasting garlic. The snow is still slanting past all the windows. Music is playing on the CD player, and such domesticity helps ease me toward the necessary transition of the end of hunting season. Three and a half days left.

Peel the potatoes, slice and seed the jalapeños, dice the onions—prep work mostly. I leave the real cooking to my wife, Elizabeth, though I do mix up some pastry dough for the dessert and set it aside to rise. And then it's time to go up onto the mountain, and B.J., who is feeling a hundred percent better, is able to accompany me.

This is the pace I like, at this time of year—the cresting and the building. It makes no sense—the equinox has come and gone long ago, all harvest should pretty much be laid in, and any sane or balanced individual would be taking it easy, altering his or her rhythms to adjust to the foreclosure of both the days' light as well as the disintegrating year itself—but I love to keep pushing on, filling the shorter days with more energy and motion than it seems they should be able to hold. The glutton. It seems astounding to me that yesterday B.J. was mucking around up to his ankles in Texas flood-waters, pulling carpet and stacking boxes and making calls to the landlord, etc., and that since that time, he has flown halfway across the country, and then taken a train through the snowy darkness, across the northern tip of three states, and then ridden up and over the summit, and has napped at my house, and is now getting out of the truck, high in the silent mountains, with no traffic out anywhere, and that we are starting up the trail, hunting in the wilderness. Or in what passes for wilderness, in this day and age. What should remain wilderness, now and forever.

We cut fresh buck tracks less than five minutes into our walk. They are huge tracks, so new and fresh that we cannot be more than a few minutes behind him. He must have been standing here in the forest and heard us drive up and get out, must have heard our truck doors opening and closing, must have heard our voices.

His tracks turn around and head back up the mountain, disappearing into the dense forest like a ghost. Except that now he cannot disappear, not entirely; and we follow him, and disappear ourselves into that seemingly impenetrable forest, passing through snowy fronds of cedars, and slipping sideways between the upright bars of lodgepoles, laboring up the hill, invisible now to the rest of the world—entering the forest as a key enters the gears and tumblers of any one lock: This is what I wanted B.J. to see. My Thanksgiving is already complete.

We hurry along behind the deer, silent in the new snow. Maybe the buck will think we will not find his tracks. Maybe he will think that we are not going to follow him. As long as he does not hear us or scent us, maybe he will not know that he is prey.

He is not running. He is only walking, and for a while, we're excited, thinking we've got the drop on him, because he's passing through some fairly open areas—places where, if we were close enough behind him, I might have a good shot.

The wind is quartering from south to north, from left to right, and so we try to follow his tracks and yet at the same time tack northerly to help prevent him from slipping downwind of us. We keep drifting to the right, trying to get out ahead of him, and looking back into the wind, hoping to catch a glimpse of him standing stock-still in all that timber, watching us, even if only for a couple of seconds. That's all we need.

The fantasy we have of possibly sneaking up on him undetected, as if coming upon him while he is merely out for a stroll in the woods on this fine stormy day, lasts for about six minutes. Perhaps he heard a stick snap, or the thumping of our hearts, or felt the heat of our living bodies radiating through the falling snow. How do big deer like that know anything?

Soon enough, his trail veers directly into the gnarliest tangles of lodgepole blowdown and cedar available to him—ridiculous obstacles of wind-sprung root wads, and the bristling dry spires and branches of trees long-ago dead. There are those who view our forests as compartments or agriculture, who believe that only a tidy, upright stand of young and quickly growing trees is of any use to either man or wildlife; but in trying to manage for such forests, these agrarians would take away yet another of the mysteries that has helped craft such rare but durable individuals as the spiny-antlered old hog that is leading us confidently on a game of cat-and-mouse, just a hundred yards ahead of us.

We play his game anyway. He has led us already into a black hole of blowdowns where the only way out would be to turn around and go back down the mountain; and so we follow him, trying to be as quiet as we can, climbing over and under and through, but unavoidably snapping the little twigs as we do so, and making little slithering sounds, little leafy and brushy sounds—and yet even though we know now, beyond certainty, that he knows we're behind him, we persist in the myth of the stalk, as if observing some extraordinarily formal code of manners.

We continue to whisper, as if our presence—our pursuit—is still a secret, and likewise, as if obeying that same strict and formal code, the deer does not panic, does not break and run, but instead continues to calmly thread us deeper and deeper into the matrix of the most difficult—the wildest—route available to him.

Is it a waste of a sentence to say that I know we are not going to sneak up on him—that he is playing us like a yo-yo at the end of his string?

It's wonderful anyway. I want B.J. to see, revealed in this new-falling snow, the inner workings of this deer's mind. The deer is smarter than we are, and stronger, and more graceful. Of course we want it. What would it look like—perhaps seen from above, or a great distance—to see that huge deer threading his way over and through 50 yards ahead of us now, but so completely in control of the situation that perhaps he is even stopping from time to time to look back and listen to our earnest but awkward pursuit?

The deer calmly evaluating the mountain around him—knowing the mountain around him, knowing each crevice and gully as well as if it were his own body, or his own mind, magnified a millionfold.

Our mother died when I was 33, when B.J. was 17. I often feel aware of a breath, a pulse, of her-in-me, encouraging me to keep an eye on him, to help finish the job—the job that is never finished—and though I can feel that she doesn't care in the least whether we get this deer or not, I can feel also that she is looking down with pleasure at her two boys trailing that deer through the snowy wilderness on a Thanksgiving afternoon, as unseen to the rest of the world, in that forest jungle, as she is now to us.

What it is like, sometimes—what happens, sometimes—is that the hunt becomes like a living thing itself, breathed into a life of its own, there on the mountain, or in the forest, and occupying the space between the hunter and the hunted. And that is what happens this day, as we labor, to the best of our abilities, to stay up with the big deer just ahead of us, this deer which is so clearly our physical and intellectual superior, on this mountain at least.

A young mountain lion slips in between us, somehow, coming in from downwind—catching the scent of mule deer buck, and of the humans climbing right behind him. The tracks suddenly before us show where the lion has come in from the north and joined in on the stalk, maneuvering itself into that compressed space just behind the deer, but just ahead of us: the newly pressed white snow glistening with heat. The lion belly-wriggling under the low boughs of yew and cedar and hemlock, and with its big padded feet, and the litheness of its spring-steel muscle, surely as silent as any single strand or current of water within a larger river, and nearly as silent as any one thought, over the entire course of a day.

For a while, the lion follows the deer directly, riding silently in that space between man and deer like a leaf riding raftlike on that flowing river; but then the lion appears to make up its mind about something—as if having adjusted itself to the pace of both the pursued and the pursuers—and shifts its course out to the side, downwind, and lengthens its stride. It seems clear to us, with the back-knowledge of the tracks beneath us, that the lion is trying to capitalize on the deer's focus on us.

The tracks are so fresh. We strain, listening for the possible sounds of struggle, just ahead. A big deer, two men and a lion are all jammed in together, all gathered within a 100-yard sphere on this mountain, and none of them can see one another; and three of the four parties know of the existence of all the others, though it seems certain, by the deer's casual gait, that he does not yet know of the lion.

Seen from above, would it look like a parade? The great deer, with his huge crown of antlers; and behind him, the lion, threading the same course; and behind the lion, the two men?

And behind us, what? A single raven, perhaps, following silently, flying coal-black and ragged through the falling snow?

In the buck's snowy tracks, it's easy to see when time fractures, like placid water stretching suddenly over a span of stony riffles. The buck never panics, but he must have finally glimpsed or scented or heard or somehow sensed the lion, for he suddenly abandons his leisurely, wandering game of cat-and-mouse and begins ascending the mountain directly, climbing straight up the steep face not like a deer now, but like a mountaineer. Not lunging or running but climbing straight up and out, traveling up a mountain face so steep that no trees grow from it; climbing through waist-deep snow, belly-deep snow; and the tracks before us indicate that, once busted, the lion follows for but a short distance before abandoning the hunt, choosing instead to conserve its calories, and to try again at a later time, once it has regained the element of surprise.

We indulge in the luxury of not being bound by any such limitations—of being able to be ceaseless not just in our desires, but in our pursuit of them—and we continue on up the steep slope, warming now, in our exertions, and with hearts hammering, and breath coming hard.

We follow the deer for the rest of the afternoon. We push hard, floundering in the deep snow, thinking always that we'll see him just over the next ridge, and our labors are made all the more tantalizing by the fact that he is out in the open now, passing across wide steep-tilted parks and meadows; and still his tracks are new-cut in the storm, still he is no more than a minute or two ahead of us; and we surge to rejoin him, to close the distance, like one river seeking the confluence of another.

But the land, and time, will not yet have it.

Our spirits lift, at one point, when—nearing the top—the buck's ascent begins to flatten out, as if he is finally growing weary.

He begins sidehilling, clearly tiring; but like a magician, he keeps the perfect distance between us and him. The snow is coming down harder, so that he's granted extra protection beneath that cloak, and he heads around to the southern end of the mountain, and then climbs up and over the final windy ridge, and travels straight down the back side of the mountain, down into the dark timber of his home, as if trying now not just to escape, but to break our spirit—we cannot help but think of how hard the climb back out will be, and with a Thanksgiving dinner engagement awaiting us, shortly after dark—but still we follow him down into the next valley, almost hypnotized.

It's as if some madness or obsession has come over us, to be following him down the back side like that—into the deeper timber, and into the darkness. At one point, his tracks head straight into those of another herd of deer, trying to blend amongst theirs—and this last gives us a bit of confidence that he might be wearying (as are we), and that he might soon make a mistake.

We must have closed the distance considerably, over the course of our afternoon-long pursuit—30 seconds behind him now? 20?—because his tracks now show where, for the first time all day, he has begun to run, bounding straight down the near-vertical slope in the high-prance stot of his species. Still we follow, like wolves, as quiet as we can, down a slope so steep that the snow barely clings to it. To lower ourselves down, we grip leafless alder and willow with our gloved hands, as if rappelling.

Perhaps, in so doing, we have called his bluff. There is only half an hour of light left, and a dim cold blue light, at that—but finally, he ceases his descent and begins angling to the north, sidehilling his way slowly back up to the ridge.

We are a long way from our truck.

We're getting tired and sloppy, and losing our hunter's edge, I think, at a time when it should be growing sharper, with not very many minutes left in the day. We're looking into the dark canyon below, and at the snowy crags in the blue distance, as night slides in over the wilderness; and it seems to us, in the way that the icy spits of snow are striking our faces, and in our exhaustion, that we are somehow in a much wilder place than when we started out, and that it is all the more beautiful, for that extra or added wildness. We stop and rest, pausing to admire the sight of such wild country before the night takes it away.

We can see where the buck has stopped to rest, also, and even where he must have sighted us, for his walking tracks will suddenly disappear, punctuated by 20-foot leaps, for which the only possible explanation, particularly given the state of his own fatigue, can be that he waited, looking back, to see finally the face or name of the thing that was following him, and glimpsed it, two upright creatures moving slowly through the dimness, 50 or a hundred yards behind . . . walk and run, walk and run; we close the distance, with our brute endurance, but he opens it back up again, stretches it farther once more. We never see him—only the places where, looking back, he has seen us—and finally, though it is not quite yet dark, it is time to head on back, so far are we from our truck, and home. It's been a great hunt, with every single minute of it filled with the possibility of making game—saturated with the possibility, and at times even the likelihood, of making game—and we have no regrets.

We pause one more time to look out at the mountains, and then we turn back toward home, no longer hunting, but merely trudging through the deep snow, passing through the forest: In my mind, there is a feeling like I have released the buck; as if, in my letting-go—my grateful letting-go—I have snipped some thread or leash that has connected us, all afternoon.

I have gotten what I needed; I have gotten what I came for. It's snowing harder. We pass out of a grove of dark lodgepole and into a small opening, and I look downslope, and see, in the dimness, nearly 200 yards away, a doe mule deer peering out from behind a tree—she too is about to pass on into the same clearing—and then I see the buck just behind her.

It's almost as if in this last wedge of light, and with us having worked so hard, she has appeared to lead him to us.

He is facing us, looking upslope, and has his head lowered, in the way that big mule deer bucks will sometimes do, when evaluating something. Unthinkingly—as if with the momentum of desire, rather than the previous burning essence of it, I raise the rifle to put the scope on him. Even at this distance, I can tell he's big—that it's the deer we've been following—but I can't find him in my scope, I've forgotten to keep it clean, in the fog and snow, and I've got to lower it and rub it clear with my sleeve.

I lift the gun quickly—desire has now resumed its path with mine—and even at this distance, the target of his heart-and-lung space looks ample, and I squeeze the trigger.

He is gone, vanished immediately. The doe that was standing next to him is still there, prancy now—after a second, she whirls and trots away—and the snow begins coming down harder, as if the sound of the rifle shot somehow punctured some reserve or restraint; and I watch and wait, wondering where the buck went. There is the chance that the bullet struck him and that he is poleaxed, sleeping already the sleep of eternity—but there is the chance too that I missed him cleanly, especially at that distance. And there is the chance also, regrettable but ever present, that he is only wounded—perhaps fatally, perhaps not—and that if B.J. and I wait quietly, he will lie down to rest, unpursued, and will die quietly in the falling snow.

I don't have a clue.

Under normal conditions, we'd sit down and wait. Rushing down there isn't going to change anything: If he's dead, he's dead.

But if he's hurt, I want to know it. In this falling snow, we're not going to have the luxury of letting him lie down to die quietly. We'll have to stay with him, following him—and any spotted trail of blood he might leave—through the night, before the falling snow can obscure the sign of his path.

As if we might be destined to follow him forever, like a set of constellations eternally wheeling across the winter skies, their distance never varying.

We wait about five minutes, to see if he might come back out into the opening—sometimes a startled or even slightly injured deer will retreat to the edge of the woods and then stand there for a long while, as if betranced, before finally resuming whatever he had been doing before the shot, as if intent upon completing his goals. As we begin to walk, I measure the distance, counting the paces.

It is 175 yards to the place where he was standing. We examine his tracks—the doe ran north, while he turned and bounded down the mountain, to the west—and I can find not a fleck of blood, nor even any hair.

When a bullet exits a deer, it will cut hair on the way out. There'll almost always be a fine spray of blood, bright upon the snow; but always there is hair, long hollow deer hair that reminds me of larch or pine needles.

There is no hair, no blood, only air, space, white snow, absence. I thought my aim was good; I felt good about the shot.

I examine the tracks more closely. They look awkward to me, in a way I can't explain: not the usual choreographed dance steps of whirl-and-bound alarm, but something else, some indecision or confusion charted in the snow—or so it seems.

We follow the tracks down the hill. Even though I saw nothing, in the blink that followed my shot, I feel as if I should have hit this deer. That I did hit this deer.

Out in the middle of the steep clearing, there is one lone bush, a large leafless willow, limbs and branches stark against the snowy evening.

"Look," B.J. says, pointing to the base of the tree, where there are branches, wide branches, beneath the other branches, and a dense dark sleeping body that is already being covered with snow.

He's heavy. It takes both of us to pull him into the forest, for shelter from the snow, where I gut him quickly, and peel the cape of his hide back, to help cool him down. The bullet never exited, which is why I never found any hair or blood.

We tuck the deer in tight beneath a big lodgepole, so that he won't be buried by snow overnight. I wrap one of my jackets around him, so that lions and coyotes and lynx and wolverines will be less likely to fool with him—hopefully the bears are all sleeping, this late in the year—and I scrub my hands in the snow, wipe them on the green bough of a lodgepole, thank the mountain and the deer for one of the best hunts ever, thank B.J. for being part of it, and for helping with the tracking, and for spotting the big old deer dead under that willow tree—and then, in the darkness, we start up the long slope to the ridge, and back down the mountain toward our truck.

The next day, we will sleep in, until eight o'clock, and then return to quarter and debone and pack out the deer, both of us struggling beneath loaded packs, and each dragging a deer shoulder behind us as well, like a sled—and the day after that, B.J. will return to Texas, and I will begin butchering and wrapping the deer for the freezer. But that evening, even though we have many more chores ahead of us, the hunt feels wonderfully complete, almost magically so; and all the way down the mountain in the darkness, I keep exclaiming to B.J., "Man, what a wonderful hunt that was!" and, alternatively, "I so love to get an animal on Thanksgiving!" until I'm sure he must wonder if perhaps I haven't turned into a bit of a simpleton, to be made so euphoric by such a simple act, the taking of one animal.

And except for the fact that he was there, he might think it so. But he saw it, and felt it; and though he cannot know of the other 364 days, he knows of this one and understood, by the way I kept repeating it, that it wasn't just the one day I was grateful for, in being presented with that deer at dusk on Thanksgiving, but instead, the whole year; the entire year that just passed by, and the whole year to come, as we ate on that deer. Everything.

THE BEAR UP THERE

STEVEN RINELLA

The mountainside looked like an outdoor movie screen, nearly vertical and alive with movement. From our campsite, my brother Matt and I had been watching the slope for an entire June day. It was raining on and off, and so far we'd seen many of the creatures that make their homes in the mountains of southwestern Montana: redtail hawks, a golden eagle, elk, mule deer, spruce grouse, ruffed grouse, and a handful of pine squirrels. In the snow around our camp were tracks of coyotes, deer, moose, wolves, and pine martens, plus a room-size swath of land excavated by a grizzly that had been digging for wild onion bulbs. The only animal we'd seen no evidence of was the one we were looking for: a black bear.

Judging by the mountainside, it was only a matter of time. The valley was locked away beneath a winter's worth of snow, but the treeless slope above camp had been scraped clean by avalanches and now provided a smorgasbord of tender, green vegetation. In Montana, where hunting black bears with the aid of dogs and bait is prohibited, these high-mountain avalanche chutes are as much of a sure thing as you're going to find. Matt and I huddled beneath a spruce to get out of the rain. And we waited.

•••

I started hunting black bears 10 years ago, after I moved from Michigan to Montana to attend graduate school. Montana has a healthy, expanding population of 10,000 or so black bears. I liked the idea of hunting the spring season because it got me into the mountains when I'd usually be nursing a case of cabin fever. I sought bear hunting tips in local sporting-goods stores. The success rate for spring hunters is only 10 percent, and I wanted any advice I could get. The lack of reliable information surprised me. Everyone agreed that the way to hunt spring blackies was to find green, emerging vegetation. The most common source of this happened to be the clover and smooth bromegrass that the Forest Service uses to stabilize logging roads. I spent several springs walking those tracks and even managed to kill a nice boar that squared over 6 feet. I wasn't seeing many bears, however, and I felt that my occasional sightings were due more to luck than to skill.

My big break came one rainy winter day when I was buying a used Ford 4x4 from a guy who lived outside of Missoula. As he signed over the title, I looked at the hunting photographs taped to the door of his refrigerator. He had about 10 snapshots of nice blackies taken by him and his friends. All showed evidence of spring, backgrounds of vibrant green grass mixed with crusted snow. The man was tight-lipped when I asked about the pictures, but his wife did his bragging for him. She offered up that he'd seen 13 bears last spring. I pressed for information—more like begged him for it—and maybe because I was writing him a $4,000 check, he allowed me a few clues to his success: Go to the high country, up near the snow line, and hunt the southeast-facing avalanche chutes. Beyond that, he had nothing to say.

Matt and I spent the next few springs armed with backpacks and topographic maps, searching Montana's mountain ranges for areas where avalanches regularly occur. We hiked to scores of chutes and looked for bear activity as well as their favorite foods, such as glacier lily, skunk cabbage, horsetail, and various grasses.

In our first serious year of hunting chutes, we saw as many bears in three days as in the past three seasons combined. And as we came to better understand the behavior of mountain black bears, we made further useful discoveries. Black bear activity tends to concentrate around areas that have only recently been cleared of snow. As the vegetation growing on an avalanche chute matures and coarsens, the bears move to higher elevations to seek out fresh sources. These conditions are not predictable because they're subject to such wildly fluctuating variables as temperature, winter snowfall accumulation, and spring rain. A chute loaded with bear sign in mid-May of one year may be void of it the next.

Because of these factors, Matt and I were on unknown territory as we glassed the nearly vertical mountainside from our camp. Usually we'd be hunting the mountains by early May, when the majority of bears have just come out of their dens and started to wander in search of food. This year, work obligations had forced me to postpone our annual trip until early June. (Montana's spring bear season begins on April 15 and, depending on the Bear Management Unit, ends May 15, May 31, or June 15.) When we arrived at one of our trusted locales, where I'd killed a black bear the year before, we were greeted by completely snow-free mountainsides covered in mature grasses. Rather than call it quits, we decided to backpack a couple of thousand feet higher toward a network of avalanche slides that we'd identified in the heart of the Lee Metcalf Wilderness Area, a quarter-million-acre federally designated roadless area encompassing portions of the Gallatin and Madison Ranges in southwestern Montana.

After hiking a mile or two, we began to feel as though we were traveling back in time toward early spring. In the shade of the mixed evergreens, the trail was completely obliterated by crusted remnants of snow, and soon we were cursing ourselves for not bringing snowshoes. After a few hours of struggling through knee-deep accumulations and wading across swollen creeks, it was a great relief to finally set down my pack and start glassing.

The first blackie appeared just before dark. Matt watched it come over the crest of the ridge above camp and then cross one of the avalanche chutes at a downward angle before climbing over a bank of snow and vanishing into timber. When it emerged a few minutes later, cutting across another chute, it was well beyond rifle range. I was viewing the mountainside from a different angle and missed the bear completely, but Matt called me over and said that it was a good size and jet black. We waited for the bear to re-emerge in the next chute, but after 10 minutes had gone by, we still hadn't seen it.

Matt moved uphill in the same direction that we thought the bear was headed. I moved toward where the bear had last been in sight. The wind was perfect, blowing lightly downhill. If the bear continued on its path, Matt was sure to get a good look. If the bear doubled back, it would cross the chute above me. I waited anxiously, expecting to hear the crack of Matt's .270 WSM. But only the hollow call of a spruce grouse broke the quiet. At dark, I walked back toward camp. Matt came in behind me. He lifted up his palms and shrugged. The bear had done what bears are good at: disappearing.

I reminded myself to be patient. In spring, bears wander great distances in search of food. You might stake out an avalanche chute for several cold and wet days in order to have just one opportunity, and that opportunity might present itself only for a minute or two. So you've got to be willing to just sit, spy, and wait. You must be careful, however, that your patience doesn't turn into laziness. It's easier to get comfortable and watch a hillside than it is to trudge through rugged, snowy country in search of fresh sign. In the mountains, I often force myself to get up and walk around even if I'd rather kick back and enjoy the scenery.

Matt and I were faced with just such a dilemma on the third morning of our five-day hunt. We'd seen a few bears above camp, but we hadn't had any luck getting into range before they wandered off. Both of us felt that we needed to do some additional exploration. We didn't have a complete understanding of our area, and we worried that we were missing out on prime locations. Matt suggested that we get up on a ridgeline and take a look around, and we packed some food and started walking.

The northern Rockies feel lonely and raw at this time of year. Old, faded horse prints left over from the previous elk season, which had ended in November, were the only sign of humans we encountered. In the old days, explorers and adventurers sought out places that had never been visited by man. To be the first person to reach some wild place was a noble accomplishment. Nowadays, there aren't many undiscovered areas left. But being in the mountains in spring brings a similar reward: People might have been there before you but not within the last half year.

This long absence of human visitors may explain the great wildlife viewing during the spring black bear season. Animals are less on edge than they are in fall. I've watched coyotes dig for rodents in avalanche debris fields, stopping only occasionally to give me inquisitive looks. One time, a sandhill crane, a notoriously wary bird, walked through grasses within a stone's throw of where I was set up. In the Whitefish Mountains of northwestern Montana, I saw a herd of elk, a moose, several mule deer, a whitetail, and a grizzly, all on the same avalanche chute in a single day. On another occasion, while Matt and I waited for a black bear to emerge on a chute, four grizzlies foraged on the slope above us.

Now, as we made our way along an elk trail on a ridgetop, we stopped every 50 or 60 yards to glass pockets of open ground on the surrounding slopes. After a half hour or so of searching, Matt froze with his 8X Nikon binoculars turned toward the north. "There's a bear!" he exclaimed.

The bruin was feeding on the lower end of an avalanche slide. It was the biggest blackie either of us had ever seen in Montana, but we had to get much closer for a shot. A two-hour stalk brought us almost within range, but the bear walked over to a big Douglas fir and dozed off in the shade. We couldn't get a good shot at the curled-up, sleeping animal, and getting any closer would have required approaching from the upwind side. Since we hadn't eaten all day, we decided to have a bite of lunch. As the sun reached its midpoint, the wind currents started to shift, and we began preparing our stalk. The bear was still dozing, giving us no apparent reason to hustle. We piddled around for a half hour, drinking water and eating candy bars. Then, when we finally stood to make our move, the bear awoke and hustled off.

Late afternoon on our last day in the mountains, we lolled around camp feeling sorry for ourselves after putting in a hard day of fruitless hunting. The unhappy thought of going an entire year without black bear sausage and smoked bear hams was looking more and more like cold, hard reality. I couldn't shake the image of that sleeping blackie. "I wish you'd never even spotted that bear," I confessed to Matt. "That way, we wouldn't need to spend the next year thinking about how we screwed that up."

I'd swamped my boots crossing a stream, and now I had them sitting next to me in case a bear showed itself on the avalanche chutes visible from camp. In the back of my mind, though, I was thinking about my own little quandary of patience turning into laziness. If I were a real hunter, I thought, I'd hurry up and put those wet suckers on, then hike about a mile upstream. Earlier in the day, we'd cased out a promising avalanche chute up there and commented on the fact that someone should sit it for an evening. I reminded Matt about this idea.

Matt agreed. "There's no sense in both of us staring at the same slope. I'll go up there if you don't want to."

"No, no. I'll go." I downed a cup of instant coffee for extra motivation, pulled on the wet boots, grabbed my pack and rifle, and started up the slushy path.

The avalanche chute was long and narrow, like an airport runway set on its end and bordered by deep snow banks. I approached from behind a spruce tree so that I could stealthily look the slide over. Peeking up the hill from between the limbs, I caught a flash of brown cutting across the open strip of ground. I couldn't tell if it was a black bear or a grizzly, but I dropped to my belly and extended the bipod legs on my .30/06. The bear dropped into a slight depression, then climbed out again about 200 yards away.

It was a medium-size blackie with chocolate brown fur. I followed it with my scope for a few moments until it stopped to graze a patch of grass. Then I placed the crosshairs of the 3X–9X variable behind the front shoulder and squeezed the Remington's trigger. The bear fell where it was standing, then rolled down the hill along the open path that had been cleared by countless loads of sliding snow.

That night, 6 inches of wet snow dumped on the mountains. In the morning, our fingers went numb as we skinned and butchered the bear, a 5½-footer that was later aged at 15 years old. We bagged the hams and shoulders while we planned the design for a new smokehouse we were preparing to build. Halfway through the job, we stopped to build a fire to warm up and dry off. It was June, but looking around I would have sworn that we'd been blasted back in time a couple of months.

"Our plan to wind back the calendar by coming up high sure worked," I said. I did some jumping jacks to get my blood pumping and then paused to warm my snow-chilled fingers by the fire. "Maybe it worked too well."

A TRIPLE PLAY
IN THE CRAZIES

PHILIP CAPUTO

In the early-morning half light, four of us filed across a meadow toward the leafless cottonwoods fringing Lost Horse Creek. Beyond the creek, another meadow rose into the timber blackening the slopes of Montana's Crazy Mountains, snowy peaks taking on a pale peach color in the sunrise. Guides Stan Adams and Ed Auger paused, scooped up handfuls of dirt, and sifted the dirt through their fingers. The wind was still favorable, quartering into our faces, and we rock-hopped over the creek and started a cautious hike up the second meadow, making for the pines above. A whitetail buck materialized and ran up a ridge, where he stopped to strike a photogenic pose.

Harold Trask, my hunting partner for the day, looked at him longingly—Trask had yet to fill his deer tag—but we were after elk.

This was my second season hunting with Adams and Auger, who have about 80 years of guiding between them. Adams, a sandy-haired man with a drought-dry sense of humor, stands about 6 feet 1, and half of that is leg. Auger is shorter and darker, a Vietnam veteran and a New Englander by birth who came west decades ago and stayed. Both are in their 60s, but years of ranging through the mountains has made them as fit as men half their age.

In my previous trip with them, I had gotten a 5x5 elk and a 3x3 mule deer with a tip-to-tip spread of 28½ inches. This time, I'd set myself a goal of bagging an elk, a mule deer, and an antelope. Mule deer abound in the Crazies (so named, according to one legend, for a pioneer woman driven insane after Crow Indians massacred her family), and I shot a decent buck on the second day. Antelope, not as numerous and much warier, proved more challenging, but on day four, after a difficult belly-crawling stalk, a 12- to 13-inch buck was in my sights, about 100 yards away on an open plain. He was no trophy, but he was good enough for me. He was, however, masked by two other animals in the herd, and I had to wait for what felt like an hour before he moved into the clear.

He offered only a quartering shot, but I took it and dropped him, feeling all gushy with pride when Auger said, "Man, you are one shootin' son of a bitch!" It was the fourth animal I'd taken with him and Adams, and I'd used just four bullets, thus acquiring the nickname "Old One-Shot." Well, it's always nice for a sport to win the admiration of his guides, but as I was to learn, there is a danger in believing in your own legend.

Having scored with two of the three, I had a devil of a time with the third, wapiti, the grandest hooved animal in the mountains, and arguably the most elusive.

Earlier in the week, we'd watched a herd of some 700 gallop down a mountain, then surge up a draw in one great mass of beige, brown, and black, packed as densely as cattle in a corral. It was an awesome sight, made more so by the presence of a magisterial bull. You could have flown a paper airplane across his antler spread—50-plus inches, Adams estimated. The herd had plowed trails that looked like ATV tracks, but elk are magicians when it comes to disappearing, and they vanished before we could get within range. We spent the next three days looking for them without success. How had such a large number of such large animals dissolved? All we could do was keep searching and hope the elk would show themselves again.

A few had appeared this morning, the final day of my weeklong hunt. At dawn, we'd glassed a dozen bulls and cows grazing in the meadow we were now crossing. I'd expected to have a bull in my crosshairs by now, but they'd pulled off another fugitive act. We climbed into the timber, skirting southward along its edges, then stopped to glass the slopes ahead. I was a bit breathless and felt a thrumming in my chest, partly from the exertion at the 7,000-foot altitude, mostly from excitement.

This was the part of hunting that I love most: the pursuit. It's paradoxical that the death of your quarry is besides the point and at the same time the whole point. A chase without a kill as its object is like a journey without a destination; a kill without a chase employing all the hunter's craft (even if it's no more than creeping up to a stand) is killing, not hunting.

By the time we emerged from the forest, I'd worked up a good sweat. The morning was unusually warm for November in Montana. Down one ridge, up another, and then Auger dropped to all fours and waved Trask and me to come ahead. Below, and about 200 yards away, a 5x5 bull was ambling through the trees on the face of an opposite ridge, his white rump to us. That and his rack were all we could see. Above him, in a parkland studded with low firs, two spikes and several cows munched grass, unaware of our presence.

In a moment, the bull made himself invisible. He was probably working his way up the wooded slope to join his herd mates atop the ridge. When he did, he would be in the open, and mine to shoot for a couple of reasons. Trask was gunning for a trophy, like the magnificent bull we'd seen three days before; I was meat hunting because I love to eat elk, whose steaks make supermarket beef taste as artificial as the sliced cheddar labeled cheese product. Any respectable bull would do, and the one below us was clearly respectable.

I lay down behind piled backpacks, which served as a rifle rest (I was shooting a Weatherby .30/06, loaded with 165-grain boattail bullets). Auger took a reading with his rangefinder: 340 yards to the ridge crest. He whispered that although it would be something of a "long poke," it shouldn't be a problem for Old One-Shot.

Waiting for the bull to reappear, I lay on my stomach for 15 or 20 minutes, until it felt as if my crooked neck was going to snap. Too bad Doug isn't here, I thought, to distract myself from my growing nervousness. Doug Stegemoller, my nephew, had been hunting with me but had to cut his trip short to make a business meeting in Phoenix. He'd been on a couple of fruitless elk hunts in Colorado, and I'd invited him to join me in Montana, hoping to daub his forehead with elk blood in the ancient ritual of first kill. Doug had taken a fine mule deer two days after I'd shot mine, but the grand prize had eluded him, and now he was driving back to Arizona.

Adams tapped me on the shoulder. The bull had come out of the trees, but he was behind one of the spikes. Finally, he stepped out, heading for the big timber, his pale tan flanks almost white when they caught the light. The Weatherby was sighted to hit dead on at 200 yards. I centered the crosshairs on the top of his back to compensate for the bullet drop, led him ever so slightly, fired, and was stunned to watch him and the rest of the herd bolt into the forest.

Old One-Shot had clean missed.

I can forgive failure in others, which is why I never would have made a decent CEO, but cannot tolerate it in myself. Driving back to camp, I muttered that I couldn't figure out what I'd done wrong. Adams considered this and said, "You missed, that's what."

At lunch, Adams and Auger's boss, outfitter Shannon Guse, said he'd spotted an elk herd 100 strong migrating toward Gordon's Butte. It was an immense tableland corrugated by draws and pocked with bowls, affording the animals shelter from the wind, which had picked up considerably.

At about half past three, we stood on a hilltop with a gale howling at our backs. The elk, 10 or more, were down in a small basin sided by two knobs. They were so far away that they were invisible to the naked eye (mine, anyway) and looked not much bigger than jackrabbits through binoculars. The wind direction denied us a straight-ahead approach. We were going to have to make a long, circuitous stalk, and I didn't think we could get within range before dark. Adams sensed my anxiety and said in a reassuring undertone, "Remember, there's no difference between the last day and the first day."

My mind grasped that, but the rest of me didn't, and Trask was feeling the same deadline pressure. In two more hours, it would be over until next season. One of those hours had passed by the time we reached a draw overlooking the basin. Hiding behind a rock monolith, we glassed the herd and counted 13, all bulls. The problem was that they still appeared to be in another zip code. I questioned the sanity of my self-imposed objective of bagging a deer, a pronghorn, and an elk. It had been a successful hunt, everyone had had a fine time, and the sight of that vast herd of 700 with its regal bull, that alone had been worth the price of admission. What difference did it make if I shot an elk? All I knew was that it did. And let's not avoid the intrusion of selfish ego: I wanted to redeem myself, in my own eyes if not in those of Auger and Adams.

They led us on, loping over the rough terrain like a pair of two-legged wolves. Half an hour later, with the wind now in our faces, we were moving downhill toward another draw. Ahead was one of the two knobs above the basin. The plan was to climb it and shoot from there. Like most plans, it did not survive contact with the enemy, the enemy in this case being some 30 or 40 mule deer milling on the side of the knob, the bucks with rut-swollen necks. If we spooked the deer, they would likely flee over the top and alarm the elk.

We made a quick revision of strategy. We would circle around the knob and make the final stalk in a crosswind. This we did, the deer studying us warily. We tried to look harmless, full of benign intentions, walking slowly, avoiding eye contact. We did everything but shove our hands in our pockets and whistle. The muleys did not entirely buy this act, but they bought it enough not to panic. We crawled on hands and knees up a gentle rise, the setting sun in our eyes.

Then Adams went flat and whispered, "There's a big 5 right in front of us, 100 yards. Two other 5s are with him."

Trask and I fell, rather belatedly, into a hushed discussion as to who would be the first shooter. He wanted a 6x6, nothing less. "O.K." "Maybe there's a 6." "Yeah, but if—" "You go." "No, you should—"

"Damn it," Adams hissed, "make up your minds right now," and I said, "All right, I'll go."

Auger and Trask crept around to climb to the lowest point on the knob. If Trask spotted his trophy, he would shoot from that position. I could hear my heart thumping against the ground as Adams and I belly-crawled toward the top of the rise. Adams slowly raised his head. More whispers.

"There he is. See him now?"

"No."

The sun had me completely blinded. "A little farther," I said, practically kissing his ear. Another yard. The grass wasn't more than 6 inches high—it was almost like trying to sneak up on elk grazing on a golf course.

"How about now?"

"Yes, I see him." He was a blurred silhouette against the red sun. It wasn't a shot I felt comfortable with, and I shook my head.

Now Adams kissed my ear. "There's another good one off to the right, closer to us. Got him?"

I nodded.

"Take him."

There were a few inches of rise in front of me. A prone shot was out of the question because I'd be shooting into the ground. Moving slowly, I rose to one knee, the scope framing antlers, head, and finally a wind-rippled flank. A broadside at no more than 75 yards. If I blew this one I would beat my rifle into a plowshare. I held the crosshairs just behind the top of his shoulder and squeezed the trigger, and the bull went down and did not get up. Adams punched me in the shoulder.

A grand slam that wasn't as grand as I'd anticipated, elation mixed with remorse as I looked at the dead bull in the fading light. I guess the hunter who doesn't feel regret for the life he's taken ought to go to work as an assassin. To repeat, killing an animal is the whole point but is no more than killing if it isn't also besides the point.

CALLIE'S HOME

RICK BASS

One of the problems with not living forever is that time eventually runs out. Your choices and options can become diminished to the point where your imagination—as in, I think that sometime I'd like to own a flushing dog—becomes irrelevant, an artifact of younger days, in which time existed like a great expanse of unexplored field. At some point—late into the game—you realize, if you are a pointing dog person, that while all the other breeds are nice enough, and interesting, and that you can even envision hunting behind them, you're always going to be a pointer person. And if you've had the hook on your heart set long ago by German short-hairs, that's just about always going to be your next dog.

Labs, Chesapeakes, French Brittanys, golden retrievers: You can imagine owning one, but so far you haven't done it. Even setters, pointing Labs, vizslas, Weimaraners, and poodles look intriguing, but in the end, when it comes down to writing the check, there's no way you can turn away from your splendid and ruinous and magnificent addiction. Maybe you just like to blow your whistle and yell. Maybe it would be this way if you lived to be a thousand; you would forever keep on imagining a different outcome, and a different desire.

This time—this dog cycle—I almost did it. I was chasing a flat-coated retriever, swayed by enthusiastic descriptions of the breed's extraordinary sweetness as well as intelligence—but I hesitated at the last moment for two reasons: price, but also a tendency for this highly bred dog to succumb to a number of cancers and not live long. No dog lives forever, but you can at least play the odds.

When push came to shove, I went back to the breed that taught me to hunt. There are a million reasons to love GSPs—perhaps first and foremost, their year-round sweetness, their charming goofiness—but by September, for me, it is foremost and irreducibly their enthusiasm for the landscape, their mistakes of excess, their sometimes bullish belief that physicality can substitute for the cerebral. More than ever these days it seems such a quaint concept, and yet it is one they are able to pull off with brio for many long years, many good years.

As a young man, I owned males, was delighted by their tirelessness—their perverse indefatigability, the way they dived through barbwire fences and tried to keep hunting even when large squares of skin flapped on them like roof tin in a wind; and the way they ignored skunk spray, porcupine quills, snakebite, anything, to keep hunting; the way they literally chewed their way out of kennels and trucks if left behind for even a single run; the way they kept running, charging, hunting hard, even when pierced by a branch, the stob of wood still protruding from the chest.

I had heard rumors of GSPs that were gifted with great intelligence and wisdom but had never encountered one. All of mine were smart enough—talented, but talented in the blood, I think. They were instinctive geniuses more so than self-made—and strong and powerful and sweet, sweet, sweet.

So having settled on a breed, next I needed a litter and a bloodline. There are two ways to go: to pursue the lineage of a dog known to you—your own, or a friend's, or a dog you've hunted with—or, in this day and age, to brave the ether, delving into the vaporous laminae and strata of reality and myth, lies and artifice and truths and hope, trying to sort out the gossamer strands of each through phone calls, photographs, references. I never thought I'd be someone who'd buy a dog off the Internet, but once you start to slide down a slope, well, it's hard to climb back up.

In the research, you begin to construct narratives. You weed out some kennels, investigate others further: the sound of someone's voice on the phone, the photographs, the dogs themselves. You can spend a lot of time looking at pictures, reading testimonials, e-mailing people, calling them. They don't call it the Web for nothing.

The more detailed and neater record keepers seem to suggest continuity and dedication to the breeding efforts, and yet you worry they could also reflect the obsession of a mad person. It's not unthinkable to find either or both of those worlds associated with pointers.

Utah, Wisconsin, eastern Montana: My heart and hopes bounced around the country like a pinball. I finally found a kennel in Vermont that felt right. I got references. I liked that they were good retrievers, close workers—Vermont ruffed grouse, I imagined—and I liked best of all the photos of the dogs from that kennel sleeping in the house, curled up all cozy and friendly with other dogs, and other people. I put my money down on a female and waited—I was no. 3 on the list—and began making a place in my mind for the future, a future that included this unseen, not-yet-being, her.

Fate intervened. Only two females were born to a litter of nine. I got my deposit back. I set out again, searching—looking at more pictures.

Around this same time, when I was cleaning out a desk, I found a 5-year-old Christmas card from the breeder where I'd bought my last pointer. The card pictured various champions that had been trained there. My dog, Auna, had fallen to a mysterious epilepsy at the age of 5. I tried to find the bloodline anyway, yet couldn't. (I did discover that her mother had died mysteriously after giving birth to her next litter.) No pups were available anywhere I called, but I liked the photo of one particular dog on that old Christmas card, registered to an owner in Oregon. Eventually, my attempts to find him via search engines uncovered an affiliation listed with an Oregon dog club.

I got that phone number, and left a message with their treasurer on an old-school answering machine, asking if they knew where that dog's owner might be. Then I forgot about it and went out to Vermont to look at that kennel—wondered briefly about buying a mature, "started" dog, even though I knew I wouldn't—and the Oregon call came in. It was Bob Straight, telling me he'd had a litter out of a really fine dog. He gave me the link, said I could read all about it, and wanted me to check it out.

I liked how easy he sounded on the phone, how friendly and undesperate. And when I looked at the Web page, I found out why.

Straight and Brenda Abraham had bred their three-time field champion sire to the 2012 Westminster best-of-breed champion, Dancer, who I remembered seeing on the front page of The New York Times, a dog of such poise and grace that I had wondered at the time if the winner had truly been a German shorthaired pointer. She was a dog that I'd assumed was all pretty looks, and therefore no fire. Yes, I knew the dog.

I called Bob back to thank him. "I can't afford one of those pups," I said. "Not even close." People were flying in from all around the country and Europe to pick up their pups from Dancer. I felt uneasy, that I was wasting his time.

"Lookit," he said, "I'm in a unique position. I don't need any publicity." But he was intrigued by the idea of having a writer own a pup from such an amazing breed. His dogs had won all sorts of awards—but the possibility of words, ink on the page, stories, sagas, that would be a different territory for him.

"What can you afford?" he asked gently.

"I can't afford anything," I said. I wasn't driving for a deal; it was just the wretched truth.

He hesitated. He named a number then, a pittance, less than a mere consideration.

You can live a long time before luck like that happens to you. You can live maybe forever and never have it happen.

"All right," I said. "O.K. Thank you."

There still remained the matter of choosing. Unlike the Vermont breeder, Bob had a plethora of females. The breeding had been an artificial insemination, and instead of the seven or so pups they'd expected, they'd had 13, nine of which were females.

As if one had been waiting for me.

From photographs e-mailed to me almost daily, I selected the one I wanted: Arya. I began to fall in love with her from afar. In the photos—already posing like a little champion—she was the one, it seemed to me, with the most spunk, no small amount of mischief, and the most intelligence. In a strange way, the fact that they were all pretty much guaranteed to be amazing made it harder, not easier, to choose.

As the great Texas writer John Graves wrote in his elegant memoir, *Blue*, sometimes the shape of one dog's head just fits your hand right.

I drove out there in June with my youngest daughter, Lowry, both of us excited by the realization that we were passing through a gate, one of many gates in life, with so much new, once on the other side, and better.

The pups came spilling out of their neat suburban kennels like monkeys rolling and playing, tumbling, chewing, biting. I wanted them all. It was no coincidence that Arya was the runt. I've almost always picked the smallest, and I was pleased that my eye—and heart—had once again been drawn to this compactness. Bob said he had some errands to run, that he'd be gone for an hour or more, but for us to just hang out with the pups and think things over.

The three liveliest were the ones we focused on, though I wasn't really looking at the others except critically. I wanted Arya. But Lowry kept admiring another one, Lyssa, who had large polka-dot patterns; and as the pups played, Arya began to tire.

It's O.K. for a puppy to nap. That's how they grow. But the other one— Lyssa, the next-to-smallest—was still going strong.

"I want that one," Lowry said—speaking of Lyssa. "She's a good dog."

When Bob returned, I told him of my dilemma.

"Your daughter's right," he said. "Lyssa is the best dog."

We shook Bob's hand, picked her up, and like that, had a dog.

Now, a name. We would change her name half a dozen times on the drive home, and a hundred times or more in the coming weeks. Her name changed by the mile, across the dry high basalt lands of the Dalles and eastern Oregon, with summer only beginning; even the scablands glowed with a freshet of green, and as she sat in my lap, bonding, all that we were seeing and smelling was new to her, it all mattered. The world, your world, always becomes new with a puppy.

I have a friend who calls it puppy TV—the way you can sit, all day, and watch their every move. The way you can be made happy just by watching them sleep, or tear into their meal. Despite her pedigree, I don't go overboard in the training: just the basics, for 10 or 15 minutes a day. Sit. Stay. Here. Heel. No. Good dog. I reread the ancient books by Richard Wolters, which have served me well with all my other dogs. Wolters would not have been pleased that she did not yet have a name. Sometimes it's hard to reach consensus in a family. Finally, embarrassed to still be calling her "Dog" after two weeks, we settle on Callie, short for Caldonia, as a bit of her spunk is starting to show.

Caldonia, Caldonia, what makes your big head so hard?

But she's still sweet as a cat, rubs up against your leg, curls, does everything but purr. And of course, with such a dog, it takes only a day or two before we love the name, because we love the dog.

We set up a little fetch corridor in the house, tossing balls and antlers and socks, then calling her so she has no real choice but to bring it back, though this allows her the freedom of perception that she is making a choice. Obedience is all she knows, and I hope to keep it that way. It's so much easier to do that work on the front end than the back.

The summer passes with me in her thrall. My heart opens to floodgates of light as she romps, stalking, pointing, then chasing butterflies, and stares up at planes in the sky, watches movies intently with me, gets up and walks around behind the TV to see where the little people are kept, sniffs for them.

Grouse season opens early in Montana—the first of September—but I'm judicious. That's a hell of a hard bird to figure out, a bird for which there is no margin of error for youthful rambunctiousness. I ease Callie into a few covers where I know there are trusting spruce grouse, where she's hyperexcited—all rototail sniffs and flash points, the world so new!—too excited; though when I knock the bird down she's thrilled, creeps to it, points it, then retrieves it solidly, proudly, beautifully.

Still, I'm waiting on pheasants. I take her over to the east side of the state, to practice on prairie birds—to find Huns, maybe, and if she finds a pheasant to point one, though it's not quite yet the season, so I won't be able to shoot.

We find none of the former, but she crawls into a dense willow thicket, goes on point—a porcupine, I worry?—then lunges forward before backing out quickly, fiercely, holding gently in her jaws the mummified wing from a hawk-killed pheasant.

It's not quite hunting. The pieces are still coming together. If for some strange reason they don't, I'll still love her. She's such a sweet pup. Is this what middle age does to you, makes you not care as much, dulls your edge?

I wait five days, once pheasant season begins. In the old days I would've been over on the east side the night before, sleepless in a hotel room, awaiting the predawn rumble of big diesel trucks in the hotel parking lot warming up to be out in the fields at first cold light—the sound of the frigid metal halyard slapping the flagpole—but that's why those are the old days. Pheasant season is long, and having killed a fair number of pheasants in my life, I value quality over quantity. There are still places in Montana where, if you time it right, you can hunt all day and never see another hunter.

So I wait, leisurely, as if I have all the time in the world. And then one morning, midweek, after the first wave of weekend hunters has pulsed through, I say aloud, Maybe we will head east, walk around, and see what we can see.

You already know how this story ends, or rather, begins. I wouldn't be writing it if she didn't hammer them. It would be a different story. I would still love her—this charismatic intelligent curious princess of a show dog—but it's not rocket science. Water flows downhill, and pointers follow, and point, pheasants.

She slays them. As if guided by some benevolent destiny, I stumble cluelessly into the perfect setup. I go back to where she found that mummified rooster wing. Because it's a lazy morning start, and a few hours' drive, it's noonish before I turn her out into the field. An early-season wet snow fell in the night, drifting to nearly a foot in the cattail-laden coulees where previously the pheasants had been hanging out to avoid the early-autumn heat.

By the time we get there, the snow has melted so that the grasses and sedges glisten dripping green. The scent of refreshed cottonwoods is luscious—every scent molecule clings as if with extra adhesion to those water molecules—and the south-facing slopes are drenched, so that all the birds will be up at the top of the draw, where it's drier, taking in that mild September sun. They'll be stacked there at the top of the slope like pearls in a necklace, strung along the rim.

I haven't figured this out quite yet, nor has Callie. We're just kind of noodling around.

She's working close, and when a rooster jumps from a tree branch, where it has been drying its wet wings like a vulture, she looks up at it with interest and confusion, as if knowing somehow, by the wiring of instinct, that it's not quite supposed to go this way. She wants to run after it, but I pull her away, not wanting her first wild pheasant to imprint itself thusly into her next many years, the pheasant leaping out of a tree like a hawk.

She's calming down. She's focusing. I can see the change come over her, activated by the landscape, and by my desire, behind her. She casts, slows, creeps, points, looking straight downhill, brow furrowed: frozen.

This may be the last time in my life where I know more about pheasants than she does. Any moment now the bird is going to get up. I can hear it rustling, it's a big one; only the big roosters relocate like that before flushing.

At this time of year, the hens hold tighter than ticks. The big rooster, surely a holdover from last year, doesn't want to fly; he knows my dog and I are positioned above him, everything is telling him, *Don't flush*, and yet the situation is untenable, the dog's breath is warm through the wet grass upon his feathers, and surely, he can see me behind the dog, visible against the sky from his perspective looking up through the lattice of his deep cover.

There's another faint rustle of relocation, of pheasant despair, and Callie's muscles tense even tauter, if possible, and her brow furrows further into dark ridges. Her eyes glow like ingots as she continues to inhale the scent.

I can't believe how fast my heart is going. I've been hunting pheasants all my life, but it's as if it's my first. Any second now a rooster is going to explode from beneath her feet, from beneath my feet, as if created by nothing more than a dab of clay and spit and our luminous, fevered desire and imagination.

Drops of water will spray from the rooster's gigantic wings. He will cackle, startling me, despite our knowing he is there. Despite our already seeing him, as brilliant in our shared foreknowledge as if through prophecy, and in that illuminated moment—a kaleidoscope of color and light and motion and sound—a flashpoint will be ignited, my dog's mind will fill with all of the old recovered and long-buried knowledge that has been running in the heated river of her blood, just beneath the surface, and will connect between us and above the surface now for all the many years to come.

Shoot in front, I tell myself, wait a couple of seconds for the bird to get far enough out, and watch for the white collar. Shoot in front, I tell myself. Don't you dare miss.

ABOUT THE EDITOR

ANTHONY LICATA is a passionate fisherman and hunter. He first joined *Field & Stream* in 1998 as an Associate Editor, and is now the editor of *Field & Stream*'s magazine, online, and televised content, as well as Group Editor for a magazine family that includes *Outdoor Life, Popular Science, Popular Photography,* and many more titles. He is the 15th editor in the magazine's history, and has served as the on-air host for the *Field & Stream Total Outdoorsman Challenge* television show.

ABOUT THE MAGAZINE

As the world's leading outdoor magazine, *Field & Stream* has celebrated the complete outdoor experience, including hunting, fishing, conservation, and wilderness survival, for more than 100 years. With great stories, compelling photography, and sound advice, the magazine has been awarded numerous national magazine and writing awards while honoring the traditions hunters and outdoorsmen have passed down for generations.

ABOUT THE AUTHORS

RICK BASS is a dedicated environmentalist, an avid hunter, and a writer. Along with his contributions to *Field & Stream*, he has published over 40 books, most recently *A Thousand Deer: Four Generations of Hunting and the Hill Country*. He is a member of Montana's Yaak Valley Forest Council, working to protect the wilderness lands in the valley.

PHILIP CAPUTO began his writing career in 1968 as a general assignment and investigative reporter for the *Chicago Tribune*. He has written 19 books and published dozens of articles for *Field & Stream*'s print magazine and website (fieldandstream.com), as well as several other leading magazines and newspapers including the *New York Times*, *National Geographic*, and *Esquire*.

C.J. CHIVERS is a journalist, author, and former Marine. He is a senior writer for the *New York Times*, is a contributor to the newspaper's "At War" and "Lens" blogs, and writes for *Esquire* and several other publications. His book *The Gun*, a history of automatic weapons, was published in 2010 to wide acclaim.

SUSAN CASEY is the author of the *New York Times* bestseller *The Devil's Teeth: A True Story of Obsession and Survival Among America's Great White Sharks* and *The Wave*, which was named a *New York Times* Notable Book and a *San Francisco Chronicle* Best Book of the Year. She also helped develop the bestsellers *Into Thin Air* and *The Perfect Storm* and served as the creative director of *Outside Magazine*.

BILL HEAVEY has worked as a writer and editor for *Field & Stream* since 1993, and is well known for the magazine's back page column, "A Sportsman's Life." His humorous writing on the outdoors has been collected and published in two volumes: *If You Didn't Bring Jerky, What Did I Just Eat?* and *It's Only Slow Food Until You Try to Eat It*.

NATE MATTHEWS is *Field & Stream*'s digital director and online editor, and has contributed dozens of articles and blog posts, along with hundreds of photos, to fieldandstream.com.

THOMAS MCINTYRE has been to every continent except for Antarctica, and has been writing since the mid-1970s. Hundreds of his articles have been published in *Field & Stream* and dozens of other publications, including *Men's Journal*, *Outdoor Life*, and many more. He has written scripts for more than 750 outdoor television program episodes, has authored several guide, fiction, and documentary books, and has edited and contributed to the outdoor story anthology *Wild and Fair*.

DAVID E. PETZAL has been with *Field & Stream* since 1972, and is the magazine's Rifles Field Editor, having begun writing about shooting in 1964 during his service in the U.S. Army. A benefactor member of the NRA and a life member of the Amateur Trapshooting Association, he has hunted in the United States, Canada, Africa, Europe, and New Zealand. He is the co-author of *The Total Gun Manual* and the art book *Gun: 100 Great Firearms*.

STEVEN RINELLA is the author of *The Scavenger's Guide to Haute Cuisine* and *American Buffalo: In Search of a Lost Icon*, and contributor to the anthologies *Best American Travel Writing* and *Best Food Writing*. He has written articles for *Outside*, *Field & Stream*, *Bowhunter*, and several other publications, and is the host of the Sportsman Channel show *MeatEater*.

"Castaway in Deer Paradise" by Bill Heavey originally appeared in the October 2009 issue of *Field & Stream*.

"Horn of the Hunter" by David E. Petzal originally appeared in the June 2011 issue of *Field & Stream*.

"Mortality" by Thomas McIntyre originally appeared in the February 2013 issue of *Field & Stream*.

"People of the Caribou" by Bill Heavey originally appeared in the January 2011 issue of *Field & Stream*.

"How I Came to Be Filled with New Zeal and Enthusiasm" by David E. Petzal originally appeared in the May 2010 issue of *Field & Stream*.

"An Improbable Elk Hunt" by Susan Casey originally appeared in the January 2007 issue of *Field & Stream*.

"Trailing a Dream" by Nate Matthews originally appeared in the October 2009 issue of *Field & Stream*.

"The Totem Bear" by Anthony Licata originally appeared in the April 2010 issue of *Field & Stream*.

"Persistence" by David E. Petzal originally appeared in the February 2013 issue of *Field & Stream*.

"Just One More Hunt" is © Philip Caputo and originally appeared in the August 2007 issue of *Field & Stream*.

"The Wire" by David E. Petzal originally appeared in the April 2009 issue of *Field & Stream*.

"Adventures of a Deer Bum" by Bill Heavey originally appeared in the October 2007 issue of *Field & Stream*.

"Pain" is © C.J. Chivers and originally appeared in the February 2013 issue of *Field & Stream*.

"The Badlands Pack" by Steven Rinella originally appeared in the November 2011 issue of *Field & Stream*.

"Stalking the Highlands" by Bill Heavey originally appeared in the July 2007 issue of *Field & Stream*.

"The Perfect Elk" by Rick Bass originally appeared in the December 2012–January 2013 issue of *Field & Stream*.

"Moose Misery" by David E. Petzal originally appeared in the January 2011 issue of *Field & Stream*.

"The Land of Giants" by Thomas McIntyre originally appeared in the January 2006 issue of *Field & Stream*.

"A Hunter's Heart" by Bill Heavey originally appeared in the March 2007 issue of *Field & Stream*.

"The Trail" by Keith McCafferty originally appeared in the January 2009 issue of *Field & Stream*.

"Seventeen Guys, One Old School Bus, and More Guns Than We Can Count" by Bill Heavey originally appeared in the January 2009 issue of *Field & Stream*.

"Ghosts of Sheep River" by Steven Rinella originally appeared in the September 2009 issue of *Field & Stream*.

"Fowl Territory" by T. Edward Nickens originally appeared in the November 2012 issue of *Field & Stream*.

"Trouble" by Mike Toth originally appeared in the February 2013 issue of *Field & Stream*.

"Bear Down" by Steven Rinella originally appeared in the March 2012 issue of *Field & Stream*.

"The Long Stalk" by Rick Bass originally appeared in the January 2008 issue of *Field & Stream*.

"The Bear Up There" by Steven Rinella originally appeared in the May 2007 issue of *Field & Stream*.

"A Triple Play in the Crazies" by Philip Caputo originally appeared in the January 2011 issue of *Field & Stream*.

"Callie's Home" by Rick Bass originally appeared in the April 2013 issue of *Field & Stream*.

weldon**owen**

President, CEO Terry Newell
VP, Publisher Roger Shaw
Associate Publisher Mariah Bear
Editor Bridget Fitzgerald
Creative Director Kelly Booth
Art Director William Mack
Production Director Chris Hemesath
Associate Production Director Michelle Duggan

Weldon Owen would like to thank Ian Cannon and
Katharine Moore for additional editorial assistance and
Mindy Schied for additional design assistance.

FIELD & STREAM

Executive Vice President Eric Zinczenko
Editor-in-Chief Anthony Licata
Executive Editor Mike Toth
Managing Editor Jean McKenna
Deputy Editors Dave Hurteau, Colin Kearns, Slaton L. White
Copy Chief Donna L. Ng
Senior Editor Joe Cermele
Assistant Editor Kristyn Brady
Design Director Sean Johnston
Photography Director John Toolan
Deputy Art Director Pete Sucheski
Associate Art Directors Kim Gray, James A. Walsh
Production Manager Judith Weber
Digital Director Nate Matthews
Online Content Editor David Maccar
Online Producer Kurt Shulitz
Assistant Online Editor Martin Leung

2 Park Avenue
New York, NY 10016
fieldandstream.com

Field & Stream and Weldon Owen are divisions of
BONNIER

FRi i-1/968